Arians and Vandals of the 4th-6th Centuries

Arians and Vandals of the 4th-6th Centuries:
Annotated translations of the historical works
by Bishops Victor of Vita (*Historia Persecutionis
Africanae Provinciae*) and Victor of Tonnena (*Chronicon*),
and of the religious works by Bishop Victor
of Cartenna (*De Paenitentia*) and Saints Ambrose (*De Fide
Orthodoxa contra Arianos*), and Athanasius (*Expositio Fidei*)

By

John R. C. Martyn,

Preface by David O'Brien

Cambridge Scholars Publishing

Arians and Vandals of the 4th-6th Centuries: Annotated translations of the historical works by Bishops Victor of Vita (*Historia Persecutionis Africanae Provinciae*) and Victor of Tonnena (*Chronicon*), and of the religious works by Bishop Victor of Cartenna (*De Paenitentia*) and Saints Ambrose (*De Fide Orthodoxa contra Arianos*), and Athanasius (*Expositio Fidei*), by John R. C. Martyn, Preface by David O'Brien

This book first published 2008

Cambridge Scholars Publishing

12 Back Chapman Street, Newcastle upon Tyne, NE6 2XX, UK

British Library Cataloguing in Publication Data
A catalogue record for this book is available from the British Library

Copyright © 2008 by John R. C. Martyn

All rights for this book reserved. No part of this book may be reproduced, stored in a retrieval system, or transmitted, in any form or by any means, electronic, mechanical, photocopying, recording or otherwise, without the prior permission of the copyright owner.

ISBN (10): 1-84718-991-1, ISBN (13): 9781847189912

TABLE OF CONTENTS

Historical Preface xi
Introduction xxiii

A. Victor of Vita *Historia Persecutionis Africae*
Preface.. 1
Prologue.. 3

Book One
Chapter 1: Entry of Vandals into Africa...................................... 5
Chapter 2: Vandal Savagery.. 6
Chapter 3: Demolition of Buildings 7
Chapter 4: Destruction of Carthage 9
Chapter 5: Expulsion of Clergy 10
Chapter 6: Faith of Sebastian... 11
Chapter 7: Heavy Persecution 13
Chapter 8: Virtues of Deogratias 14
Chapter 9: Thomas the Confessor... 16
Chapter 10: Maxima, other Martyrs and Confessors................. 16
Chapter 11: Completing their Martyrdoms................................. 18
Chapter 12: Persecution Worsens... 20
Chapter 13: Martyrdoms of Reader and Others.......................... 20
Chapter 14: Remarkable Event... 21
Chapter 15: Confessor Mascula, Master of Mimes 23
Chapter 16: Faith of Saturus... 23
Chapter 17: End of Geiseric's Persecution 25

Book Two
Chapter 1: Beginning of Huneric's Reign 26
Chapter 2: Bishop's Consecration Allowed................................ 27
Chapter 3: Virtues of Eugenius 28
Chapter 4: Start of Persecution... 29
Chapter 5: Huneric Treats his Family Savagely 30
Chapter 6: Visions before Persecution 32
Chapter 7: Heavy Persecution 34
Chapter 8: Faithful Forced into Exile 35

vi Table of Contents

Chapter 9: Young Woman's Admirable Faith 36
Chapter 10: Prison's Unpleasantness 38
Chapter 11: Ghastly Journey 39
Chapter 12: Savage treatment of Christians 40
Chapter 13: The King's Edict 41
Chapter 14: Eugenius' Reply 42
Chapter 15: King's Rejection 43
Chapter 16: Savagery against the bishops 44
Chapter 17: Great Miracle 45
Chapter 18: A Happy Martyr 47

Book Three (A)
Preface 50
Section 1: The Unity of God's Substance 51
Section 2: Proof from Scripture 52
Section 3: Father and Son are Equals 53
Section 4: Two Natures in Christ 54
Section 5: The Birth of the Son 55
Section 6: An Objection Answered 56
Section 7: Substance of Unbegotten and Begotten 56
Section 8: Indivisible Substance of God 58
Section 9: Holy Spirit. consubstant. with Father, Son 59
Section 10: Proof in the Scriptures 60
Section 11: Three Persons in One Name 61
Section 12: Their Creation is in Common 62
Section 13: Foreknowledge 63
Section 14: The Power of the Holy Spirit 63
Section 15: The Presence of God everywhere 64
Section 16: God lives amongst His Saints 65
Section 17: Proof of Father, Son & Holy Spirit 65
Section 18: Goodness of Father, Son & Holy Spirit 65
Section 19: The Dignity of the Holy Spirit 66
Section 20: The Common name of Paraclete 66
Section 21: Recapitulation 67
Section 22: A Stronger Argument 68
Section 23: The Confession of Baptism 69

Book Three (B)
Ambrose's Defence of Catholic Faith
Preface 71
Confession of Faith 72

Prologue... 73
Chapter 1 76
Chapter 2 77
Chapter 3 80
Chapter 4 83
Chapter 5 85
Chapter 6 87
Chapter 7 88
Chapter 8 90
Conclusion 96

Book Four
Victor of Vita
Chapter 1: False Accusations by Arians 97
Chapter 2: Huneric's Edict against Catholics.. 97
Chapter 3: Savagery towards Catholic bishops 102
Chapter 4: Deceived by Trickery.. 103
Chapter 5: Forced into Exile... 104

Book Five
Chapter 1: General Persecution 106
Chapter 2: Suffering of Servus 108
Chapter 3: Bravery of Victoria 108
Chapter 4: Faith of Martyr Victorian... 109
Chapter 5: Two Brothers, Confessors... 110
Chapter 6: Amazing Faith of Typasitans: Great Miracle............................. 111
Chapter 7: Vandals' Savagery to their own People 112
Chapter 8: Constancy of an Exiled Matron 112
Chapter 9: Struggles of Clergy in Carthage. Muritta's Splendid Deed... 113
Chapter 10: Clergy Forced into Exile 115
Chapter 11: Antony's Savagery towards Eugenius 116
Chapter 12: On the Holy Habetdeum 117
Chapter 13: Violent Acts by the Arians.. 118
Chapter 14: Woman's Egregious Deed 119
Chapter 15: Confessors' Deaths in Deserts 121
Chapter 16: Holy Habetdeum 121
Chapter 17: Serious Famine 122
Chapter 18: Morality of Barbarians.. 125
Chapter 19: Lamentation for Africa 127
Chapter 20: Author Invokes the Saints... 128
Chapter 21: Huneric's Reign 129

viii Table of Contents

B. Victor of Tonnena: *Chronicon 444-566* 130
Preface 130
Covering the years 444 to 566 AD 132

C. Victor of Cartenna: *De Poenitentia* 167
Preface 167
Chapter 1 168
Chapter 2 170
Chapter 3 173
Chapter 4 174
Chapter 5 177
Chapter 6 179
Chapter 7 181
Chapter 8 182
Chapter 9 184
Chapter 10 186
Chapter 11 188
Chapter 12 189
Chapter 13 190
Chapter 14 191
Chapter 15 194
Chapter 16 195
Chapter 17 196
Chapter 18 198
Chapter 19 199
Chapter 20 201
Chapter 21 202
Chapter 22 203
Chapter 23 205
Chapter 24 206
Chapter 25 208
Chapter 26 209
Chapter 27 210
Chapter 28 211
Chapter 29 212
Chapter 30 213
Chapter 31 214
Chapter 32 214
Chapter 33 216

D. Athanasius: *Expositio Fidei* 218
Preface 218
Chapter 1 218
Chapter 2 219
Chapter 3 221
Chapter 4 222

Select Bibliography 224

Appendix: *Notitia* 232

HISTORICAL PREFACE

THEOLOGICAL AND HISTORICAL BACKDROP

The Arian controversy broke out in Alexandria some time during the second decade of the fourth century and was soon to present the Church with its greatest intellectual crisis to date. Though scarcely making inroads in the west for any significant period of time, it effectively destabilized the Church in the eastern part of the Roman Empire for the next sixty years until the Council of Constantinople (381) and the vigorous anti-Arian measures of Theodosius. By the life-times of the three Victors in the fifth and sixth centuries, 'Arianism' had long been regarded as the archetypal Christian heresy: the word 'heresy' being a technical term signifying a particular theological opinion deemed to be unacceptable and dangerous to religious belief; a Christian innovation, borrowed from the polemics of the rival philosophical schools by second century writers. 'Arianism' was regarded as the archetypal heresy because in emphasizing the essential difference between God and the Son it ultimately drew into question the core tenets of Christianity regarding the nature of salvation and the long established liturgical practices of the Church.

Opponents of 'Arianism', following the polemical conventions of the day, drew connections between Arius' system and the rejected theological positions of another heretic from the previous century, Paul of Samosata, who, as far as we can tell, held to an adoptionist position, calling Jesus 'Christ' only after the baptism, at which event the Logos took up his abode in the man Jesus through the conferral of the Holy Spirit. Both heretics are said to espouse 'low and mean views' of the Son in relation to the Father. Modern readers have to be careful in accepting all descriptions of Arius' Christology. What we have of Arius' own writing is meagre, and these documents are preserved by hostile critics, who selected them to be damaging, if not actually misquoted or taken out of context. Arius had nothing to do with many of the later concerns that became known as the 'Arian controversy' (including questions such as whether the Son is like the Father or unlike him? etc). Arius' surviving letters and poem show that he regarded himself as a conservative, treading in the footsteps of pious teachers and fully in line with the doctrine of the bishop. There are two chiefly historical factors that functioned as catalysts to this intellectual crisis.

The first can be traced back to the brutal and sustained persecution of the Church in the eastern part of the empire from 303 to 313 by Diocletian and his fanatically anti-Christian successor, Galerius. Martyrdom was common in Egypt in particular, and had the effect of weakening the hierarchical authority in the Alexandrian community. The bishop of Alexandria, Peter, was martyred in 311, having been absent previously for long periods through hiding. During the vacuum caused by his absence, another bishop, Melitius of Lycopolis, ordained clergy for Alexandria without the permission of Peter, who evidently could be reached without too much difficulty, thereby causing a major schism. The second factor has to with the rather unique nature of authority in Alexandria at the time. Since the late second century, beginning with the shadowy figure of Pantaenus, but following on by the more palpable figures of Clement, and Origen, and continuing through to the fourth century, presbyters of the Churches and teachers in that city enjoyed considerable independence, with several regarding themselves as charismatic leaders. Arius himself, like several of his predecessors, claimed to be a teacher 'instructed by God', espousing the idea that the charismatically inspired teacher was more authoritative than the hierarchical leader. Arius was born in Libya and was probably already an old man when the crisis broke. He is described as a skilled dialectician and seems to have had some facility in philosophy, although this does not imply that he had received a formal philosophical education. By the end of the second half of the fourth century Arius is firmly anchored in Alexandria as a pastor of the Baukalis church, a very popular preacher famous for his asceticism. Thus, when Alexander succeeded Peter as bishop of Alexandria in 313, he inherited not only a Church fractured by schism but also a parochial system, with the bishop presiding over a college of near equals. To the rest of Egypt the bishop of Alexandria was '*papa*', in his own city he was '*primus inter pares*'.

The controversy, as best as we can discern, came to a head when Alexander, attempting to consolidate episcopal authority by means of insisting on a form of doctrinal orthodoxy, called upon several presbyters in the city to give their opinions 'about a certain passage in the divine law.' Most likely this had to do with the interpretation of *Proverbs* 8.22-31, a passage that explicitly states that God had 'created' wisdom, for the sake of his other works, before the creation of the earth, abyss and mountains. The interpretation of this passage evidently had a long history of debate in Alexandria. In the early third century Origen used the passage to refute the Sabellian blurring of the distinction between the Logos and the Father. His pupil, Dionysius of Alexandria, carried this anti-Sabellian exegesis even further, declaring 'that the Son of God is a creature and something made, not his own by nature, but alien in essence from the Father ... Being a creature, he did not exist before he came into being', an interpretation which later compelled Athanasius to perform some fancy footwork in his attempt to absolve his predecessor from any proto-Arian inclinations. For Arius himself, this text provided an interpretation crux illustrating the substantial difference between God and the Logos. His solution is elegant: if God creates the Logos, he cannot be eternal alongside God; he must exist because God wills him to exist. 'There was when he did not exist' is purported to be one of Arius' slogans.

We have a creedal statement drawn up by Arius and his supporters submitted to Alexander around 320 or 321,

> 'We acknowledge one God, the only unbegotten, the only eternal, the only one without cause or beginning, the only true, the only possessed of immortality, the only wise, the only good ... the begetter of his only Son before endless ages ... giving him subsistence by his own will ... the perfect creation of God, but not like one among other creatures...'

Arius goes on to distinguish this teaching from various heresies and errors which make God out to be a material and divisible being, by suggesting that the Logos is a ὁμοούσιος portion of divinity, or reduce the Logos to an impersonal function of God or to one among other aspects of God.

Both Arius and Alexander were influenced in part by Origen who taught that, although the Son depended on the Father, there was no interval prior to the generation of the Logos, as God's self-expressive action must be eternal. Arius' main concern was to secure the uniqueness of the Father and the contingency of the Logos on the Father's decision. Alexander, in contrast, emphasized the Son's co-eternal nature: 'always God, always the Son.' He picks up Origen's insight that there is a distinction between eternal existence and independently necessary existence: an eternal Son, sharing in all the Father's qualities without reserve, except for the single fact that the Father has no origin, is reconcilable with the fact that the Father alone is the source of all. The Son does not exist because of God's choice: he is the natural expression of God's nature, the eternal and perfect

xiv   Historical Preface

image and radiance of the Father. Arius, in turn, repudiates Alexander's argument as coming acceptably close to the 'two first principles' error.

As far as Alexander is concerned, Arius is teaching a novel doctrine about Christ. If only the Father is incapable of change, the Logos must be changeable; that is, his eternal virtue must be the result of his own free choice. This raises the uncomfortable implication that salvation depends on something other than God's grace. While nothing in Arius' writings bears this out directly, Alexander may simply be drawing out the implications of Arius' teachings, a common technique of theological debate in this period, where an opponent can be held responsible for possible implications of his teaching, even if he does not say it specifically.

The Council of Nicaea

Unfortunately, while we have several documentary remains of the correspondence between the major players, we have no means of reconstructing the sequence of events leading up to the Council of Nicaea with any certainty.

It is clear that around 318, Arius, deposed and excommunicated by a recently convened Alexandrian synod, wrote to and enlisted support from some influential Church leaders in Palestine and Asia, including Eusebius of Caesarea and Eusebius of Nicomedia. The latter Eusebius was a former pupil of Lucian of Antioch martyred a few years earlier, and one of the most learned and significant exegetes of the age. His disciples included several senior figures in the Churches of the eastern Mediterranean, and Eusebius was able to draw on their support. Arius implies that he too studied with Lucian.

An epistolary battle ensued and pressure from Eusebius of Nicomedia led to another synod, this time in Palestine, which ended up by vindicating the orthodoxy of Arius. Alexander, exasperated by the constant appeals of Arius' episcopal allies, issued a series of letters spelling out the exact nature not only of Arius' heresy, but also of his allegedly schismatic behavior and that of his supporters in Alexandria.

Some time afterwards, Constantine, having become emperor over the whole Roman Empire after his victory against Licinius in 324, became concerned about events in Alexandria. He wanted to use the Church to

Arians and Vandals of the 4th-6th Centuries

cement loyalty and unity within the State, and thus had great interest in resolving what was turning out to be a violently disruptive quarrel in the Churches. In response to extensive lobbying, probably from both sides, Constantine summoned a general Council of as many bishops as possible, from every part of the Roman Empire, which was to meet in Nicaea in early summer of 325. The exact number of bishops who attended will never be known. Earlier witnesses only give round numbers but most estimates are around the 300 mark.

We cannot reconstruct with confidence the proceedings of the Council because no account official or otherwise of the whole affair has come down to us. All we have is a number of descriptions by individuals of some events that happened in it, but we do not know the order and their significance at the time. At the time of the Council's opening, Arius had few unequivocal supporters; those who backed him were probably more concerned to rule out what they saw as the erroneous doctrines of Alexander's party. Nevertheless, it is clear that early on the Council was concerned to find a formula to which Arius' supporters could never agree.

The following is the creed that the Council drew up:

> 'We believe in one God, Father Almighty, Maker of all things, seen and unseen: and in one Lord Jesus Christ the Son of God, begotten as only-begotten of the Father, that is of the substance (οὐσία) of the Father, God of God, Light of Light, true God of true God, begotten not made, consubstantial (ὁμοούσιος) with the Father, through whom all things came into existence, both things in heaven and things on earth; who for us men and for our salvation came down and was incarnate and became man, suffered and rose again on the third day, ascended into the heavens, is coming to judge the living and the dead: And in the Holy Spirit.'

But to those who say "there was a time when he did not exist," and "before being begotten he did not exist," and that "he came into being from non-existence," or who allege that the Son of God is of another ὑπόστασις (hypostasis) or οὐσία, or is alterable or changeable, these the Catholic and Apostolic Church condemns.

The consciously anti-Arian tone of the creed is unmistakable. To say that the Son was "of the substance (οὐσία)" of the Father and that he was "consubstantial" (ὁμοούσιος) with him was controversial, and would continue to plague future attempts for a workable consensus. Nothing comparable to this had been said in any creed or profession of faith before.

Alexander himself had never described the Son's relation to the Father with *ousia* and its cognates. The word ὁμοούσιος probably had a loose meaning but there were several problems with the word not having a scriptural basis, and some historical and philosophical associations, including that of an implied materiality, which even those who were not wholehearted Arians would eventually find unpalatable.

It is reported that the creed, even though it included the terms οὐσία and ὁμοούσιος, was received by an overwhelming majority at the time of the Council. The loose nature of these terms could allow someone like Eusebius of Caesarea, who was by no means an opponent of Arius' views, to persuade himself to accept the creed. He claims, rather unconvincingly, that the emperor himself qualified the addition of consubstantial (ὁμοούσιος) by saying that:

"The Son is not to be said consubstantial (ὁμοούσιος) is the sense of any corporeal experiences, nor does he exist as a result of division or any subtraction from the Father; for the immaterial and spiritual and incorporeal nature cannot undergo any corporeal experience, and that it is right to hold such views about divine and inexpressible subjects of thought."

The other remarkable point about the creed is the condemnation in the anathemas at the end in the view that the Son is "of another ὑπόστασις (*hypostasis*) or οὐσία" from the Father. The fact is that at the time of the making of the creed there was a great deal of semantic confusion over the terms ὑπόστασις (*hypostasis*) and οὐσία indeed for many they had pretty much the same meaning. By the standard of later orthodoxy, as achieved in the Council of Constantinople in 381, it is patently heretical, allowing for a Sabellian doctrine of the successive 'modes' of divine being. Some supporters of Nicaea, notably Marcellus of Ancyra, really did teach something that approached Sabellianism.

In its letter to the Egyptian and Libyan Churches, the Council recorded its condemnation of Arius' person and views: he was excommunicated and probably degraded from his priesthood. The Libyan bishops Secundus and Theonas refused to sign the creed and shared his fate. Eusebius of Nicomedia was also banished some short time after the Council, after receiving and communicating with some Arian presbyters in his See. Within ten years they had all been restored by Constantine. Arius was able to present a non-committal creed to the emperor and his ecclesiastical advisors, where he affirmed that "the Son is begotten from the Father before all ages," but remained silent on *homoousios*. Evidently this was enough to satisfy Constantine and he was restored, although he was not reconciled with the See of Alexandria. Arius died in 336, suddenly, his opponents tell us, just prior to his being readmitted into communion, on a public toilet, after experiencing such violent diarrhea that 'his bowels came out.' As Rowan Williams succinctly puts it, 'the emperor and the city were duly shocked and edified.'

'Arianism' after Nicaea

It is important for modern readers to understand that 'Arianism' is not a coherent system, founded by a single great figure and sustained by his disciples. It is a fantasy based on the polemic of pro-Nicene writers, above all Athanasius who wish to turn 'Arianism' into a self-conscious sect, as if the boundaries of Catholic identity were already firmly set. That is why there is a trend for scholars to enclose the word 'Arianism' with inverted commas. Those bishops sympathetic to the Arian view refused to consider themselves as followers of Arius, a mere presbyter. They did not look upon Arius as a factional leader and were quick to distance themselves from him.

It was soon apparent that Nicaea did not prove to be the workable consensus that Constantine hoped for, and for the next thirty or forty years several replacement creeds were drawn up. The majority of eastern bishops had genuine misgivings about the ὁμοούσιος term in the creed. These anti-Nicenes thought of themselves as being 'Catholics,' as mainstream Christians, and regarded both Athanasius and his supporters, on one hand, and the aggressive Arians like Eunomius, on the other, as isolated extremists.

The majority saw the Logos as the perfect and internal image of God, existing independently, but in such a way as to reveal God definitively. Arius' stress on the infinite qualitative difference between God and the Logos was generally unfavorable. By the 350's there was a substantial group who took the middle ground by supporting the term ὁμοιούσιος 'of similar substance,' adding an iota to the offensive term, as a designation of the Son's relation to the Father. These were called the Homoians. Others perceived that this did not clearly distinguish the natures of the Father and Son sufficiently, but simply raised again the problem of two first principles. The latter were the Anomoians for they believed that the

Father and Son were ἀνόμοιος 'dissimilar' in substance. Since the Father was unbegotten, an essential attribute of divinity, and the Son is begotten, he could have nothing in common with the Father. By the late 350's, the Anomoians had gained a considerable power base, usually at the expense of the pro-Nicenes and the Homoians, from the support of Constantine's son and successor, Constantius.

The 360's would provide the turning point, where the creed of Nicaea would gradually begin to become more appealing to the majority. This is attributable to two factors. The first is political. In 361 the East witnessed the accession of a passionately anti-Christian emperor, Julian 'the Apostate.' Julian was evenhandedly hostile to pro-Nicenes, Homoians, Anomoians, and everyone else in the Christian world. His policy was to allow most exiled bishops to return to their Sees, so that factions could fight their battles directly, without state intervention. His hope was that they would effectively destroy each other. His accession removed the power bases previously enjoyed by any of the factions that led many to look elsewhere for alliances in this new and precarious situation.

Secondly, Nicene theology began to look attractive in such a context, largely because Athanasius (c.295-373), the successor to Alexander in Alexandria, defended it so doggedly. Athanasius was almost the sole articulate opponent not only of the Arians but also of the consensus of the Homoians, and later the Anomoians. He was a young deacon in Alexander's entourage at Nicaea and retained his convictions, even if it meant suffering the displeasure of emperors with opposing views. He was exiled no fewer than five times.

If we remember, Arius is concerned to secure the grounds for believing in a separately subsisting Logos, who reveals to us all we can know of God, and leads us to share his own adoration of the divine mystery. It is precisely because the Son is limited that he can communicate to men, who share his limitations, about God who is absolutely ineffable. Arius certainly takes the incarnation seriously, something that the Nicenes could not do as effectively. The key to Arius' soteriology is that the Logos, through God's will, suffered. The Logos is the subject of all the human experiences of Jesus.

Arius' understanding of salvation is fundamentally flawed, in the view of Athanasius. He raises the fundamental problem about how God communicates with creation, if there is an immeasurable ontological gulf:

how can even the most exalted creature help in the process? If the incarnate Son makes us sons and daughters of the eternal Father, what does it mean that the Son too has to be made a son? Does he also need a mediator? What the Son gives he must have; if he has by grace and not by nature, there must be a process by which he acquires these gifts, which introduces the risk of making salvation dependent on actions other than God's. In short, for the Son to give God's gifts, the Son must act with God's action, and not be passive to the act of grace.

Athanasius conceives of salvation in terms of divinization. His conviction is that one agency alone, God's, is involved in the work of salvation. Only if it is this agency that acts for our redemption may we be confident of our salvation. Salvation is union with the divine life, directly and without intermediary. He stands in Alexandrian tradition, especially that of Origen, which is deeply occupied with the unity of God's work: the father is eternally and naturally productive, generating the Son eternally because this is his very nature.

Perhaps Athanasius' greatest theological contribution to the theological controversies of the period is his innovation in distinguishing between *hypostasis* (person or subsistence) and οὐσία (essence or substance) during his attempt to woo the broad Homoian constituency in the 360's. He refines the sense of the ὁμοούσιος bringing it as close as possible to the ὁμοιούσιος of the Homoians, by distinguishing the substantive *hypostases* of Father and Son. This work would be taken up and completed by two brothers, Basil of Caesarea (329-79), his younger brother Gregory of Nyssa (died 395), and their friend Gregory of Nazianzen (died 390), commonly known as the Cappadocians, who devoted themselves to the task of describing how can the one God simultaneously be three eternally distinct persons, without plurality destroying the unity or the unity undermining the reality of the distinctions.

Like the Eastern majority, they emphasized in Origenist fashion the distinctions between the three persons of the Trinity, basing their concept of the Son's deity on the idea of 'image': the Son is like the Father in all things, including being and eternity. The Cappadocians are often called the neo-Nicenes, because they adapt the Nicene Creed to Origenist emphases. The Cappadocian formula of the Trinity that asserts the one substance of Father, Son and Holy Spirit, but speaks of three personally distinct hypostases, would attract a majority in the East. The Father

xx   Historical Preface

retains a certain priority as the primary cause, although the works and natures of the three persons are indistinguishable.

As has been discussed, in the generations following Constantine, the pro-Nicene cause in the East suffered under consciously anti-Nicene imperial policies. We have seen that Constantius tended to support the Anomoians and how Julian was antagonistic to all Christian factions. The anti-Nicene trend continues with Valens (364-378), who was a convinced homoian Arian and occasionally used his power to suppress other factions. This included *inter alia* banishing Gregory from Nyssa and making sure that the Arian Lucius succeeded Athanasius as bishop of Alexandria, after the latter's death in 373. Valens also sent a number of pro-Nicene clergy and monks of the See of Alexandria to work in the mines. One of his favorite devices for discouraging clergy with opposing views was to enlist them among the *curiales*, thus making them liable to considerable expenses from which his favored clergy were exempt.

Pro-Nicene fortunes changed for the better when Valens died and was succeeded by Theodosius (379-395). Theodosius, born and raised in Spain, was a son of a general with distinguished service suppressing rebellion and restoring order in Britain and Africa. He had been called from retirement by Gratian to share the burden of imperial rule. In February 380, he issued an edict known as *Cunctos Populos,* declaring the Nicene doctrine of the Trinity to be the official doctrine of the Empire. His subjects were ordered to hold to 'the single divinity of the Father, Son and Holy Spirit within an equal majesty and an orthodox Trinity.' He deposed the Arian bishops in Constantinople and Alexandria appointed under Valens. On January 10th 381, Theodosius issued an edict addressed to the Praetorian Prefect of the diocese of the Oriens, known as *Nullis haereticis*, prohibiting heretics (specifically Eunomians, Photinians and Arians), from occupying any Church building for worship, or even from gathering together within the walls of any town for that purpose. In May of that year he convened a Council in the imperial city of Constantinople to settle the ecclesiastical affairs of the Eastern Church.

Unfortunately we know even less about the proceedings of the Council of Constantinople than we do about that of Nicaea. There is no mention of the creed from Constantinople until the documents of the Council of Chalcedon in 451. We do know that immediately after the Council ended, at the end of July 381, Theodosius issued an edict with the opening words:

Arians and Vandals of the 4th-6th Centuries   xxi

"We now order that all Churches are to be handed over to the bishops who profess Father, Son and Holy Spirit of a single majesty, of the same glory, of one splendor, who establish no difference by sacrilegious separation, but the order of the Trinity by recognizing the persons and uniting the Godhead."

Several bishops spread over a wide area as possible are identified as holding this as the norm of doctrine. And anyone who refused to communicate with these bishops is now declared a heretic and is to be refused office in the Church. By this edict, Theodosius finally and decisively rendered the pro-Nicene version of the Christian faith the official religion of the Roman Empire, East and West. Naturally, prescription ought not be taken as necessarily indicative of description, but it is clear that soon afterwards certain bishops, Theophilus of Alexandria an infamous example, embarked on anti-Arian and anti-pagan purges in their Sees with ruthless efficiency with the backing of the emperor.

Now being officially outlawed, Arian influence temporally declined in the East during the late fourth and early fifth centuries. Other controversies, schisms and heresies became more pressing during this time. In North Africa, Augustine of Hippo was largely absorbed with the Donatists as his chief combatants. All this was to change abruptly and violently by what was aptly called a 'tempestuous whirlwind.'

The 'tempestuous whirlwind'

At the beginning of the fifth century, the Vandals, fleeing westward from the Huns, invaded and devastated parts of Gaul before settling in Spain in 409. During the late 420's the Vandals, under their new King Geiseric, reputedly 80,000 in number, were ferried across the straits of Gibraltar into North Africa, and reached Augustine's See of Hippo by 430, with the old bishop dying during the siege. Geiseric obtained a hasty land settlement in Numidia in 435, and took Carthage in 439. Despite abortive attempts by Theodosius II to send a fleet to control them, in 441, Vandal rule over most of North Africa received a *de facto* recognition in 442. Geiseric had taken over Corsica, Sardinia and the Balearics by 455, and on the death of Valentinian II in that year, he entered and sacked Rome. North Africa remained in Vandal control until the expedition of Belisarius in 533, after which the Vandals disappear from the pages of history.

The Vandals were ardent Arians, having accepted that form of Christianity under Valens during the third quarter of the fourth century. However, the

xxii   Historical Preface

Vandals did not see themselves as Arians, but regarded themselves rather as 'reformed' Christians. Their persecutions of Roman Catholics in Africa were at times fierce, particularly during the last years of the reign of Geiseric's successor, Huneric (reigned 477-484). North Africa was a province long accustomed to religious persecution. The Vandals applied the same punishments to Catholics as Augustine had proposed against the Donatists. Under Vandal rule, Catholic bishops were punished with deposition, exile or death. Other people were excluded from office and frequently suffered confiscation of their property. The following treatises by the three Victors are first hand accounts of those who lived under their rule and who suffered for adhering to their Catholic faith.

David O'Brien
Lecturer in Theology, Trinity College, Melbourne

INTRODUCTION

This work is primarily an English translation of three works of the fifth and sixth centuries written in North Africa, by three different Bishops Victor, texts that will provide some interesting historical evidence for that period, concerning events and schisms taking place there, mostly unknown or poorly covered hitherto by contemporary documents. The first, the *Historia Persecutionis* by Victor of Vita, is far the best known of these three works, although it had to wait until 1991 for a translation into modern English, by John Moorhead.[1] When they are combined, these three works will help both historians and archaeologists to discover more about the history of North Africa and the Mediterranean area during the fifth and sixth centuries. Further new information can be obtained from my English version of all of Pope Gregory's letters, and my version of the Greek biography of Bishop Gregory of Agrigento, whose life was very closely linked with that of the Pope, and was largely spent in Sicily and in North Africa.[2]

The translations will include some notes, but most will explain the Biblical quotations, and a few Classical ones. With three such different works, it

---

[1] John Moorhead's trans., notes and introduction to *Victor of Vita: History of the Vandal persecution* was vol 10 in Liverpool Univ. Press' *Translated Texts for Historians* (1991). The translation has useful notes, but unfortunately it very often omits words and distorts the sense of the Latin. For this work, to which I am indebted, an *M* will be used in the notes hereafter. Other poor or very dated translations in German (1883 and 1884), in Italian (1859), in Dutch (1568), in Polish (1930) and in French (1563, 1664 and 1921) are briefly noted by Christian Courtois in his *Victor de Vita et son Oevre*, p. 89. For Courtois, *CVV* will be used for his work on *Victor de Vita*, and *CA* for work on *les Vandales et l'Afrique*. For his praise and others' criticism of Courtois' works, see *M* p. ix.

[2] For Pope Gregory, see John R. C. Martyn *The Letters of Gregory the Great*, tr. with intro. & notes, in 3 Vols, (PIMS, Toronto, 2004). For Bishop Gregory, see John R. C. Martyn *A Translation of Abbot Leontius' Life of Saint Gregory, Bishop of Agrigento*, tr. & comm. (Edward Mellen, Lampeter, 2004). Note also that a new *Association pour l'Antiquité Tardive,* at the C.N.R.S. Paris, has just released a vol. of 506 pp. on *L'Afrique Vandale et Byzantine*, Tome 10, 2002, with a 2nd volume due this year. See my review in *Parergon* 21.1, 2004, 155-7.

xxiv   Introduction

would take many months for all the relevant primary and secondary scholarship to be assessed and incorporated in each section, adding many pages to what is essentially an attempt to reveal relatively unknown texts in English, not to provide a definitive historical or editorial work. For Victor of Vita's history, several notes will cover textual matters, where readings affect the logic of a passage, a normal requirement for a translator. The chronicle of Victor of Tonnena covers 120 years, replete with controversial religious and political history; a few hundred pages would be needed to annotate it in full. Basic notes are included.

The identity of Victor of Vita is unclear.[3] Moorhead suggests that he was a priest based in Carthage, where he had access to the See's archives and witnessed the persecution, while somehow avoiding exile or worse. If so, he would have become a bishop later on, perhaps filling the vacant See of Vita, whose bishop (also called Victor) was marked as absent from the Council held in Carthage. But it seems much more probable that he was already bishop of Vita (the two Victors are most unlikely), who kept a very low profile during the Council. The text shows him in later years still interviewing victims who had survived the persecution, suggesting that it was completed in 489, as he himself claims (60 years after the invasion in 429 by the Vandals), if not several years later, but not in 484 as was proposed by Moorhead.[4] Victor thus had the status to interview Archbishop Eugenius and to check the King's documents and other archives, and perhaps he was able to avoid the swords of the Arian priests as an official and impartial historian.

In the prologue below, Victor describes Eugenius as venerable and clever, taught by the most praiseworthy scholar Diadochus, and an equal to Timothy and Luke, and Victor is writing his work on Africa at his instigation. So it seems that Victor was an early disciple of Eugenius, and became an official historian at his request.[5] This would suggest that most of Victor's research and interviews would have followed the Council, the destructive plague and the death of Huneric. Without a reasonable delay, historical perspective would have been impossible. The historian's success lies in his ability to bring alive the passions of the great Council, and the bishops' quandary outside the walls of Carthage, and the many

---

[3] See *CVV* pp 5-10, and *M* note 15, p. xv.
[4] See *M* p. xv for Victor as priest, and xvi-xvii for his work's completion in 484.
[5] See *CVV* 17-22 and *M* p. xvii. Both rightly support this hypothesis. To judge from his quotes from Cicero, Juvenal, Lucretius, Ovid and Virgil (*Aen.* and *Gcs*) and reference to Sallust, it is likely that he had a basic education in the Classics.

horrific but admirable martyrdoms. It should be added that Victor had to bribe the Moors so that he could enter the black hole where so many believers were enclosed without a toilet, like the Jews' carriages on the way to the Nazi death camps. Bribing Moors to see the victims within suggests a well-funded and specially treated historian, and his ready access to the King's documents reinforces this view.

The delay in its publication can be backed up by several comments in his narrative. In 4.10, 'Carthage now worships the choir of twelve boys as the twelve apostles,' boys who survived being kidnapped and beaten under Huneric, and were not likely to be worshipped before the King's death. The dating of the tongue-less Reparatus incident in 4.6 is uncertain, but it seems quite late in Zeno's reign, in the mid 480s. Victoria in 4.3 is roasted and her arms are torn out of their sockets, but she reported to Victor afterwards that some virgin had restored her to good health. The 'afterwards' suggests after 484. In 2.12, the tombs of the new Saints rise up erected along the highway, showing the very large number of victims, but not at once, again suggesting a row of post-Huneric memorials. In 1.11, the nun Maxima, a young virgin 'still alive today,' has become an abbess 'well known to me also.' A gap of several years is certainly suggested. Finally, in 1.10, a man who had witnessed a miraculous recovery from exposed entrails 'testified before me on oath that this miracle had taken place.' This also suggests a later date, when such research was far easier. Short reports may be filed during hostilities, but the history of any campaign needs some years for a full study of events and their sequel.

There has also been some uncertainty over the identity of the second Victor, who wrote the *Chronicon*, and seems to have suffered the same sort of life as the young Sicilian Bishop Gregory. As a youthful bishop of Tonnena, this Victor was first imprisoned and beaten in Alexandria, and was then carted off in 564 to Constantinople, with five other rebellious bishops, to be imprisoned in local monasteries until they were all ready to accept the Catholic Church's position on the divisive Three Chapters issue, that figures so extensively in his *Chronicon*, and in Pope Gregory's letters, and caused such trouble for the Emperors. Victor reappears in North Africa as the reinstated bishop of Tonnena in the letters of Pope Gregory, dated September 601 (*Epp* 12.3, 8 and 9), sent about thirty seven years after his departure to Constantinople. How long he had been back in Africa before the Pope's letters reached him is unclear. But by then he was supporting the orthodox position and was ready to condemn the Three

xxvi   Introduction

Chapters, following the lead of the inspiring and persuasive new Pope, Gregory the Great. In his final years, Victor became a very senior bishop, in fact the Primate of Numidia.[6]

If he was 33 when appointed bishop in 564 (Gregory became bishop of Agrigento when aged 31), this Victor would be nearly seventy in 601, certainly not an unusual age for bishops at that time, when they remained in their Sees until death, even when very sick in body or even in mind, and Saint Augustine helped in the defense of Hippo against the Vandal attacks when he was seventy six years old (1.3). Otherwise, Victor's successor would have to be another Victor, Primate of Numidia, known only in the Pope's letters, which again seems singularly unlikely. Victor's *Chronicon* runs down to 566, although he must have written and published it well after his release from the monastery. The terminus of his history at the death of Justinian in 566 may well suggest a return then to full duties, with his ever wider pastoral care, rather than an approaching death as has been commonly believed hitherto, and he welcomed a far less oppressive rule under Justin II. The *Chronicon* certainly does not break off in mid-stream, as scholars have argued, but is neatly rounded off with the death of the great Justinian and young Justin's accession, and a final count of the years between Adam, Jesus and Justinian.

Victor, bishop of Vita, made use of a great many biblical quotations in his history of the Vandals, especially from the *Psalms* (15 times) and for his own lamentation in chapter 19, ten being taken from *Lamentations*.[7] Victor clearly took part in the Catholic opposition to the cruel and unending attack on his fellow priests and their churches by the tyrannical Kings Geiseric and Huneric, and for most of the dramatic scenes he was clearly an eyewitness. He also did all he could to collect information from the many clergy and laity whose sufferings and extraordinary courage were later described by him in his history of the Vandals. Like a reporter or a photographer in a modern war, he must have faced many crises himself, risking his own life while investigating the deaths and exiles of so many of his friends. He was strictly orthodox himself, as is revealed by

---

[6] He is called 'Primate among you' in *Letter* 12.8, to Columbus, Bishop of Numidia.

[7] *Psalms* (in the Vulgate): 16, 17, 34, 37, 38, 41, 48, 58, 68 (2), 74, 77 twice 105 and 143. *Lamentations*: 1.2, 1.3, 1.4, 1.6, 1.10, 1,11, 1.12, 1.17, 1.19, 2.3, 2.16, 4.1, 4.5. See note 74 on his use of the Greek Septuagint, the Vulgate and his own adaptation.

Arians and Vandals of the 4th-6th Centuries

xxvii

his eulogies of Catholic martyrs, and by his description of the Catholic faith in chapter three.

With this chronological history I have also included my English translation of the tract *De Fide Orthodoxa contra Arianos* ('On the Orthodox Faith, against the Arians') composed by Saint Ambrose, a very interesting document when compared with the not much later work by Victor, bishop of Vita, and I have added at the very end my version of Athanasius' *Expositio Fidei* (Ἔκθεσις Πιστέως). By including this work of Athanasius, or pseudo-Athanasius, I have provided readers with the three main defenses of the Catholic faith over two hundred years, the first against a contemporary Arius, the second against his later followers, and the third against the even more destructive Arian Vandals.[8]

A full comparison between these three defenses of the Catholic faith during this period of about three hundred years would be of great interest, but would better suit a theologian's research. From the point of view of their quotations, Eugenius' *De Fide* (18 pp) has the following sources, with those from Ambrose's *De Fide* (22 pp) in brackets: *Matthew* 8 [0], *Luke* 0 [1], *John* 31[21], *Acts* 6 [1], *Romans* 0[1], *I Corinthians* 6[10], *II Corinthians* 5[0], *Galatians* 1[0], *Ephesians* 0 [1], *Colossians* 0[3], *I Timothy* 1[0], *II Timothy* 2[0], *Hebrews* 2[0], *I Peter* 1[0], *I John* 5[0] (68[38] Greek Scriptures), *Genesis* 4[3], *Exodus* 2[7], *Numbers* 1[1], *I Kings* 1[0], *Job* 1[0], *Psalms* 14[6], *Proverbs* 0[1], *Wisdom* 1[3], *Sirach* 0[1], *Isaiah* 3[4], *Jeremiah* 4[2], *Ezekiel* 1[0], *Daniel* 1[0], *Joel* 0[1] (33[29] Hebrew Scriptures). Total: 101[67]. The absence of *Mark* and *Luke* is noteworthy, as is the extensive use of *John*, and, as usual, of the *Psalms*. Saint Ambrose uses the Hebrew Scriptures more, expanding predictions of the Trinity, whereas abstract material in Victor makes more use of the two *Corinthians, Matthew* and *I John*. Athanasius' text is short compared with the other two (5 pp long), but in it he makes use of the Greek Scriptures (13 quotes) more than the Hebrew ones (5 quotes), most

---

[8] For the Latin of Victor's history, see Migne: *Patrol. C. C.* Vol. 17, 1058, *De Viris illustribus* 77. The founder of the Arians' heretical sect, Arius, lived c.250 – c.336, and after studying in Antioch was ordained in Alexandria, by its Bishop Alexander, who later excommunicated him for teaching the subordinate position of Christ. Condemned at the Council of Nicaea (325), but forgiven and recalled, he died in a street in Constantinople. Orthodoxy prevailed, except for the Teutonic tribes, which used Ulphilas' Gothic bible and liturgy, heretical versions to Victor of Vita. See the preface above for the wide and long-term impact of Arianism.

xxviii   Introduction

from the gospel of *John* (5), *Proverbs* (3), *I Corinthians* (2), *Colossians* (2) and *Jeremiah* (2), with one from *Luke, Acts, Hebrews* and *I John*.

The third Victor was the bishop of Cartenna, and he lived from 428-477 in North Africa, where he wrote a quite lengthy book of thirty-three chapters (pp. 1060-1094 in Migne) on 'Penitence' (*De Poenitentia: Liber Unus*). See below for his interesting and often quite original work. Besides Saint Ambrose's defense of the faith mentioned above, I shall finally provide, as stated, a translation of the Greek Defense of the Faith ("Εκθεσις Πίστεως) credited to Athanasius, archbishop of Alexandria (328-373), who spent most of his life (even when in exile) attacking the heretical bishop, Arius, and his misguided followers, and thwarting the vigorous encroachments by the dominant Melitians.[9] I have also included the *Notitia*, possibly based on interviews and note-taking by Victor of Vita himself. The names still need some work on them, for modern equivalents in particular, but at least they are available here, and are relevant to Victor's text.

---

[9] Most modern scholars argue against Athanasius having been the author, despite a very similar style, language and approach. For the Saint's output on the first of these schisms, see his *Orationes contra Arianos* (356) and *Historia Arianorum ad Monachos* (358). For an interesting study of Athanasius' relationship with heretics and four emperors, see Henric Nordberg's 'Athanasius and the Emperor.' I made use of Nordberg's Greek text as the basis for my version of the 'Defence' by pseudo-Athanasius. See the preface to this Greek defence in (E) below and the Preface to this book.

A. VICTOR OF VITA

Preface to his *Historia Persecutionis Africae*

The bishop of Vita's account of the Vandals' persecution of the Catholics in North Africa has been written with great skill and great descriptive ability, and includes plenty of drama, variety and pathos. Clearly there are many exaggerations, and most of the miracles that end the grisly tortures and killings of the Catholics suggest a *Deus ex machina*. Victor was a participant in the main events and admits that he had talks then and afterwards with many of those who survived the onslaught. He seems to have composed his account during or fairly soon after the events described, and some of the martyrdoms are recorded elsewhere, as with the burning of Laetus. But it was inevitable that plenty of Catholic propaganda would be used in the blackening of almost all the Vandals and of their bloodthirsty Arian priests.

A translation of the third book, that sets out to defend the Catholic faith, has been included, although its author is not certain. But I shall show that Victor of Vita has the strongest claim. Certainly in its literary style and vocabulary, it suggests the same author as in the historical account that incorporates it.

This document (book 3a) is said to have been written by the bishops for the king's synod, some time beforehand, and then presented by the archbishop of Carthage, the saintly Eugenius, as Bishop Victor himself pointed out: *ante nostri praevidentes, libellum de fide conscripserant* ('our bishops had foreseen this beforehand and had written a pamphlet on faith'). It may possibly have been the work of the ten bishops chosen to represent the rest, but they had little chance to do so before the finale. More probably the earlier author was a single person, the erudite bishop of Vita, who describes himself as an observer. With his many other duties, it is unlikely that the pious Archbishop Eugenius could have written it before the proceedings. But if the first draft did by any chance derive from the ten bishops or from the archbishop or from the mass of bishops, the bishop of Vita certainly expanded and revised it for publication. This statement of faith deserves to be included now, anyway, as an interesting description of the Catholic faith at a very important time of subjugation and schism in the fifth and sixth centuries. It should be noted also that at the beginning of book 4, the pamphlet is referred to as *noster libellus* ('our booklet') and this certainly suggests Victor, who mainly used the first person plural in referring to himself. If the selected ten bishops or the archbishop himself had written it, a third person plural or singular would have appeared (with *episcoporum,* or *Eugenii*). Biblical quotations abound in the statement, to show that the Catholic faith is fully endorsed by both the prophets and the evangelists. In it most quotations come from *John, Matthew* and the *first* and *second Corinthians,* and from the *Psalms* and *Genesis*. In the rest of the history, there are far fewer quotations, but they too mostly come from *Matthew, John* and the *Psalms* (and in his lament over Africa's fate, many come from *Lamentations*). In both areas, the author seems to work from memory, and often adapts the original to suit his argument. In both sections the Latin is very similar in its structure and vocabulary. This suggests that Bishop Victor certainly played a major part in its preparation, if not the sole part.

At the end of this statement, four bishops, two from Numidia (Januarius and Villaticus) and two from Byzacena (both called Boniface) are given the unenviable task of presenting it. These four are not said to have composed it, but were used as representatives of all the Catholic bishops in their presentation of this defense of their orthodox faith to the king.

A HISTORY OF THE PERSECUTION OF THE PROVINCE OF AFRICA IN THE TIMES OF GEISERIC AND HUNERIC, THE KINGS OF THE VANDALS, WRITTEN BY THE HOLY BISHOP VICTOR, WHOSE NATIVE PLACE WAS VITA

Prologue[1]

1. In times past the ancients, due to their strong desire for wisdom, did not desist at all from examining and carefully enquiring into what or what sort of things might perhaps have happened beneficially or otherwise in the provinces, places or regions. As they sharpened the pen of their intelligence over these matters and within them, to the ignorant they would offer baskets full of history with the perfumed flowers of their teaching, gratuitously, and ensured that what had been done somewhere should in no way remain totally hidden. But being puffed up by the arrogance of worldly love, those men longed for the glory of their pride to be made known with high praise far and wide.

2. By contrast, as the venerability of your intellect inquires into this, you order me[2] to compose a history with a similar passion, indeed, but with a different sort of love. The ancients wrote so as to be praised in this world, I myself wrote, so that you may appear glorious in the world to come, and may say: 'My soul shall make her boast in the Lord; let the humble hear

---

[1] This typical prologue was rightly considered authentic by *CVV* p. 19 and *M* p. 1.
[2] No object is given for the transitive *jubens*, modestly, and it must be *me*, and *ipse*, in contrast to *illi*, is first person, for as is revealed clearly in section 4, Victor is dedicating his history to the venerable Eugenius, Archbishop of Carthage. *M*'s version suggests here that Eugenius is writing the history. But he rightly accepts the originality of this revealing prologue.

4   Victor of Vita, Prologue

thereof and be glad.'[3] You will be able to do what you want, you say, because you have received from Heaven 'every good gift and every perfect gift,'[4] having been taught by such a great bishop, the blessed Diadochus,[5] who deserves to be extolled with every sort of praise, whose very many written records of Catholic dogma still survive, like glowing stars. And it is enough for you that you are equal to your teacher in learning, because 'it is enough for the disciple that he be as his master.'[6]

3. I see another Timothy, 'brought up from the cradle of his infancy in the Holy Writ,'[7] and also a Luke, among the others sublime and alert, a doctor by profession and a disciple of the Apostle Paul, the teacher of nations.[8]

4. For I shall submit my neck obediently to the control of the one who orders, and I shall try to show gradually and briefly what happened in the regions of Africa, as the Arians raged without control. And like a country worker, I shall extract gold from hidden caves, until my arms are worn out, but I shall not hesitate to hand over what still appears unrefined and blended, for the skilled craftsman to assay in the fire, able to produce mint gold coins.[9]

---

[3] *Psalms* 34.2 (33.3).

[4] *James* 1.17.

[5] Diadochus, bishop of Photice (in N.W. Greece) wrote on *Spiritual Perfection* (in 100 chapters, that still survive). *M* rightly sees his pupil, Eugenius, as the prologue's probable addressee, an easterner brought to Carthage together with Zeno's legate (Bk 2, 2-3). For his provenance, see *CVV* pp 21f and *M* p. 2.

[6] *Matthew* 10.25. *M* wrongly applies the quote to the main sentence.

[7] *II Timothy* 3.15.

[8] *M* omits Paul's epithet (*gentium doctoris*).

[9] Victor's gold mining imagery is most effective, with Eugenius as the craftsman.

BOOK ONE

Chapter 1: Vandals' Entry into Africa

It is clear that this is now the sixtieth year (487) since that cruel and savage people of the Vandal race reached the boundaries of unfortunate Africa. They crossed over the straits of the sea with an easy passage,[1] where between Spain and Africa this vast and spacious ocean compresses itself into a narrow strait, twelve miles across.

And so the whole mass crossed over, and to create a terrifying report of his race, its cunning leader, Geiseric, decided that the entire multitude should be counted at once, including anyone born from the womb into the light right up to that time. They included old men, young men, children, slaves and masters, eighty thousand in number. When news of this was published, the ignorant accepted that this was the number of armed men, right up to today, although now their number is small and weak.

And so, finding the province peaceful and quiet,[2] their unholy troops attacked the beautiful pastures flowering all over the land,[3] wherever they turned, devastating and stripping the land of its people and exterminating

---

[1] May 429. The strait of Gibraltar is about 10 miles across at its closest, so Victor came nearer than most. King Geiseric led them (either *dux* or *rex* was possible - Victor was well aware of his rank; *contra*, see *M* n.24, p. xvii). Repeated trips by fishing boats could have transported the 80,000 and their gear as they reached the south coast of Spain. See *CA* pp 215-7; he rightly explains it as a migration, camp followers included, just as Victor describes it.

[2] J. D. Fage (ed) *Cambridge History of Africa* vol 2, p. 480 argues fancifully that nomadic tribesman were causing havoc there at that time. J. D. Randers-Pehrson *Barbarians and Romans* (Croom Helm, 1983) pp 152-3 rejects theories that the Vikings were invited to help Count Boniface against Placidia, or to help Sigisvult against the Count, rightly stating that when Geiseric became sole king, he decided to show his mettle by invading what was clearly a poorly defended North Africa. For the crossing, he recalls the British army saved from Dunkirk in 1940 (p. 153).

[3] Reading *impetebant* ('they attacked') in Migne. Halm's *impendebant* adopted by *M* (p. xix) could only mean 'threatened,' and they went far beyond threats.

6 Book One

them all with fire and murders. Nor did they spare the fruit-bearing orchards at all, in case those hidden by mountain caves or steep cliffs or secluded places might feed themselves on those fruits after they had passed by. Thus, as they raged like that again so cruelly, no place remained immune from their contagion.[4]

They raged so much more wickedly against churches and saints' basilicas, especially, and cemeteries and monasteries, that they burnt down the houses of prayer with larger fires than they used against cities, as well as all the towns.[5] When they had happened to find the doors of a sacred courtyard closed, blows from their hatchets competed with each other to force an entry, so that it could rightly be said then: 'They cut down its doors with hatchets, and cast down a thicket of trees with hatchet and axe. They burnt your sanctuary to the ground; they defiled the tabernacle of your name.'[6]

Chapter 2: Vandal Savagery

How many famous bishops and noble priests were put to death then by the Vandals, with different types of sufferings, forcing them to hand over any gold or silver of their own or of the Church! And until they might more easily extract what riches there were, with the pressure of torture, they put pressure on those offering them, again with cruel tortures, affirming that just some part of their riches had been offered, not the whole lot. And the more they handed over, the more the Vandals believed that they had something extra. In the case of others, they forced open their mouths with levers made of stakes, and pushed stinking mud down their throats to make them confess about their money. Others the Vandals tortured by twisting cords around their foreheads and shins, until they cracked.[7] They mercilessly offered seawater for most, for others vinegar, the dregs of olive oil or fish-sauce, and many other cruel drinks, placed on their

---

[4] It must have taken them three months to travel the 700 kms to Carthage, living off the land (for fruit, corn and vegetables) as they wound their way there (their 'contagion'). See Randers-Pehrson p. 153.

[5] Possidius argued that only three churches survived intact, in Carthage, Hippo and Cirta. (*Vita Augustini* 30). See *M* p. 4 n. 4. Exaggeration is more likely.

[6] The quote is very close to *Psalms* 75(4). 5-7, but the text has *dejecerunt eam* and *in terra; polluerunt*, for the Vulgate's *exciderunt* and *in terra polluerunt.*

[7] The *nervis remugientibus* suggest a cracking sound (of both cords and bones), lit. 're-echoing.' The participle is onomatopoeic (a creaking noise).

mouths as if from water-bottles.[8] Neither the weaker sex, nor consideration of nobility, nor priestly reverence softened their cruel hearts. In fact, on the contrary, where they saw dignified men of honour, their passionate anger was heightened. Nor can I describe on how many priests, how many high officials they loaded enormous weights, as if they were camels or other beasts of burden. And they used iron goads to force them to walk, and some of them lost their lives miserably beneath their burdens.[9]

The maturity of old age and distinguished grayness, that whitens the hair on men's heads like bright wool, granted them no pity from their visitors. But in their barbaric fury they even tore babies from their mothers' breasts and dashed the innocent infants on the ground. Others held the babies' feet wide apart, and split them from their quite natural orifices right up to their heads at the top. Then perhaps captive Zion sang: 'Mine enemy said he would burn my boundaries, and slay my youth, and dash my little children on the ground.'[10]

Chapter 3: Demolition of Buildings

In some buildings consisting of great temples or grand houses, where the employment of fire had been less effective,[11] after totally removing their roofs, they leveled their beautiful walls to the ground, so that that ancient beauty of the cities did not now remain at all as it had been. But there were a great many towns also that were occupied by few or no inhabitants. For even if some towns survive today, they are frequently desolate, just as in Carthage, where due to the Vandals' hatred, they totally destroyed the theatres, the temple of Memory and the road of

---

[8] Not the 'while full wineskins were placed' in *M*; rather, *quasi* 'as if' from *utribus imbutis* 'from damp skins' or 'water-bottles,' with the fresh water awaited in vain by an increasingly thirsty mouth.

[9] The *fasces* were in early times the axe and rods symbolizing a magistrate's power of life and death, but they were also used simply as 'burdens.'

[10] Adapted very freely from *II Kings* 8. 12. Our text reads: *Dixit inimicus incendere fines meos, interficere infantes meos, et parvulos meos se elisurum ad terram*, for the Vulgate's *Ille dixit Ō civitates eorum munitas igne succendes, et juvenes eorum interficies gladio, et parvulos eorum elides*. There will be many more quotations like this, but most minor variations in the Latin will be omitted.

[11] Besides leaving out *ministerium* ('employment'), *M* rightly translates *valuerat* ('had been of less service'), but reads the perfect subj. *valuerit*, not wanted here.

8   Book One

Caelestis.[12] And to say what needs to be said, with tyrannical license they subjected to their own religion the church of the Ancestors,[13] where the bodies of the holy martyrs Perpetua and Felicitas were buried, and the Church of Celerina and of the Scillitani, and others which they had not destroyed. But when some fortresses were seen that could not be stormed by the hostility of their barbaric fury, then as a countless throng congregated in a circle around the fortress, with their deadly swords they butchered them, so that when the corpses had rotted, with the stench of the putrefying bodies they could kill those they could not reach, due to the defensive walls that protected them. Who will be able to describe how great and how numerous the priests were who were tortured at that time by them? For then the venerable bishop of our city also, Papinian, was scorched all over his body by burning plates of iron,[14] and similarly Mansuetus, bishop of Urusi,[15] was also burnt to death at the Porta Fornitana.[16] At that time, the city of Hippo Regius was also under siege. It was governed by its bishop, Saint Augustine, the writer of many books, and so worthy of every praise. But then that river of eloquence, which ran plentifully through all the Church's plains, was dried up by fear itself,[17] and his sweet charm, provided so pleasantly, changed to bitter wormwood, as the saying of David aptly observed: 'While the wicked were before me, I was dumb and humiliated, and held my peace from good.'[18] Up to that time he had already finished two hundred and thirty two books, plus innumerable letters, his exposition on the entire Psalter and Gospels,

---

[12] *M* omits *odii causa* ('due to their hatred'), but rightly draws attention to over literal interpretations, and to the temple of Caelestis, destroyed before the Vandals' arrival. Augustine attacked these two unholy temples in *De Civ. Dei* 2.26. See *CVV* pp 42-4. For other omissions, see 1.8 *virtutes*, 2.5 *crudeli*, 2.18 *et persecutionem*, 3.6 two sentences, 3.17 quote from *Psalms*, 4.1 *confortavit*, 4.2 *ali* and *penitus* and 5.10 *profuturum*.

[13] *M* rightly adopts the *maiorum* in Colb., rather than *maiorem* in Migne. For this church, see Frend 'The early Christian Church in Carthage' (1977), pp 25-6.

[14] *M* suggests that Pampinian was then bishop of Vita. Possible, as he was an early victim, but in the *Notitia Provinciarum* Victor is Vita's bishop, and no Bishop Pampinian is mentioned. He was probably a bishop in Carthage, his adopted city.

[15] Mod. Henchir Sougga. Hippo Regius became Hippone and is now Annaba.

[16] Modern Henchir d'Aïn-Fourna. See *CVV* p. 46.

[17] *M* accepts Pitkäranta's *meatu* ('in mid course'), but it was hardly 'mid course' for the very elderly Augustine, and the dramatic *metu* better suits 'wormwood.'

[18] *Psalms* 39.1-2(38.2-3).

Arians and Vandals of the 4th-6th Centuries 9

and popular sermons that the Greeks call 'homilies.' To work out their number is quite impossible.[19]

Chapter 4: Destruction of Carthage

Need I say more? After these atrocious and impious acts of madness, Geiseric took over and entered the very great city of Carthage itself, and reduced to a state of slavery that city's ancient, inborn and noble freedom. For his captives included a very large number of the city's senators. And then he published a decree that whatever each one of them had of gold, silver, jewels and precious apparel, should be brought to him. And so in such a short time, using such diligence, this robber purloined the wealth of their ancestors and parents.[20]

He disposed also of each single province, reserving for himself Byzacena, Abaritana and Gaetulia, and part of Numidia. However, for his army's use, he divided up with a bond of inheritance the Zeugitana and proconsular province. Valentinian, who was still Emperor, was defending the remaining provinces, although they were already devastated. After his

---

[19] The text includes an *Epitaphium S. Augustini* in his honour, probably by Victor:
  Hic posuit cineres genetrix castissima prolis,
  A most chaste mother placed here her son's
  Augustine, tui altera lux meriti.
  ashes, another deserved light,Augustine..
  Qui servans pacis caelestia iurasacerdos,
  You serve the divine laws of peace as priest
  commissos populos moribus instituis.
  teaching the people in your care morality.
  Gratia vos manet, gestorum laude coronat.
  Grace awaits you, crowns you with praise for
  Virtutum mater felicior subolis.
  your acts, mother blessed by a child's virtues.
As bishop of Hippo Regius, from 396-430, Augustine played an important part in the defense of his city, under Duke Boniface, although he was in his mid 70s, and he died during the Vandals' siege. In fact he wrote as many as 59 books as dialogues and 57 on biblical subjects, and about 220 letters. His influence on the Church cannot be measured, although a great many works have tried to do so. Soon afterwards Pope Gregory showed in his writings how this brilliant African theologian had influenced him, both in his language and biblical interpretations.
[20] For damning details of the Vandals' cruelty, see the *Vita Augustini* by Possidius of Calama. See C. Courtois *Les Vandales et l'Afrique* (Aalen, 1964[2]) (*CA*), p. 165.

10   Book One

death,[21] Geiseric captured the whole periphery of Africa, and he also appropriated for himself, with his customary arrogance, the greatest of the islands, Sardinia, Sicily, Corsica, Ebusa,[22] Majorca, Minorca, and many of the others. And one of those, namely Sicily, he later granted to Odovacer, king of Italy,[23] by the right of tribute; through which Odovacer paid tribute to Geiseric as its owner, on fixed occasions, while reserving some part of the island for himself

Furthermore, Geiseric did not hesitate at all in ordering his Vandals to force the bishops and noble laymen to flee from their churches and mansions totally naked. But if, when the choice was given them, they were too slow in leaving, they would remain as their slaves perpetually. And this occurred in very many cases, for we know that many bishops and laymen, men famous and highly honoured, were slaves of the Vandals.

Chapter 5: Expulsion of Clergy

Then indeed the king ordered that the bishop of the aforesaid city, namely Carthage, a man well known to God and mortals, called Quodvultdeus, and a very great crowd of clergy, be placed on board some broken-down ships and be expelled, naked and despoiled. But God, with the mercy of his goodness, allowed them to reach the city of Naples in Campania after a favorable voyage.

As for the senators and highly honoured men, at first he contrived a cruel exile for the majority of them, and afterwards expelled them to lands across the ocean.[24] For[25] with the bishop expelled, as we have described above, together with his venerable clergy, Geiseric at once subjected the church called Restituta to his own religion, in which there had always been bishops, and he removed every church inside the walls of that city, including their riches. But he also occupied whatever churches he wanted outside the walls, especially the two splendid and spacious ones of the

---

[21] Valentinian III was killed in Rome on March 16th, 455.

[22] Ebusa, situated next to Majorca, the modern Ibiza. Some early editors omitted it, but it appears at the end of the *Notitia* with Opilio as its bishop.

[23] Odovacer ruled Italy (including Sicily) from 476, until the Ostrogothic King Theoderic killed him in 493.

[24] For these exiles, see *CA* pp 281-3, and *M* n. 17, p. 8.

[25] The connective *namque* was omitted. Likewise *enim, autem, forte* and *etiam* repeatedly, although often needed (but not always) in the English.

Arians and Vandals of the 4th-6th Centuries   11

holy martyr Cyprian,[26] one where he had shed his blood, the other where his body was buried, a place called Mappalia ('The Sheep-cotes'). But who could bear this and remember without tears when he ordered the bodies of our dead to be taken for burial in silence, without the solemnity of hymns? He added further that the few clergy who remained were to be driven into exile also, as a punishment.

And while these things were taking place, the high priests and distinguished men who had survived in the above-mentioned provinces, divided up by the Vandals, decided to approach the king to implore his favor. And when he had came out as usual on the shore of Maxula,[27] which is commonly called Ligula ('the tongue'), these men who had already lost their churches and wealth, had the audacity to confront Geiseric. They begged him that, although the Vandals were now ruling, they at least be given a chance to live there, so as to console the people of God. Geiseric is said to have replied through a go-between with a furious look: 'I have decided not to send away anyone with your reputation and birth, and yet you dare to make such demands!'
He even wanted to drown them in the nearby sea at that instant, and would have, if his men had not asked him for a long time not to do so. And so they returned worn out by grief and misery, and began to celebrate the holy mysteries as best they could, and wherever they could, as their churches had been removed. But thereafter, as his reign was enriched with wealth, his arrogance also began to increase all the more.

Chapter 6: Faith of Sebastian[28]

I shall now describe a deed that was done at the same time. There was a certain Count called Sebastian, sharp in counsel and strenuous in war, and son-in-law of that famous Count Boniface. And Geiseric, just as he considered his advice to be necessary, even so was afraid of his presence, and wanted to get rid of him, so he sought an excuse for his death over a

---

[26] This reference to Saint Cyprian is of interest. He lived from c. 200 to 258, and like Saint Augustine, he started as a pagan rhetorician, but he finally converted to Christianity in about 246, becoming bishop of Carthage in 248. After escaping from Decius' persecution, he was martyred under Valerian's. These two brilliant scholars and theologians were the brightest lights in the North African sky, and among the brightest throughout the civilized world. The removal of all churches is an exaggeration. See *M*, pp 8-9, notes 17, 18 and 19.
[27] Modern Radès. See *CVV*, p 46.
[28] For Sebastian's career, see *PLRE* 2, p. 984. See also *M* n. 22, p. 10.

12   Book One

religious matter. The king thought that it would suit Sebastian, so with his own bishops and courtiers present he said: 'Sebastian, I know that you have sworn faithfully to be loyal to us, and your labors and vigilance demonstrate the truth of that oath. But so that your friendship should always remain linked to us with a close union, we have decided in the presence of our own priests, that you become an upholder of that religion which both we and our people venerate.'

Sebastian, finding an answer both admirable and necessary for many people, replied to the king cleverly in the circumstances:

'I ask for this, my lord and king, that a very pure loaf made of fine white flour be brought before me now.'[29]

Since Geiseric had no idea of Sebastian's coming victory, he ordered the loaf to be brought at once. And so, as Sebastian held the perfect loaf, he spoke as follows:

'For this loaf to reach such beautiful whiteness as to be considered appropriate for the royal table, the course bran was sifted, sprinkled from a pile of fine white flour and passed through water and fire, and for that reason it is thought fair in its appearance and pleasant to eat. In the same way I also was ground in the mill of my Catholic mother[30] and purged by the sieve of examination, like pure, fine white flour, and moistened with the water of baptism, and baked by the fire of the Holy Spirit. And as this bread arises from the oven, even so I also have arisen through the offices of the Holy Sacraments, purified by the font, with God as its creator. But may my proposal be carried out, if you agree. Have that loaf broken into pieces and soaked in water, and then molded again and placed in the oven. If it comes out better, I shall do what you suggest.'

When Geiseric had heard this proposition, with all those present, he was so confused that he was totally unable to find a solution. For that reason

---

[29] The *similagineus* ('of fine white flour'), found in other editions, seems somewhat preferable to the *similaceus* in Migne, only used here. Only the wealthy could afford such bread, the rest having gritty brown or black loaves that soon wore down the teeth. See P. V. Glob *The Bog People* (London, 1969), pp 42 and 61.

[30] Mother 'Church' of course. The stress here is on orthodox baptism. The death of Sebastian was in 450.

Arians and Vandals of the 4th-6th Centuries 13

he murdered the warlike man afterwards, using a different sort of argument.[31]

Chapter 7: Heavy Persecution

And let us return from where we digressed. He terrified us with deadly orders, so that in the midst of the Vandals our people could scarcely breathe, and no allowance was ever made for those sadly asking for prayers or the sacrifice of Mass, so that the prediction of the prophet was clearly brought to pass:

> 'We have in our day no prince, no prophet, nor a leader, nor a place to sacrifice to your name,'[32] since every day malicious prosecutions were plentiful, even for those priests who were active in the regions that paid tribute to the king's palace. And if perchance someone, as is the custom, while warning the people of God, should have mentioned the name of Pharaoh or Nebuchadnezzar or Holofernes, or someone similar, he would be charged with having said such things against the person of the king, and he would be forced into exile at once.[33]

This sort of persecution was being carried out, here quite openly, elsewhere secretly, so that such deceits might destroy the very name of the pious. For that reason we know very many priests who were exiled then, like Urban, the bishop of Girba, Crescens, the metropolitan of the city of Aquitana and the superior of one hundred and twenty suffragan bishops, Habetdeus of Teudalis, Eustratius of Sufes. and two bishops from

---

[31] The Latin is confused, but *alio* seems preferable to *alius* in the text. It was in fact that King who finally achieved his malevolent aim. I suggest that we read: *Quare alio genere argumenti* ('Therefore, with another kind of argument'). It is very odd otherwise: 'Another man killed him ... with the argument of his birth.' The *alio* is accepted by *M* ('on some other grounds').

[32] Quite freely adapted from *Daniel* 3.38. The text has *in hoc tempore princeps aut propheta vel dux neque locus ad sacrificandum nomini tuo* for the Vulgate's *tempore hoc ... et dux et propheta neque holocaustum, neque sacrificium ... neque locus primitiarum coram te.* It seems that Victor knew his Bible off by heart. Some of his quotes are altered to suit his argument, but most have minor changes. There are no quotes at all from the Bible in the *Chronicon*.

[33] Holofernes was an Assyrian general, who was enlisted by King Nebuchadnezzar to subdue Judaea, and the Pharaoh was synonymous with an autocratic King. For their part in sermons, see *CA* p. 286 and *M* n. 25, p. 11.

14 Book One

Tripolitania, Vicis bishop of Sabratha and Cresconius, bishop of Oea,[34] and Felix, the bishop of the city of Hadrumetum, for the reason that he had brought a monk called John from across the sea. There were many others also, but it would take me too long to name them. But when death came upon them while they were in exile, other bishops were not allowed to be consecrated in their cities. But amid all this, the people of God remained steadfast in their belief, and like a swarm of bees building its wax hive, they were strengthened as they grew with honeyed tendrils of faith, to fulfill that maxim: 'The more they afflicted them, the more they multiplied and grew too strong.'[35]

Chapter 8: Virtues of Deogratias

But after this, it happened that, at the request of the Emperor Valentinian, after a long silence of desolation, a bishop was consecrated for the church of Carthage, called Deogratias.[36] If anyone should try to set down in detail all the virtuous acts[37] of that man that the Lord did through him, words would begin to fail him before he could start to describe them. And so, when he had been made bishop, it came about that, thanks to our sins, Geiseric captured that once most noble and most famous city, Rome, in the fifteenth year of his reign, and at the same time he took away from there the riches of many kings together with its people.[38] And when this multitude of captives reached the shore of Africa, the Vandals and Moors divided up the very large number of people, as is customary with barbarians, separating husbands from their wives and children from their parents.

---

[34] Sabratha and Oea (Sabrata Vulpia, and Tripoli) were two notable towns at that time, and appear in the *Notitia*. The notes found in Migne's edition show how they lay under the *Vices Sabratenum* in the Latin text. Leo is named as the bishop of Sabratha in the *Notitia*. Sufes is now Sbiba. See *CVV*, p. 47.

[35] The quote was adapted from *Exodus* 1.12 with *invalescebant nimis* for the Vulgate's *crescebant*. Lorichius' emendation *claviculis* ('tendrils') seems a distinct improvement on the commonplace *calculis* ('stones') in the text.

[36] He was consecrated in the Basilica of Faustus on October 24th, 454, his festival being on March 22nd. See below where it houses the Romans rescued by the archbishop, and in 2.17, Eugenius celebrates Epiphany therein. It had replaced the old cathedral, Restituta, taken over by Arians. See *CVV*, p. 44; *M* n. 30, p. 13.

[37] The *virtutes* were omitted by *M*.

[38] See Victor of Tonnena ch. 15 for the sack of Rome in 455, and *M* n. 28, p. 12.

Arians and Vandals of the 4th-6th Centuries 15

At once that man Deogratias, full of God and dear to him, was quick to sell off all the golden and silver vessels of Mass and to buy their freedom from barbaric captivity, so that the marriage bonds should remain and children should be returned to their parents. And because there were not any places big enough to hold such a large multitude, he allotted two well-known and spacious churches, of Faustus and of Novae, equipped with beds and bundles of straw, deciding how much each should receive each day according to what was deserved. Because the unaccustomed voyage and the cruelty of their captivity had afflicted most of them, no small number of them were ill, and that blessed bishop, like a pious nurse, every now and then went around them as their doctor.[39] Food followed, so that, in his presence, each of them should be given what was needed, once their pulse had been checked. Not even in the hours of night did he have a break from this work of mercy, but he went on hurrying from bed to bed, asking how each person was feeling. For he had dedicated himself so totally to this hard work that he spared neither his weary limbs nor his already withered old age.[40]

As a result, the Arians were inflamed with envy, and quite often sought to kill him all the more, with all the tricks they could.[41] I believe that our foreseeing Lord wished to liberate his sparrow quickly from the hawks' claws. The Roman captives lamented his departure, especially as they then thought that they would be more likely to be handed over to the hands of the barbarians, once he had reached Heaven. But he exercised his priesthood for three years. The people were so eager with love and desire for him that they might have snatched the limbs from his worthy body, if he had not been buried on good advice without the multitude's knowledge, while they were busy with customary prayer.[42]

---

[39] Reading *vice medici* ('in the manner of a doctor') rather than the *medicis* ('with doctors') in the text (and in *M* p. 13). He was nursing them and trying to cure their illnesses, without any likelihood of a team of doctors being supplied.

[40] For *cariosa senectus* ('withered' old age, not 'decayed' in *M*) see Ovid *Amores* 1.12.29.

[41] The comparative *saepius* has the sense of 'more' or 'quite often', and 'many' misses the *quam plurimis* ('as many as possible'). Idiomatic usages like these are regularly missed by *M*, like *quin etiam* ('what's more'), *utique* ('anyway'), *quod si* ('but if'), *quin immo* ('nay rather'), *etiam tunc* ('even then'), *tanquam* ('as if') and *adhuc* ('thus far').

[42] Deogratias died before the end of 457. *M* omits the 'customary prayer' during his burial.

16 Book One

Chapter 9: Thomas the Confessor

One should not remain silent forever about the wicked deeds done by heretics, nor will it be possible for one to feel ashamed of what contributes to the praise of the sufferer. Even so, there was a priest, ordained long ago, called Thomas, and he was quite often handicapped by their heathen traps, but a time came when they flogged the venerable old man over his shoulders in public view.[43] But he counted that not as a disgrace, but as payment for his glory, and he rejoiced in the Lord.

Wherefore, after the death of this bishop of Carthage, it came about that Geiseric banned any new bishops from being consecrated for the province of Zeugitana and for the Proconsular province. Their number was one hundred and sixty four, but they gradually died away, and now, if they are in fact alive, there seem to be just three, Vincent of Zigga, Paul of Sinnari, truly a Paul in merit and name, and the third, Quintianus, who is now fleeing from persecution and is living in Edessa, a city of Macedonia, as a foreigner.

Chapter 10: Maxima, other Martyrs and Confessors

But it is clear that there were a great many martyrs even then, but of confessors there was a far greater number, and I shall try to tell the stories of some of them. There were at that time slaves of a certain Vandal, and this Vandal was one of those whom they call 'company commanders'.[44] The slaves were Martinian and Saturian, and their two brothers. There was also a fellow slave girl, a splendid nun called Maxima, beautiful in both her body and her heart.[45] But he counted that not as disgraceful, but as a payment for his glory, and he rejoiced in the Lord. And because Martinian was an armourer and seemed quite acceptable to his master, and Maxima was governing the whole household, the Vandal believed that to make the above-mentioned servants more faithful to him, he should join Martinian with Maxima in marriage. Martinian, according to the custom

---

[43] The editors who read *publica,* agreeing with *facie,* may be right, but it is odd Latin, and I prefer *publici* ('in public view'). By itself, as in the text, *facie* is meaningless. The Greek origin for the word for 'shoulders' is post-classical (the word *catomus* was used by a scholiast on Juvenal *Satires* 2.142).

[44] Lit. 'the commanders of a thousand troops.'

[45] The Latin *Christi ancilla* ('handmaiden of Christ') was usual for a 'nun'. Likewise 'convent' or 'nunnery' is the normal translation for *monasterium puellarum.*

Arians and Vandals of the 4th-6th Centuries

of young men of his day, was keen on the marriage, but Maxima, who was already consecrated to God, was opposed to human matrimony. But when the time came for them to approach the silent privacy of their bedroom, and Martinian, not knowing what God had decided about him, desired to sleep beside her, as his wife, to carry out the marital pledge, the above-mentioned nun replied to him with a spirited voice:

'Brother Martinian, I have dedicated the limbs of my body to Christ, and I cannot take part in a human marriage, as I am already betrothed to a heavenly and true being.[46] But I will give you some advice. If you should want it, you will also be able to bring it about for yourself, while it is allowed, that you too may delight in serving Him whom I have desired to marry.'

It thus turned out, with the Lord's protection, that in obeying the virgin, the young man also enriched his soul. And so, while the Vandal knew nothing about the spiritual secret they shared, Martinian was remorseful and a changed man, and he even persuaded his own brothers to share the treasure that he had found together with him, as they were his true brothers. He was thus converted with his three brothers, and accompanied by the nun also, they left the house secretly during the night, and the men joined the monks of the monastery of Thabraca,[47] over which Andrew was then abbot, a noble pastor. And the nun went to live in a convent not far away.

When, therefore, the barbarian tried to find out about this with plenty of cross-examinations and bribes, what had been done could not be hidden. And so, finding out that they were no longer his slaves, but were servants of Christ, he threw them into chains and inflicted various tortures on these servants of God, forcing them not only to have sex together, but what is more serious, to befoul the ornaments of their faith through the filth of rebaptism. This matter finally came to the notice of King Geiseric, who ordered their master to be implacable and to afflict his slaves continually until they succumbed to his will.

---

[46] Their master clearly did not realize that Maxima was a nun. In Pope Gregory's letters, he is ready to accept married priests, provided they are abstinent after their ordination.

[47] Modern Tabarka. See *CVV*, p. 47.

18   Book One

He ordered that, just as with wild animals,[48] thick, knotted clubs with spikes like palm-trees should be applied, and as these beat their backs, they not only broke the bones, but sharp spines also remained, boring their way inside their flesh. As the flesh was torn off, the blood flowed out of them, and their entrails were laid bare, but on the next day, with Christ as healer, they were rendered permanently unharmed. This was done quite often and over a long time, but no traces of the beatings were visible, as the Holy Spirit cured them at once.[49]

After this they were totally restricted by a harsh imprisonment, and were stretched, with their legs cruelly fettered, but there was no shortage of monks visiting them,[50] but as they all watched, the strength of the great wooden beams was broken as the wood rotted. This miracle was also celebrated by the voices of all of them, and the man responsible for their imprisonment testified before us on oath that this had taken place.[51]

Chapter 11: Completing their Martyrdoms

But when the Vandal failed to recognize their divine virtue, the avenging anger of God began affect his home. He himself died at the same time as his children, and all the best of his household and animals perished simultaneously. And so his lady remained a widow, destitute of husband, children and fortune, and she offered the servants of Christ as a present to a relative of the king, called Sersao. When they were offered to him and he had received them with excessive thanks, a demon began to severely upset his children and household, with various disturbances, due to these Saints. In turn, that relative of his described to the king what had happened. The king at once decreed that they should be sent in exile to a certain heathen king of the Moors, whose name was Capsur. But he was confused and overcome by the nun Maxima, and let her go at her request. Indeed that virgin is still alive today, an abbess in charge of many nuns,

---

[48] *M* has 'in the manner of saws' reading *serrarum* rather than the mss *ferarum*. But spikes, not edges, do damage (and spikes/spurs were usual with animals).

[49] The king's knotted clubs had sharp spikes protruding, designed to tear right into the flesh of the victims. The agreeing *quatientes* in *Colb* 1 is preferable to the verb's intransitive use in the ablative absolute in the text. Their recovery with exposed entrails was certainly miraculous.

[50] For Maxima to be held over a spear point as in *M* is too far-fetched and lacks a precedent. The reading in Migne makes far better sense, with the wood's miraculous rotting, and all the slaves unhurt while suffering (*eos*, not *eum/eam*).

[51] The later testimony under oath by a jailor suggests a post-Huneric date.

Arians and Vandals of the 4th-6th Centuries   19

well known to me also.[52] But the rest reached that place and were handed over to the aforesaid king of the Moors, who was staying in part of the desert called Caprapicta.

And so the disciples of Christ, when they saw many illegal forms of sacrilege at the pagans' sacrifices, through their preaching and way of life began to invite the barbarians to an understanding of the Lord our God. In this way they enriched Christ our Lord with a great multitude of heathen barbarians, where before nobody had mentioned the name of Christ. Then they next considered what should be done, so that the field, already cultivated and cleared of grass by the ploughshare of preaching, might receive the seed of the gospel and be irrigated by the rain of holy baptism. They sent legates along the wide-spreading tracks of the desert, and they finally reached the city of Rome. The Bishop of Rome was asked to send a priest and deacons to a people who were believers, and the Pope fulfilled their request with joy A church of God was built and a very great multitude of barbarians was baptized at one time, and from one-time wolves a fruitful flock of lambs grew in number.[53] But Capsur informed Geiseric of this in a report of his.

With rising ill-will over this matter, Geiseric gave orders that the monks should be tied by their feet behind fast-moving four-horse chariots, to perish together among the thorny parts of the woods. And that the bodies of these innocent men were to be dragged forwards and backwards among the prickly wooded bushes, so bound that they might see each other's deaths in turn. When they were tied up, and the untamed horses were galloping and the Moors were lamenting, they looked at each other in turn, and each said farewell to the rest at the brief moment of his flight, with these words:

> 'Pray for me, my brother. God has fulfilled our desire. In this way one may reach the kingdom of Heaven.'

---

[52] Translating *propriae voluntati* in the text, but other MSS have *propria voluntate* ('at his own wish'), which is equally possible. A report from the surviving abbess well known to Victor would provide typical source-material for his history; the 'today' suggests research after the end of Huneric's oppressive reign (post 484).

[53] It is hard not to take *civitas Romana* as Rome (for Africa *urbs Romana* or *oppidum Romanum*), and the *pontifex* must be the Pope, best able to send over its clergy, and always keen to spread the good word. *M* takes it as the first Roman town they reached in Africa; why then *tandem* ('at long last')?

20 Book One

And so by praying and singing psalms they gave up their holy souls, as the angels rejoiced. And right up to this day our Lord, Jesus Christ, does not cease to do great miracles there. For Faustus, the once blessed bishop of Buruni, bore witness to me that a certain blind woman[54] had received her sight when he himself was present there.

Chapter 12: Persecution Worsens

After this Geiseric was burning with anger against the Church of God. He sent a certain Proculus to the province of Zeugitana, to force the priests of the Lord to hand over the holy utensils and all their books, so as to strip them of their weapons, firstly, and then the artful enemy would more easily capture them when unarmed. When the priests cried out that they could not hand them over, the Vandals stripped them of all those things with their greedy hands. And from the altar-cloths (what a crime!) they made themselves shirts and breeches. However, Proculus, the man who carried this out, ate his own tongue bit by bit, and shortly afterwards he died a most shameful death.

Then also orders were given that the holy bishop of the city of Abensa,[55] Valerian, as he had bravely struggled not to hand over the holy sacraments, should be driven out of his city on his own. And it was ordered that nobody should allow him to inhabit his house or field, and so he lay for a long time on the public street, under the open sky.[56] And he was more than eighty years old, and although unworthy, I was privileged to greet him while he was suffering such an exile.

Chapter 13: Martyrdom of the Reader and Others

At one time the festival of Easter was being celebrated, and when our men were unlocking a church for themselves that had been shut up, in a place called Regia, for the service of Easter Sunday, the Arians found out. At once one of their priests, called Anduit, gathered a band of armed men by his side and incited them to storm the crowd of innocents. They entered with their two-edged swords drawn and seized arms. Others climbed up the building also and shot their arrows through the windows of the church.

---

[54] Modern Henchir el Dakhla. See *CVV*, p. 46.
[55] Bordj-Hamdouna today. See note above.
[56] Migne reads *nudus* ('naked') but the idiomatic *nudo aere* in other mss for 'open air' suits the context much better.

And at that moment, it happened that as the people of God were listening and singing, a reader was standing in the pulpit singing the Alleluia chant.[57] At that moment he was struck in the throat by an arrow, and as the book fell from his hands, he himself fell down dead after it. For it is known that they killed very many others with their arrows and javelins in the middle of the altar precinct.[58] For those not killed then with swords were tortured afterwards, and almost all were killed at the king's command, especially those of a more mature age.

For elsewhere likewise, as happened at Tunuzuda, Gales and Vicus Ammoniae,[59] and in other such places, at the very time when the sacraments were being offered to the people of God, the Arians entered with the greatest of fury, and scattered the body and blood of Christ all over the floor, and trampled on them with their polluted feet.

Chapter 14: Remarkable Event

For Geiseric himself had given orders, when persuaded by his priests, that only Arians should be appointed to various ministries within his court, and those of his sons. Among others they then came to see our Armogas. Over a long time they frequently bound his ankles by tying them with swelling cords, and bound his forehead, on which Christ had fixed the standard of his cross, which was creased rather than wrinkled, as the cords split it and twanged, and the bonds broke like spiders' webs, as the Saint looked up to Heaven. But when the torturers saw that the sinewy cords were broken, they brought in many more and stronger cords and hemp ropes, but they all fell apart as he simply called upon the name of Christ. But while they hung him with his head downwards by one foot, all thought that he was sleeping, as if on a feather-filled bed. Then the king's son, Theoderic, who was his lord, since the punishments had no power, gave orders for him to be beheaded.

But his priest, Jocundus,[60] prohibited this, saying to him:

---

[57] For the Easter Alleluia chant see Augustine *Serm.* 252.9.9.

[58] This is reminiscent of Thucydides' grim account of the massacre in Corcyra, where arrows were shot downwards through the roof (*Pelop. War*, Bk 4)

[59] Gales is the modern Henchir el-Kharrouba. See *CVV*, p. 46.

[60] For the public burning of Jocundus, because of his close links with Theoderic that are revealed here, see 2.5 below.

22   Book One

'You will be able to kill him with various afflictions. For if you kill him with a sword, the Romans will begin to preach that he is a martyr.'

Theoderic then condemned the bishop to dig ditches in the province of Byzacena. Afterwards, as if for a greater disgrace, he ordered him to be a cowherd not far from Carthage, where everyone could see him.

During this, the bishop saw from a revelation by the Lord that the day of his final sleep was close at hand, and he summoned a venerable Christian called Felix, who was the steward of the house of the king's son and who revered Armogas as an apostle. He said to Felix:

'The time of my release from life is approaching. I beg you, by the faith that we both hold, to deign to bury me beneath this oak tree, and if you fail to do so, you will render an account thereof to our God.'

It was not that he was worried about where or how his body might be buried, but to demonstrate what Christ had revealed to his servant.

Felix replied, saying:

'Far be this for us, venerable confessor of the faith.[61] But I shall bury you in one of the churches with the triumph and grace that you deserve.'

The blessed Armogas said to him:

'No! But you are going to do what I told you.'

Felix was afraid to upset a man of God and promised faithfully that he would do what he had ordered. Soon after, within a very few days, he departed from this life partaking in a good confession.[62]

And so Felix hastened to dig his grave under the tree, as ordered. The tangled roots and the hardness of the dry ground delayed him, and he was distressed that the limbs of the holy body might be buried too late with the work. But when he had finally cut out the roots and had hollowed out the ground much more deeply, he caught sight of a sarcophagus of most

---

[61] The confession in this context was restricted to the true Christian's 'confession of faith,' and was not an admission of sin.

[62] In the Roman martyrology for 29th March, Armogas was given the rank of Count from this passage, but in the context it is simply used with the sense of *cum*.

Arians and Vandals of the 4th-6th Centuries 23

splendid marble, prepared for Armogas, such as perhaps no king at all had ever had.[63]

Chapter 15: Confessor Mascula, Master of Mimes

But I ought not to pass over a certain Master of Mimes, called Mascula.[64] When he was under pressure through many tricks to give up his Catholic faith, the king himself invited him afterwards with worldly words of flattery, promising that he would be loaded with many riches, provided he was willing to do what the king wanted. But as he remained brave and invincible in his faith, the king ordered him to suffer a sentence of death. But he cleverly advised the king secretly to this effect. In that moment of the sword being brandished, if he was terrified of the blow, he should be killed all the more, so that he would not become a glorious martyr. But if he saw him brave in his confession, he should be spared the sword.[65] But Mascula was made strong, like an immovable pillar built on the foundation of Christ, and returned as a glorious confessor of the faith. Although the envious enemy was unwilling to make him a martyr, yet he could not injure our confessor.

Chapter 16: Faith of Saturus

I knew another man also at that time, called Saturus, who had been an illustrious member of the Church of Christ, and with a Catholic's free speech he frequently condemned the depravity of the Arians. He was the steward of the house of Huneric. A deacon, called Marivadus,[66] who was

---

[63] The difficulties for the excavation are well described, with the most surprising and miraculous finale.

[64] These names are uncertain, as is often the case in this work. But the name of this *archimimus* goes better with the name *Mascula* than the two proper names, and makes the confession more pointed. It should be noted that mimes were very popular in the Vandal court. See Procopius *Bell. Vand.* II. 6,7 and Riché, Pierre *Éducation et culture dans l'Occident barbare, 6ᵉ-8ᵉ siècles* (Éditions du Seuil, 1962) trans. Contreni J. J., *Education and Culture in the Barbarian West, sixth through eighth centuries* (Univ. of Carolina Pr., 1976), p. 64.

[65] His clever two-way advice seems to have confused the king. If he was terrified, Mascula would become a martyr (to be avoided by the king), if he were brave, he would be spared, so as not to become a martyr.

[66] *M* suggests (n. 47, p. 21) that Marivadus may be the deacon attacked in a work by Vigilius of Thapsus. Victor damns him as an informer and favourite of Huneric.

24   Book One

highly honoured by the infamous Huneric, accused him, and it was agreed that Saturus should become an Arian. Honours and a great deal of wealth were promised if he would do so, and dire punishments were prepared if he was unwilling to join them. This choice was proposed, that if he disobeyed the royal commands, first an examination would be held, then before his eyes his home and fortune would be lost, and all his slaves and children would be sold, and in his presence his wife would be handed over in marriage to a camel-driver.[67]

But he was full of God, and so that this would come about more quickly, he provoked the impious men. For that reason his wife, without her husband's knowledge, was seen to have sought a truce from these who were carrying this out. Another Eve, she came to her husband, taught by a serpent's counsel. But he was no Adam, who would taste the enticing apples on the forbidden tree,[68] for he was not called 'Indigent' but 'Saturus' ['filled'],[69] filled with the richness of the house of God, and he had drunk from the stream of his delights. His wife came to the place where her husband was praying on his own, with her clothes torn, her hair hanging free, and the children accompanying her, as she held in her hands a young baby girl still breast-fed. Throwing the child at the feet of her unsuspecting husband, she also grasped his knees herself with her arms, hissing with the voice of a snake:

'Have mercy on me, my darling, and on yourself at the same time. And have mercy on the children we share, and whom you see before your eyes. Do not let them be subjected to the status of slaves, when our family's descent has made them illustrious. Do not let me be subjected to an unworthy and base marriage, while my husband is still alive, for among the women of my age I often congratulated myself on my Saturus. God knows that what you are about to do, you do unwillingly, which quite a few may have done voluntarily.'

He replied to her with the voice of Job:

---

[67] Huneric is certainly inventive in his punishments. Here his threat leads to a dramatic confrontation between husband and wife.

[68] See *Genesis* 3.6. This Eve is damned (as ever) as she becomes the hissing snake, with about 26 sibilants.

[69] The word-play is on *saturus*, not on *indigens* (as in *M*, p. 22).

'You speak as one of the foolish women.'[70] I should be afraid, woman, if there was only bitter sweetness in this life. Wife, you are serving the devil's cunning. If you loved your husband, you would never drag your man to a second death. Let them sell my children, separate me from my wife, take away my possessions. Secure in the promises of my Lord, I shall follow his words: "If any man shall not send away his wife, his children, his fields or his home, he will not be able to be my disciple." '[71]

What more? His wife departed with the children, after being refuted by him. Saturus was strengthened for his heavenly crown, while he was broken, despoiled, worn out with punishments, sent off as a beggar and denied any chance of going outside. They removed all of his possessions from him, but they could not take away his baptismal stole.

Chapter 17: End of Geiseric's Persecution

After this, Geiseric ordered the Church of Carthage to be closed, its priests and deacons being scattered and dispersed through various places of exile, because there was no bishop. And yet it was reopened, with difficulty, through the patrician Severus,[72] after a request from the Emperor Zeno. And so all of its priests returned from exile.

But those who suffered miserably there will describe better in their own words of mourning what he did in Spain, Italy, Dalmatia, Campania, Calabria, Apulia, Sicily, Sardinia, Bruttium, Lucania, Old Epirus and Greece.[73] But now let this bring our persecution to an end, carried out with equal arrogance and cruelty by Geiseric, whose reign lasted for thirty-seven years and three months.

---

[70] Adapted from *Job* 2.10.

[71] Very freely adapted from *Luke* 14.26.

[72] His mission was in 474, as the Vandals' assault on the Catholics in North Africa aroused the Byzantine Emperor to take some action. See *M* n. 51, p. 23. In post-classical Latin, *princeps* was regularly used for the emperor.

[73] For Geiseric's pillaging, see Procopius *BV* 1.5.22 (Sicily, Italy and Greece), 1.7.26 (whole Roman domain) and 1.22.16-18 (Peloponnese, Zacynthus – bodies of 500 notables cut into pieces and thrown into Adriatic sea). See *M* n. 52, p. 23.

BOOK TWO

Chapter 1: Beginning of Huneric's Reign

And so, at the death of King Geiseric, Huneric succeeded his father, being his oldest son.[1] In the first part of his reign, with the usual subtlety of a barbarian, he began to act more gently and with more moderation, and especially concerning our religion, so that even meetings of a congregation could be held, whereas before under King Geiseric, it had been decided[2] that no spiritual gatherings should take place. And to show that he was religious, he decided that the Manichaean heretics[3] should be hunted out more earnestly. He burned many of them, but most he sold off for ships going overseas. He found that almost all of the Manichaeans belonged to his own religion, and especially the priests and deacons of the Arian heresy. Due to that, the greater his embarrassment, the more intensely he raged against them. Of these heretics, one was found called Clementian, a monk of theirs, who had written on his thigh: 'A Manichaean disciple of Jesus Christ.'[4]

Because of this, the aforesaid tyrant appeared quite praiseworthy, but in one matter he gave no pleasure. For he burned more strongly with

---

[1] Far the most successful of all the Vandal kings, Geiseric obtained control of both Hippo and Carthage by 439, and took Rome in 455, while dominating the sea and consolidating his land empire in North Africa, Sicily, southern Italy, Corsica and Sardinia. Alaric's death in 410 when setting out for Africa left him a clear field. For the fates of Geiseric's other two sons, Theoderic and Genton, see ch. 5 below.

[2] Reading *praedicatum* as in other manuscripts rather than the *praejudicatum* in the text. The Vandal King had no need of a judge or judgment.

[3] Mani was born in Ecbatana, and lived from c. 215-276, and founded the new religion at the court of the Persian king Sapor I. Its adherents were known as Manichaeans, and after their founder's murder in 276, they spread their faith over the Mediterranean area, with its dualist doctrine, especially in Egypt and North Africa. Even intellectuals like the young Augustine of Hippo were won over by its solutions to all things human and divine.

[4] The Latin *Manichaeus discipulus* suggests a 'Manichaean disciple' not 'Mani, the disciple' as in *M* (p. 24).

insatiable greed, and burdened the provinces of his kingdom with various false accusations and taxes, so that it was said especially about him: 'A king in need is a great calamity.'[5]

Following the requests of the Emperor Zeno and of Placidia, widow of Olybrius, the king allowed the church of Carthage to ordain for itself whichever bishop was wanted. It had now been deprived of such an ornament for twenty-four years.[6]

Chapter 2: Bishop's Consecration Allowed

And so he sent the illustrious Alexander to the church, bearing a legation to this effect, that in his presence the Catholic people was to look for a worthy priest for itself, and he also sent an edict through his notary, called Vitarit, to be read publicly, containing this measure:

'Our Lordship has ordered you to be told that the Emperor Zeno and the most noble Placidia have written through the illustrious man Alexander, seeking that the church of Carthage should have its own bishop of your religion. He commanded this to take place and wrote back to them, and ordered it to be said by those legates sent there, that you should consecrate a bishop for yourselves of your own choice, as they have sought. Under this approach, bishops of our religion who are in Constantinople and in the other Eastern provinces, should from his command have a free choice in their churches to practice with their congregation and follow Christian law in whatever language they wanted; just as here, and in the other churches established in the provinces of Africa, you will have a free choice in conducting masses in your churches,[7] and in practicing and in doing what is prescribed by your law in whatever way you want. For if this request is not observed concerning this free choice, an order will be given to both consecrated bishops and their clergy, as well as to other bishops and their clergy who are in the provinces of Africa, to be sent among the Moors.'

---

[5] The general *calamitas* accepted by the earlier editors is preferable to the more limited *calumniator* ('false accuser') in Migne, adopted by *M*.

[6] Placidia, a daughter of the Emperor Valentinian III, sister of Eudoxia and wife of Huneric, was brought over to Africa by Geiseric when he had captured the city of Rome, in 455, and she was sent to Constantinople in about 461. See *PLRE* 2, 887. Zeno reigned from 474 to 491.

[7] Migne has *habetis*, but the future in other MSS, adopted by *M*, is preferable. The present is just too unreal. The use of local languages is of interest.

28 Book One

While this edict was read out in my presence, on the eighteenth of June, for the universal Church, we began to groan, muttering that men who harbored evil plots had prepared a persecution in the future. And it is well known that we spoke thus to the legate:

'If this is so, this Church is not pleased to have a bishop with the inclusion of these dangerous conditions. Let Christ govern the Church, who has always deigned to govern it.'[8]

The legate failed to accept this suggestion. At the same time the people too flared up angrily, demanding action at once. Their shouting was unbearable, and they could not be settled by any reasoning.

Chapter 3: Virtues of Eugenius

And so Eugenius was consecrated as their archbishop,[9] a holy man acceptable to God, and sublime happiness was born, and the Church of God was filled with joy. The Catholic multitude was exultant over the consecration of a restored bishop, under the barbarian rule. For the greatest number of young men and young girls rejoiced in common among themselves, swearing that they had never seen a bishop sitting on the throne there. Furthermore, that man of God and priest, Eugenius, due to his life of good deeds, began to be thought venerable and worthy of reverence, even by those who were outside the city. And he was so agreeable to everyone that, if it had been right, they would all have been pleased to lay down their lives for his sake.

The Lord also allowed him to give alms of such a sort that it seemed incredible that he contributed so much, when the Church, with the barbarians holding all its goods, was known to have no means of paying a cent.[10] If someone should begin to praise the humility in him, and the love and divinely bestowed piety, he would be unable to describe it all. It is agreed that money never remained in his possession, unless perhaps it was

---

[8] The jussive subjunctive *gubernet* in *al* is needed, to allow Christ to take over from the State, yet Migne's *gubernat* was accepted as 'governs' by *M*.

[9] See note 11 above. Eugenius appears as the only candidate, sent from Byzantium by the emperor, with plenty of funds, it seems, and the blessing of the historian he had chosen. He arrived in 480/481 filling the see vacant since the death of Deogratias in 457. For the exemplary Christian mission of Deogratias, see ch. 1.8 above.

[10] The Latin *nummus* denoted a very small silver coin, 'a cent' or 'farthing.'

Arians and Vandals of the 4th-6th Centuries   29

offered at such an hour as when the day's sunshine was now completing its course, and was giving its order and place to the shadows of darkness. He kept as much as sufficed for the day, not all that greed would have procured, as our God then gave him great income and greater every day.

But when his fame was celebrated and well known everywhere, as a result the Arian bishops began to be tormented by sore envy over this, and attacked him every day with false accusations, especially Cyril. Need I say more? They suggested to the king about him that he should in no way sit on his throne, nor preach to the people of God in the usual way. Then they also ordered that he should prohibit any men and women he saw going inside the church in Vandal dress. He replied as was fitting: 'The house of God is open for all; no man will be able to turn away those entering.'[11]

This was said most of all because there had been a huge multitude of our Catholics entering the church in their Vandal attire, for the reason that they were servants of the royal household.[12]

Chapter 4: Start of Persecution

But when the king received such a reply from the man of God, he decided to station torturers at the Church gates. Whenever they saw a woman or a man entering in the clothing of their race, they at once threw small stakes with hooks on their heads, and drew their hair on to them and twisted them quite violently, and dragged all the skin off their heads together with their hair. And some of them, while this was being done, at once lost their sight, and others died just from that pain. In fact some women after this punishment were paraded through the streets before the gaze of the whole city, with their heads bare of skin and a herald going before them. But they counted it the greatest benefit the more they suffered this on their bodies. And I knew most of them, and do not know any of them forsaking the straight and narrow even when they were pressed with punishments at that time.

---

[11] The future in *poterit* appears in *M* as 'should.' The moods are often astray, and some purpose and result clauses, and *dum* with subj., are misrepresented.
[12] For discussions of this special Vandal attire, see J. Kleemann 'Quelques réflexions sur l'interprétation ethnique des sepultures habillées considérées comme vandales' and P. von Rummel 'Habitus Vandalorum? Zur Frage nach einer gruppen-spezifischen Kleidung der Vandalen in Nordafrika, in *Antiquité Tardive,* pp 123-130 and 131-142.

30   Book One

But when he could not in that way break through that wall of faith, he decided that men of our religion appointed to his court should receive neither their ration of corn nor their usual stipends. In addition, he also decided to wear them out in rural work, and sent quite delicate, freeborn men to the plain of Utica,[13] to cut out clumps of wheat under the heat of a burning sun. But they all went there with joy, rejoicing in the Lord.

Among their company there was a man with a withered hand, over which he had had no control at all for a great many years. And when he quite truthfully excused himself as being unable to work, he was ordered to proceed, all the more violently. But when they came to the place and they all lamented, praying on his behalf especially, through divine piety, that withered hand was restored intact for the confessor of the faith.

But now, from this time on, the persecution by Huneric commenced our grief and our travail.

Chapter 5: Huneric treats his family savagely

This man who for some time now had shown himself lenient to all men, desiring to leave his kingdom to his own sons after his death (although it did not happen[14]), began to attack his brother Theoderic and his children cruelly, and the children of his brother Genton no less so. He would have let none survive, if his death had not removed the fulfillment of his desire. First, he knew that the wife of his brother Theoderic was astute, and I imagine that he suspected her, in case she armed her husband perhaps or her eldest son, as seemed prudent and wise, with fiercer resolve against the tyrant. He laid a charge against her, and ordered her to be executed with a sword. Afterwards that eldest son, who had received a higher education,

---

[13] Modern Utique. See *CVV*, p. 47. On p. 6, Courtois notes that a Victor of Utique was once considered a possible author o f this history.

[14] For the king's family tree, see *CA*, pp 390, 405-9. In fact when Victor was finishing his book off in about 487-9, Hilderic took over the throne, as the son of Huneric and Eudoxia, after the deaths of Guntamund and Trasamund. This note may have escaped his notice in his final work on the history. It seems that Geiseric died in 477, after 37 years and 3 months on the throne, although Procopius gives 39 years and Isidore of Seville and Victor of Tonnena have 40 years. Most agree that Huneric's reign lasted 7 years and 10 months, ending 484.

Arians and Vandals of the 4th-6th Centuries   31

was also killed.[15] According to the will of Geiseric, he had the greatest right to the throne amongst the nephews, since he was the oldest of them.

Huneric was eager to perpetrate something even more cruel. As the common people stood in the center of the city before the steps of the new square, he gave orders for a bishop of his religion called Jocundus, whom they called their patriarch, to be burnt alive on a pyre, for the reason that he was considered most acceptable in the household of the king's brother, Theodoric. It was with his support that the above-mentioned family might perhaps obtain the throne.[16] But in this impious crime, we foresaw an evil future coming upon us, as we said in turn to one another:

'As he has shown himself so cruel towards his own priest, will that man ever spare our religion, and us?'

Next he exiled with a cruel banishment[17] the eldest son of Genton, called Godagis, together with his wife, without the service of a slave or a slave-girl. Likewise indeed he exiled his brother Theodoric, in a state of nakedness and destitution, after killing his wife and son. After his death, the king placed the son who was left, a little baby, and his two grown-up daughters, on the backs of donkeys, and sent them far away to suffer affliction. But he also pursued with false charges a great many counts and noblemen of his race, due to the fact that they supported his brother, burning some of them and slaying others with a sword. He proved himself to be an imitator of his father Geiseric, who had drowned the wife of his own brother, throwing her in the well-known river Amsager at Cirta,[18] with heavy rocks tied to her. And after the death of their mother, he also killed her children.[19]

But when his father Geiseric was dying, he also recommended many people to his son, and they sealed it with an oath. But Huneric forgot his promise and violated their oath, and butchered them with various tortures and burnings. For one was a certain Heldicas whom his father had made governor of the kingdom, now an old man and full of years. The king

---

[15] The *litteris institutus* is surprising, suggesting boys' training in the Classics in Carthage or Rome. See Riché, *Les Écoles* 1976, p. 64.

[16] For the influence of this important priest on Theodoric, see chapter 1.14 above.

[17] The emotive adjective *crudeli* was omitted by *M*.

[18] Modern Constantine; the river is the Suffegmar.

[19] They were the wife and children of Gunderic, who died in 428 and was succeeded on the throne by Geiseric.

32   Book One

beheaded him with dishonour, and burnt his wife, with another lady called Theucaria, in the middle of the city. He ordered their bodies to be dragged through the lanes and streets, and they lay there all day, until his own bishops asked him not to, and in the evening he reluctantly allowed the women to be buried. He could not kill Gamuth, the brother of Heldicas, because he had taken refuge in one of their churches. But he shut him up in a filthy hole, a cesspit, and made him stay there for a long time. Afterwards he condemned him to dig ditches for vines, with a goatherd and a peasant to help him. He also lacerated them with cruel whips twelve times a year, namely, once a month, allowing them next to no water and coarse meal bread. They suffered this for five or more years.[20]

These punishments could have given them the benefit of an eternal reward, if they had been Catholics, and had put up with that treatment for the good of their faith. But we could not pass over that fact in silence, no less than we should silently omit the king's impiety towards those of his own faith. For he not only burnt on pyres his own bishop, Jocundus, but also burnt a great many of his priests and deacons, that is, Arians, and even delivered them up to wild beasts.[21]

Chapter 6: Visions before Persecution

And so, after cutting down all those he feared in a short time, and consolidating the kingdom for his own use (as he thought, its future being brief and fleeting), being in every way free of concern and secure, he directed all the weapons of his fury towards persecuting the Catholic Church, as a roaring lion.[22]

---

[20] Besides the cesspit, and that hard labor and all those whippings, and very menial companions, the aristocrat had to eat what was left when the fine white flour, his normal diet, had been removed. The King again proves extremely imaginative in his punishments. No doubt peasants received equal treatment.

[21] These *bestiae* were a regular part of the Roman gladiatorial games' butchery, and this interesting comment may be a reference to a similar use of wild animals in Carthage's games. For the amphitheatre's survival in Carthage until Arab attacks, see Lachaux, J.-C. *Théâtres et amphitheatres d'Afrique proconsulaire* (Aix en-Provence, 1979). The 'roaring lion' was a favourite with the crowd.

[22] See *Psalms* 22.13[21.14] for 'as a ravening and a roaring lion.' For a summary of his reign, more ruinous for the Catholics than his father's, see Victor of Tonnena's account below, chapters 28, 30 and 50 especially.

Arians and Vandals of the 4th-6th Centuries

But before the calamitous persecution,[23] many forewarning visions and signs had revealed the impending evil. Almost two years before it took place, someone saw the church of Faustus glittering with its usual ornaments and with shining candles also, and glowing red with the white robes[24] and bright lanterns. And while he rejoiced at the brightness of such great splendour, suddenly, he said, the brilliance of that highly desirable[25] light was extinguished, and as darkness ensued, a foul smell arose and filled his nose, and all of that company of white-robed priests was driven by threats out of doors, expelled by some Ethiopians. And he lamented at once for the reason that he did not see the church restored again at all to its former brightness. For the man had described that vision to the holy Eugenius, in my presence.[26] And a certain priest saw that church of Faustus filled with crowds of countless people, then after a short time it was evacuated, and filled with a multitude of pigs and nanny goats.

Likewise another saw a threshing-floor of wheat ready for winnowing, the grains still under the control of the winnower and not yet separated from the chaff, and while he wondered at the size of the great heap, although mixed together, behold, there suddenly appeared a tempestuous whirlwind, and it began to make its presence felt with a rising blast of wind, as the dust flew up.[27] When struck by it, every bit of that chaff flew away, while the grains of corn remained. After this a tall man came with a splendid face and gleaming with bright attire, and he began to throw away the lean and empty grains, by purging those unfit for fine white flour. After examining them for a long time, he reduced the greatness of that heap, once tested, to form barely a tiny pile.

Similarly another man said:

'A certain very tall man was standing on the mountain that is called Ziquense, and he cried out to the right side and to the left: "Depart from here, depart."'

---

[23] For *tempestatem* the metaphorical 'calamity' is preferable to the 'time' in *M* p. 30. For a neutral 'time,' *tempus* would be usual. Victor of Tonnena says that it began in 466, two years after he became king (ch. 30).

[24] The white woolen *pallia* were worn almost only by archbishops, but here they seem to stand simply for the priests' white robes, reflecting the glowing candles.

[25] The rare word *concupiscibilis* had appeared in Jerome's *Quaest. in Paral.* 1.1.

[26] Note that Victor was with the archbishop as these ominous reports came in.

[27] The powerful 'rising blast' of *sonivago* is a post-Classical compound.

34   Book One

Another saw sulphurous clouds in a rumbling and turbulent sky, and huge stones raining down. And when these stones had fallen on the ground, they were more alight and burned with greater flames, and entering the inner rooms of houses, they set alight all the people they found. But the person who saw this says that when he had hidden himself in a bedroom, through God's mercy, the flame could not reach him. I think that that prophecy was being fulfilled: 'Close your doors and hide yourselves for a brief moment, until God's anger passes.'[28]

The venerable Bishop Paul also saw a tree stretching right up to the Heavens with flourishing branches, and with its shade it covered almost all of Africa. And when all men were rejoicing at its great size and beauty, behold, a violent ass suddenly came forward, he said, and rubbed its neck over its strong roots, and as it pushed there was a great crash, and it forced that wonderful tree to fall on the earth.

But even the honourable Bishop Quintianus saw himself standing on some mountain, from where he could see a flock of countless sheep, and in the middle of the flock there were two cooking pots bubbling vigorously. But some butchers appeared, who sank the sheep's flesh in the boiling pots. When this was done, the whole of that huge flock was consumed. I myself think that those two pots were the two cities of Sicca Veneria and Lares,[29] in which the first multitude had congregated and from which the fire took its beginning. Or else they were King Huneric and his bishop, Cyril. But let this suffice for the many visions, because we must show concern for brevity.

Chapter 7: Heavy Persecution

What next? The tyrant decided first of all, with a terrible judgment, that nobody in his palace should be a guard, nor anyone carry out public functions, unless he had become an Arian. A great many of these officials showed invincible strength, and gave up their temporal office to avoid losing their faith. Afterwards he forced them out of their homes, stripped them of all their goods and banished them to the islands of Sicily and Sardinia. What is more, he hurriedly decreed that throughout the whole of Africa he could claim for himself as his own funds the income of our deceased bishops. And any successor to a dead bishop would not be

---

[28] This is again a very free adaptation, of *Isaiah* 26.20.
[29] The towns are Le Kef and Henchir Lorbeus. See *CVV*, pp 46-7.

Arians and Vandals of the 4th-6th Centuries

consecrated unless he had contributed five hundred sovereigns into the king's purse. But as the devil strove to construct this edifice, Christ at once deigned to destroy it. His courtiers made this suggestion to the king, saying:

'If your order were to remain, our own bishops, who are established in parts of Thrace and other regions, will begin to suffer worse things.'

Then he ordered the holy nuns to be brought together, directing the Vandals with midwives of their race to inspect and feel their private parts, contrary to the laws of decency, with neither their mothers nor any of the Catholic matrons present.[30] And they tortured them, by hanging them painfully and binding huge weights to their feet, and placing red-hot plates of iron on their backs, stomachs, breasts and flanks. And amid these punishments the Vandals kept on saying: 'Admit that the bishops are making love to you, and to your clerics also.'

We know that very many of them were killed by the harshness of their punishments. Others who survived were given curved backs through the parched nature of their skin. For the nuns were striving to find the way,[31] and through its opening, to publicize the persecution that had been carried out. And in doing this, Huneric still could not discover in any way how he might dishonour the Church of Christ.

Chapter 8: Faithful forced into Exile

With what rivers of tears shall I recount how he sent into exile in the desert bishops and priests and deacons, and other members of the Church, totaling four thousand, nine hundred and seventy six?[32] Among them there were a great many with gout,[33] and others deprived of their bodily

---

[30] The Vandals supervising this inspection were certainly male (*Vandalos*), even if their midwives were female. The 'Catholic' was omitted by *M*. The nuns thus had no family or Church support.

[31] The nuns were finding the 'true way' to Heaven (*M* makes Huneric the subject, taking *nitebantur* as singular). Although the king shamed and coerced the nuns, none admitted a liaison.

[32] Exaggerated, it seems. Victor of Tonnena has 'about four thousand.' See ch. 50 of the *Chronicon*, and *CVV* pp 38-39.

[33] This appears to have been a very common ailment at this time, its famous victims including Pope Gregory the Great, and his very close friend, the sadly

36 Book One

sight due to their old age. Among their number was the blessed Felix, bishop of Abbir,[34] who had now been in his bishopric for forty-four years, and as he was struck by a paralyzing disease, he did not feel anything and could not speak at all. We gave him a great deal of thought, as he could not be carried on a beast of burden, and we suggested that the king might be asked by his men to give orders that, as he was soon to die, he should at least stay in Carthage, as he could in no way be carried into exile.

The tyrant is said to have answered this in a state of fury:

'If he cannot sit on an animal, untamed bulls must be yoked together to take him where I have ordered, dragging him along, tied to them with ropes.'

We carried him the whole way tied on a mule crosswise, like a log of wood.

Chapter 9: Young Woman's admirable Faith

They were all brought together in the cities of Sicca[35] and Lares, so that the Moors could meet them there and lead those handed over to them into the desert. Then two Counts came up with damnable cleverness, and they began to deal with the confessors of God with persuasive words:

'For what reason are you so obstinate, and do not submit to the orders of his Lordship at all, you who could be honourable in the king's sight if you hurry to do his will?'

At once they cried out with a loud voice, saying: 'We are Christians! We are Catholics! We confess the one indivisible God in the Trinity.'

They were shut in a prison, certainly more oppressive, but the largest so far, where I was given an opportunity to go inside and give a word of

---

misjudged Emperor. The Pope was godfather to Maurice's eldest son and heir, Theodosius.

[34] It is called Henchir el-Khandak today. For this and subsequent modern versions, see *CVV*, pp 46-7.

[35] For the importance of this border town see Procopius *Build* 6.7.10, noting that Justinian built defensive buildings there against the Moors. See *M* p.33.

warning to our brethren, and celebrate the holy mysteries.[36] There were also a great many baby children there, and those who had given them birth were following them with maternal affection, some of them rejoicing, others saddened and others dragging them back. Some were rejoicing that they had given birth to martyrs, while others were striving to retract from their confession of the faith those who would be as good as dead with the water of re-baptism.[37] Enticements overcame none of them, nor did ties of the flesh force them to submit.

I am delighted to recall briefly what a certain old woman did there. While we were making our way accompanied by the army of God, and were traveling more at night, as it happened, because of the heat of the sun, we caught sight of an unfortunate woman bearing an old bag and other clothes, and holding a poor little child by the hand.[38] And she consoled him with these words: 'Run, my lord. Do you see how all the saints are going forward and are hurrying joyfully to their crowns?'

We rebuked her, as it appeared inappropriate for her either to join with men or to associate with the army of Christ, on account of her sex, and she replied: 'Bless us, bless us, and pray for me and for that poor little grandson of mine. For although I am a sinner, I am the daughter of the one-time bishop of the city of Zura.'

We asked her:

'And why do you walk so abjectly, and what reason do you give for having gone so far on such a long journey to this place?'

She replied: 'I am going into exile with this poor little servant of yours, so that the enemy does not find him alone and recall him from the way of truth to his death.'[39]

---

[36] The 'we' suggests that Victor was there, and able to celebrate Mass for them. See also chapter 10 below. The great risk he took suggests a modern reporter's courage under fire.

[37] *M*'s *moriendos* ('should be dead') is far better than the text's *moliendo*, lacking an object and missing the point of the fatal re-baptism into the Arian faith. See the note on the baby below. The sense of 'submit' is suggested by 'bow to the ground'.

[38] The use of five '*diminutives de tendresse*' here (*mulierculam, sacculum infantulum* and *parvulo* twice) is clearly designed to heighten the pathos of this very dramatic episode.

[39] See above for their 'death' even in enforced re-baptism.

38   Book One

At these words we were filled with tears and did not want to say anything, except that God's will be done.

Chapter 10: Prison's Unpleasantness

Perhaps our enemy was saying now: 'I shall share the spoils, I shall have my fill of them, I shall kill with my sword and my hand shall rule them.'[40] Yet he could not catch anybody. So he searched for narrow and very grim places, to enclose the army of God in their recesses. Then the enemy even denied them the consolation of a human visitor,[41] and they were punished by the guards' clubs, and were seriously hurt.[42]

The confessors of Christ, held in by the prison's narrowness, were in turn thrown on top of each other, like hordes of locusts, or rather, to put it properly, like the most precious grains of wheat. In such a dense crowd, there was no space for one to step aside for a call of nature, but when forced by necessity they made a place there for excrement and urine, so that then that horrible stench surpassed all other types of punishment. Finally we were just allowed to go in to them secretly, while the Vandals slept, after giving the Moors a large bribe.[43] As we went in, we began to sink up to our knees, as if we were in a sea of dung, and we then saw that those words of Jeremiah had been fulfilled:[44]

'Those who were bred in saffron have embraced their dung.'[45]

What next? They were warned by the Moors shouting on all sides to be prepared for the journey to where they had been allocated.

---

[40] Again this is a free adaptation, of *Exodus* 15.9.

[41] Like Victor himself, able to provide them with Mass.

[42] Reading *custodum* 'the guards' clubs.' The *custodes* in the text were certainly not being struck. *M* reads *ponuntur* ('guards were placed'), but without a prep. *fustibus* is not connected with 'placed'.

[43] Note the large amount of money carried by Victor, to cover bribes like this.

[44] The first person plural is regularly used by Victor for himself, but there must have been others with him (a slave at least) for this disgusting episode.

[45] *Lamentations* 4.5, freely adapted.

Chapter 11: Ghastly Journey

And so they left on the Lord's Day, their clothes and faces and heads smeared with excrement, and the Moors were threatening them, and yet they were singing this hymn to the Lord with exultation:

'This is the glory for all his saints.'[46]

At this time the blessed Bishop Cyprian was present there, the bishop of Unizibir, and he consoled them splendidly, cheering up individuals with pious and fatherly affection, not without a steady flow of tears. He was prepared to 'lay down his life for his brethren,'[47] and to make himself a volunteer for such sufferings, if he were allowed. And all that he owned, he then spent on his impoverished brothers in that time of need. For he was looking for this opportunity, and he joined with the confessors of Christ, being a confessor himself in courage and virtue. Afterwards, through many trials and the foulness of prisons, he reached with great joy the exile that he had desired.

And the roads and paths could in no way hold the crowds of people coming to them, showing what great multitudes of people visited the martyrs of God from that time on, from different regions and cities. Countless crowds of Christians hurried together over mountain crests and through the depths of valleys, and came down carrying candles in their hands and casting their young children at the feet of the martyrs. And they cried out those words: 'To whom do you leave us wretched people, while you go to claim your crowns? Who will baptize our babies in the font of perennial water? Who will confer on us the benefit of penitence, and who will free us when bound by the chains of our sins, through the absolution of reconciliation? For it has been said to you:

'Whatsoever you shall free on earth, shall be freed in Heaven also.'[48]

And when we die who will bury us with solemn prayers? Who will present the usual rite of the divine sacrifice? We too should be delighted to go with you, if it were allowed, so that in this way sons need not be separated from their fathers.'

---

[46] *Psalms* 149.9.
[47] *I John* 3.16.
[48] *Matthew* 18.18.

40 Book One

For all these words, tears and praises, no comforter was still allowed to go with them, as the multitude was forced to hurry on, to occupy a labor farm where a cellar[49] had been prepared. And when the old ones' strength was failing, as with others who were young but happened to have delicate bodies, the Moors began to beat them with the points of their spears, to make them run, and struck them with stones. As a result, the weaker they became, the more they were fatigued.

Chapter 12: Savage treatment of the Christians

But afterwards, the Moors ordered that those who could not walk should have their feet tied together and they should be dragged along, like the carcasses of dead animals, over hard places, rough with stones. At first their clothing was torn, and afterwards each of their limbs was ripped off. On the sharp edges of the rocks one had his head crushed, others had their sides split open, thus breathing out their lives in the hands of those dragging them. We could in no way work out the total of these victims, prevented by their very great number. But their graves speak, as the simple tombs of those saints rise up all along the public highway.[50]

The remaining ones with greater strength reached the places in the desert where they were quartered, and were given some barley for their meal, fit for cattle.[51] And such a great number of poisonous animals and scorpions are said to exist there, that it would seem incredible to those who do not know about it, that the poison of the venom by its breath alone affects even those who are placed far away. For they say that nobody has ever survived when struck by a scorpion, and yet, with Christ's defense, not one of his servants appeared to have been harmed by their savage virulence up to the present time. But while they were being fed there with grains of barley, afterwards even this was withdrawn, as if God, who had

---

[49] In medieval authors *cannava* had the sense of a *cavea* ('enclosure' or 'cage') or *cella vinaria* ('wine cellar'), as here. See Du Cange *Glossarium* vol 2, p. 77. *M*'s 'lowly lodging where some poor accommodation had already been prepared' suggests a backpacker's retreat – not these slave quarters thrust upon them.

[50] If these were actual tombs, it would have taken several years after the persecution for the erection of so many. The list of Uppena (*C.I.L.*, VIII.2304) seems to be too early for these martyrs. See *CA* n. 7, p. 295, and *M* n. 19, p. 37.

[51] Then and now *hordeum irregulare* was grown in Northern Africa, mainly for animals and for the poor to consume.

Arians and Vandals of the 4th-6th Centuries 41

once rained manna on the Fathers,[52] could not feed those who were now banished into the same sort of exile.

Chapter 13: The King's Edict

The king thought of fiercer action against the Church of God, as if after cutting off some of its limbs, he would destroy the whole body by tearing it apart. For on the day of the Lord's Ascension, in the presence of Reginus, emissary of the Emperor Zeno, he sent to Bishop Eugenius an edict to be read in the middle of the church, written as follows. He also sent it over the whole of Africa through speedy couriers.[53]

THE EDICT OF KING HUNERIC

To Eugenius of Carthage and to the rest of the Catholic bishops appointed throughout the whole of Africa, it is directed that they should come to Carthage to give an account of their faith.

Huneric, king of the Vandals and Alans, to all the consubstantialist bishops.[54]

'It is well known that your priests have been prohibited not once, but quite often, from celebrating any meetings in the Vandal territory, in case they should subvert our Christian souls with their seductive message. Very many had rejected this advice and have now been found holding masses in Vandal territory contrary to the ban. They claim that they observe the correct rule of the true Christian faith. And because in the provinces conceded to us by God we do not want there to be any inducement to sin,[55] for that reason know that, by the providence of God and with the consensus of our holy bishops, we have decided that on the day of the calends of February that comes next,[56] you must forgo any excuse of being

---

[52] For the manna, see *Exodus* 16.14-18 and *Numbers* 11.6-9. The impersonal verbs in this chapter suggest that Victor was unable to join them in the desert.

[53] Reading the *veredariis* in Migne, the 'couriers,' not 'post horses' as in *M*, p. 37.

[54] Using the Greek word ὁμοούσιος as before for the Latin *consubstantialis;* this technical term is usually restricted to the Trinity. But see ch. 3 for its regular use. For the king's title (Vandals and Alans) see *M* n.24, pp 37-8.

[55] The sense of *scandalum* is a 'stumbling-block' or 'temptation,' not a 'scandal' as in *M*.

[56] The date for this event, February 1st, allowed them about eight months after May 20th to prepare for the ordeal. Huneric's father died in 477.

42   Book One

afraid, and come to Carthage, all of you, so that you may enter into a debate with our venerable bishops over the interpretation of faith, and may prove properly from Holy Writ the faith of your consubstantial bishops that you defend, so that it may be decided if you hold a true belief. And we have sent the gist of this edict to all of your bishops ordained throughout the whole of Africa.'

Given on the thirteenth day of the calends of June, in the seventh year of the reign of Huneric.'[57]

Chapter 14: Eugenius' Reply

When those of us present learnt this and at the same time read it, 'our hearts were at once faint and our eyes grew dim,'[58] and truly 'the days of our feast were turned to mourning, and our songs into lamentation,'[59] as the contents of the edict indicated the fury of a future persecution. And this was especially so when he said:

'In the provinces conceded to us by God we do not want there to be any inducement to sin,' it was as if he said: 'In our provinces we do not want there to be any Catholics.'

We discussed what should be done. The imminent calamity found no remedy, except that the holy Eugenius should make a reasonable suggestion, if the barbarian heart might be mollified, written with a text like this:

THE REPLY OF THE HOLY EUGENIUS

A suggestion made to King Huneric by Eugenius, archbishop of Carthage, that bishops be summoned from overseas also to have a conference on the question of a common faith.

'Whenever the question of the soul and of eternal life and of the Christian faith is dealt with, it is necessary that one should suggest without fear (as the king has wisely promised) what is appropriate. Recently his royal power deigned to advise my poor self through his notary, Vitarit, who

---

[57] That is, May 20th, 483.
[58] Based on *Lamentations* 5.11.
[59] *Amos* 8.10.

Arians and Vandals of the 4th-6th Centuries   43

expounded the king's edict concerning the merit of our religion and faith in our church, in the presence of its clergy and people. From its theme we learnt that the royal edict had been circulated similarly to all of my fellow bishops, demanding that they come on the arranged day for a discussion of the faith. And we suggested reverently that they should accept this. But my Humility suggested to the aforesaid notary that he should acknowledge the faith of all those countries overseas also, that agree with us in our one religion and communion, because they all submit to his rule everywhere, especially as it is a question for the whole world, not just for the provinces of Africa only.

Since I promised that I would present what should be suggested[60] in a second reply, as a suppliant I beg your Magnificence to see fit to bear my suggestion just mentioned to the ears of his lordship and most merciful king. May his Clemency thus recognize courteously that we in no way decline or shun the discussion of holy law,[61] with God's help. But without universal consent, we should not undertake cases for the defense of our faith. So we ask that through his kindness, whereby he is so great, and through the justice of his wisdom, he may deign to accept our plea.'

Given by Eugenius, archbishop of the Catholic church of Carthage.

Chapter 15: King's Rejection

But when the blessed Eugenius offered this suggestion, the man who had 'already conceived misery,' was urged to 'give birth to even worse iniquity.'[62] And so it appears that he sent this order to the holy man, Bishop Eugenius, through Obadus, a governor of his kingdom:[63]

'Subdue the Universe for me, so that all the world is in my power, and then I shall do what you say, Eugenius.'

---

[60] Du Cange suggested that Victor used a unique noun *suggerendam*, with the sense of a 'suggestion' or 'proposal.' See his *Glossarium* vol. VI p. 430. I am sure that this noun was in fact the neuter gerundive *suggerenda* ('things that should be suggested'). Dittography explains the unwanted *m* (*-endam me*). The normal noun *suggestio* appears just below.

[61] The *legis* suggests [holy] law, not religion as in *M* p. 39.

[62] Based on *Psalms* 7.15.

[63] Obadus is only known as a Vandal governor here. See *CVV* p. 54 for these otherwise unknown officials (Heldicas, Vitarit, Armogast, Felix, Saturus and the judges Elpidofor and Proculus).

44   Book One

To this the blessed Eugenius replied as best he could, saying:

'What is irrational should not have been said. It is like saying of a human being that he may be carried through the air and fly, which is contrary to human nature. For I said, if the king's power desires to know our faith, which is the one and true faith, let him send word to his friends, and I shall write also to my brethren, so that my fellow bishops may come, who may show you our faith together with us, especially the Church of Rome, which is the head of all the churches.'

Obadus replied to this:

'You then and his lordship my king, are you similar?'

Bishop Eugenius said:

'I am not similar to the king. But I said: "If he wants to know the true faith, let him write to his friends, to direct our Catholic bishops, and I am writing to my fellow bishops, as there is the common concern of a universal Catholic faith." '[64]

This is what Eugenius did, not because there was nobody else in Africa who might refute the objections of our adversaries, but so that those bishops might come who were free of their dominion, and who might at the same time report back to all the lands and peoples about the falsehoods about our oppression.[65]

Chapter 16: Savagery against the bishops

However, as he was contriving deception, the king was unwilling to listen to reason, and introduced an unending stream of arguments to harass whichever of the bishops he had heard were erudite, using various insults. He had already sent Secundianus Vibianus into exile, after subjecting him to a hundred and fifty strokes with a cudgel,[66] and also Praesidius, bishop

---

[64] The present *scribo* neatly suggests that Eugenius is already backing up his argument with action, as he attempts to force the Vandals' hand.

[65] Eugenius suggests a Council of all Western bishops, for a chance to argue for the orthodox faith, and spread the word about Vandal atrocities. The king quickly rejected it.

[66] On the *Notitia,* in the province of Byzacena, Secundianus of Mimiana is listed as having been exiled.

Arians and Vandals of the 4th-6th Centuries 45

of Sufetula,[67] a bright enough man. Then he beat to death with cudgels the venerable Mansuetus, Germanus and Fusculus, and many others likewise.

While he was doing this, he gave orders that none of his priests should share a table with men of our religion, nor should they eat at all with Catholics. But while this rule provided no benefit for them, it brought very great profit to us. For if their speech, as the apostle says, 'is accustomed to creeping like a cancer,' how much more will a table of food in common be able to infect us, when the same apostle says: 'Do not have food in common with the wicked'?[68]

Chapter 17: Great Miracle

But with the fire of persecution now burning and the flame of the destructive king blazing everywhere, our God revealed a miracle through his servant, the faithful Eugenius, which I should not pass over. There was in the same city, that is, in Carthage, a certain blind man very well known to the citizens and the city, called Felix. The Lord visited him, and in the night he was told through a vision, as the day of the Epiphany was dawning:

'Arise and go to my servant, Bishop Eugenius, and say to him that I have sent you to him. And at the hour when he blesses the font, to baptize those coming to the faith, he will touch your eyes, and they will be opened and you will see the light.'

Although informed by such a vision, thinking that he was deluded by a dream, as often happens, the blind man was unwilling to get up. But when he was again deeply asleep, he was similarly forced to go to Eugenius. Again he ignored it, but on the third occasion he was rebuked quickly and severely. He woke up the slave boy who normally assisted him, and went with all speed to the church of Faustus. He offered prayers, and approaching with a great flow of tears, he suggested to a certain deacon, called Peregrinus, that he announce him to the bishop, indicating that he had some sort of secret to make known. Hearing this, the bishop ordered

---

[67] Modern Sbeitla. See *CVV*, p. 47.

[68] The first quotation was adapted from *II Timothy* 2.17 *et sermo eorum ut cancer serpit* and the second freely adapted from *I Corinthians* 5.11 *cum eiusmodi nec cibum sumere.*

46   Book One

the man to enter. At this time, because of the solemnity of the festival, nocturnal hymns were already resounding throughout the whole church, as the people sang. The blind man indicated to the bishop the sequence of his vision, and said to him:

'I shall not let you go unless you give me back my sight, as you were ordered to do by the Lord.'

The holy Eugenius told him:

'Depart from me, brother, for I am an unworthy sinner,[69] and a wrongdoer above all other men, seeing that I was reserved for times like this.'

But Felix held his knees, saying nothing else, except what he had already said:

'As has been commanded, restore my eyes to me.'

So Eugenius, considering the man's shameless credulity,[70] as time was now pressing, went with him to the font, accompanied by the clergy on duty. There he knelt down with a great groan, piercing Heaven with his sobs, and then blessed the font's rippling bowl.[71] When he had finished his prayer and had arisen, he answered the blind man:

'I have already told you, brother Felix, that I am a sinful man. But let the Lord who has deigned to visit you look after you according to your faith, and let him open your eyes.'

At the same time the bishop marked his eyes with the sign of the cross, and at once the blind man recovered his sight, restored by the Lord. And the bishop kept him with him there until they had all been baptized, to prevent the crowd from being over excited by such a great miracle, and crushing the blind man who had regained his sight.

---

[69] Based on *Luke* 5.8.

[70] The adj. *inverecundam,* used by Jerome (*Ep* 128.2) well suits the *credulitatem* ('credulity') of the very persistent blind man. Eugenius had other things to do. This is misunderstood by *M* with his 'reverent trust.' (p. 42).

[71] The font's *alveum* is a 'bowl' rather than a 'pool' (as in *M*), and despite the 'rippling' it does not suggest total immersion. Groaning, he blessed and shook it.

Arians and Vandals of the 4th-6th Centuries 47

But afterwards this was revealed to the whole church. The man who had been blind proceeded to the altar with Eugenius, as was the custom, to make an offering to the Lord for his cure. The bishop accepted it and placed it on the altar. As the congregation was aroused by joyfulness, an uncontrollable burst of noise arose.

A messenger went to the tyrant at once. Felix was seized, and was asked what had happened, and how he had regained his sight. He told him all about it in detail, and the bishops of the Arians said:

'Eugenius did this through sorcery.'[72]

And they were overcome by confusion and could not hide this ray of light, for the reason that Felix had often been seen and was well known to the whole city. But they wanted to kill him, if it were lawful, just as the Jews wanted to kill Lazarus when he was raised from the dead.[73]

Chapter 18: A Happy Martyr

Now that the future day of February 1st was drawing close, a day of treachery arranged by the king, there were gathered together bishops not only from the whole of Africa, but also from many islands, men worn out by affliction and grief.[74] There was silence for many days, until he had meanwhile separated all the most experienced and educated men, who were to be killed once false accusations had been brought against them. For one of that group of the men of learning, called Laetus, an active and very intelligent man, after the long-lasting squalor of imprisonment, was burnt to death on a pyre.[75] The king thought that by striking fear with such an example, he would crush the rest of them.

---

[72] A common charge when miracles were observed. In the bogus charges brought before Pope Gregory against Gregory, bishop of Agrigento, magic (from his studies in Egypt) and adultery were the main ones. See my translation of his biography.

[73] See *John* 12.10: 'the chief priests consulted that they might put Lazarus also to death.' Very apt! *M* (n. 30, p. 42) wrongly suggests a misreading of *John* 11.45-53.

[74] For the bishops and priests present, and their later treatment, see the *Notitia*.

[75] In 474, the eloquent intellectual, Bishop Laetus of Nepta (in Byzacena) visited the Emperor Justinian, and successfully appealed for his military help for the Catholic Church, against the Arian king of the Vandals. This appeal was certainly dangerous for Laetus when he returned to Carthage, determined to endure his

48   Book One

Finally we all came to the conflict of debate, of course to a place chosen by our adversaries. And so our bishops, to avoid the tumult of shouting (in case the Arians might perhaps say afterwards that the large number of our clergy over-ruled them), chose ten from our number to reply on behalf of all of us. Cyril with his followers arrogantly placed a throne for himself on a high platform, while ours stood before them. And our bishops spoke:

'That meeting is always pleasant where the proud superiority of power is not dominant, and what is true is recognized when it comes from a common consensus, with the judges making a decision from the pleas of each party. But who will be the judge now, who the cross-examiner, so that the scales of justice may either confirm a sound argument or refute an erroneous assumption?'

And when they were saying such things and others, the king's notary replied and said:

'Let the Patriarch Cyril speak.'[76]

At that title, arrogantly and illegally usurped by him, our bishops cursed him and said:

'Inform us who has allowed Cyril to assume that title for himself.'[77]

And from then on our adversaries stirred up a great din and began to accuse our bishops falsely. And our bishops requested that if they were not allowed to cross-examine them, their sensible group should at least be allowed to look on. Because of this, all the sons of the Catholic Church who were present were ordered to receive a hundred blows from a cudgel. Then the blessed Eugenius began to cry aloud:

---

martyrdom, it seems. He played a key rôle in the *Chronicon* also. He was clearly a most courageous and impressive man, martyred when burnt to death in 479.

[76] This comment has led to several weak emendations. I suggest that *dicat* ('let him speak') was corrupted into the very common word in dialogue, *dixit*.

[77] Cyril's title of 'bishop' appeared in 2.3 ('especially Bishop Cyril'), and in 2.6 ('Huneric and his Bishop Cyril'), here five times and in 5.6 below ('an Arian bishop, previously a notary of Cyril') that suggests considerable power. Gregory of Tours was wrong not to give him the title of 'bishop' (*Hist Franc* 2.3). The title here of 'patriarch' may have been correct, bestowed by the king, although the Catholics certainly would not admit it.

Arians and Vandals of the 4th-6th Centuries   49

'May God witness the violence that we suffer, may He know the affliction and persecution[78] that we endure from our persecutors.'

Turning to Cyril, our bishops said to him:

'Explain what your intentions are.'

Cyril replied: 'I do not know Latin.'

Our bishops said:

'We know for certain that you have always spoken Latin. Now you should not excuse yourself, especially as you have stirred up a controversy over this matter.'

And seeing that the Catholic bishops were better prepared for the debate, Cyril was all too ready to use various sophistries to refuse a hearing. But our bishops had seen this beforehand, and had written a short work on the true faith, composed aptly enough and not too long, saying:

'If you want to know our faith, this is the truth that we uphold.'

---

[78] The 'and persecution' (*et persecutionem*) was omitted by *M*.

BOOK THREE (A)

Preface

As stated above, this document is said to have been written by the bishops some time beforehand, and then presented by the archbishop of Carthage, the saintly Eugenius, as Bishop Victor himself pointed out: *ante nostri praevidentes, labellum de fide conscripserant* ('beforehand our bishops had foreseen this and had written a short work on faith'). This may have been the work of the ten bishops chosen to represent the rest, but they had little chance to do so before the finale, and only one could have written the final version. Quite possibly the earlier author was the erudite bishop of Vita, who was clearly a trusted observer (as we have seen in his work with Eugenius and his prison visitations). With his many pastoral duties, it seems quite unlikely that Eugenius could have written so long a statement before the proceedings began.

But if the first draft did perhaps derive from the ten bishops or even from the archbishop, the bishop of Vita certainly expanded and revised it for literary presentation. It deserves to be included now as an interesting description of the Catholic faith at this important period of occupation and schism in the sixth century. It should be noted also that at the beginning of book 4, the pamphlet is referred to as *noster libellus* ('our little book') and this certainly suggests Victor, who regularly used the first person plural to describe himself, and the author's self-depreciatory diminutive *libellus* suggests him also. If the selected ten bishops or the archbishop himself had written it, a third person plural or singular would have been used (*episcoporum*, or *Eugenii*). In fact the self-depreciation continues as Victor describes the Catholic defense in a lukewarm manner as *satis decenter sufficienterque conscriptum* ('composed aptly enough and not too long'). He would have been far more eulogistic, if his hero Eugenius or the courageous bishops had in fact written this very polished statement.

For a comparison, my translation of Ambrose's *De Fide Orthodoxa Contra Arianos alias De Filii Divinitate et Consubstantialitate* will be included after this one as book 3 (b).

Arians and Vandals of the 4th-6th Centuries 51

The Profession of the Faith of the Catholic Bishops as offered to King Huneric.

Section 1: The Unity of God's Substance

'We are ordered by the king's command to give an account of the Catholic faith that we hold, and for that reason we undertake to describe briefly what we believe and what we preach by virtue of our meager powers, but relying on divine assistance.

First, therefore, we know that we must explain about the unity of the substance of the Father and the Son, called 'consubstantiality' by the Greeks.[1] And so we profess the Father and Son and the Holy Spirit in the unity of divine nature, in such a way that we admit with a faithful confession that the Father subsists as a distinct person, and the Son exists no less in his own person, and the Holy Spirit retains the distinctiveness of his personality. But we do not assert that the Father is the same as the Son, nor do we admit that the Son is the same as the Father or the Holy Spirit. Nor do we accept that the Holy Spirit is the same as either the Father or the Son. But we believe that the unbegotten Father and the Son begotten from the Father, and the Holy Spirit proceeding from the Father and the Son, are all three of one substance and essence,[2] since the unbegotten Father and the begotten Son and the derived Holy Spirit have one divine nature in common, but they consist of three distinct persons.

And a heresy has arisen against this Catholic and Apostolic faith, introducing a new interpretation, asserting that the Son was not born from the substance of the Father, but from no existing thing, that is having substance from nothing. A Greek word 'ὁμοούσιον' ('consubstantiality') has been coined to refute and totally abolish this impious proposition, that has arisen against our faith, as it is interpreted as 'being of one substance and essence,' and it signifies that the Son was not born from nothing, nor came from any substance other than the Father.[3] But anyone who thinks

---

[1] As observed above, this very important word at this time (written in Greek three times below), translates the key concept of consubstantiality in the text.
[2] Migne reads *de Patre et Filio*, as found in most mss. *M* omits it, as an argument of 'later theology.' But see section 21 below: *de Patre procedit Spiritus sanctus*, but it both creates and has prescience *cum Patre et Filio*.
[3] Accepting the negative *ex nullis* read in other manuscripts, to be consistent with the argument above, although the text's *ullis* looks all right at first sight.

52   Book Three (A)

that 'consubstantiality' should be removed wants to assert that the Son was born from nothing. But the Son is not from nothing, without doubt he is from the Father, and the Son is rightly consubstantial, that is, of one substance with the Father.

Section 2: Proof from Scripture

That He is born from the Father, that is, of one substance with the Father, is supported by these testimonies, as the apostle says: 'Who being the brightness of his glory and the express image of his person, and upholding all things by the word of his power.'[4] And again God the Father himself, while chastising the perfidy of the unbelievers, who were unwilling to listen to the voice of his Son preaching through the prophets, and continuing in his substance, said: 'They heard not the voice of my substance.' Rebuking those who despise the voice of his substance with a terrifying statement, He speaks to the same prophet: 'Accept weeping over the mountains and over the paths of the desert accept grief, because they have given up, for the reason that there are no men there; they heard not the voice of my substance, from the fowl of the air right down to the cattle.'[5]

And again he upbraids those who declined to admit one substance and were unwilling to stay in the same substance of faith, saying: 'If they had stood in my substance, then I should have turned them from their evil way, and from their very wicked thoughts.'[6]

And again it is declared most openly that the Son is to be confessed as not being outside the substance of the Father, but is to be considered to be in the same substance, by a faithful eye, as the prophet says: 'Who has stood in the substance of the Lord, and has seen, and has heard his voice?' It was proved long ago by prophetic oracles that the Son is the substance of his Father, as Solomon says: 'For you showed your substance and the

---

[4] *Hebrews* 1.3 (with *gerens* for *portans*).

[5] The whole verse in *Jeremiah* 9 appears, but it is greatly adapted. The original (in the James version) is: 'For the mountains will I take up a weeping and wailing, and for the habitations of the wilderness a lamentation, because they are burned up, so that none can pass through them; neither can men hear the voice of the cattle; both the fowl of the heavens and the beast are fled; they are gone.'

[6] *Jeremiah* 23.22. There is just a change in word order. The following quote comes four verses earlier in *Jeremiah* (but with *substantia* for the Vulgate's *consilio*).

sweet love that you have for your sons,'[7] a substance that seems to have flowed forth from Heaven for the people of Israel, in the figure and the image of the heavenly bread. The Lord himself explained this in the gospel, saying: 'Moses gave you not that bread from Heaven, but my Father gives you bread from Heaven.' And he shows himself to be the bread anyway, when he says: 'I am the living bread which came down from Heaven.' On this, the prophet David says: 'Man did eat angels' food.'[8]

Section 3: Father and Son are Equals

For so that the unity of the substance of Father and Son may be still more evident, and the equality of their divinity may be revealed, He himself says in the gospel: 'I am in the Father and the Father is in me.' And: 'I and my Father are one.'[9] And this refers not only to unity of will but also to one and the same substance, because he does not say: 'The Father and I have one will,' but 'we are one.' For the assertion of paternal unity is declared not so much from what they will but from what they are. John the evangelist says the same: 'Therefore the Jews sought to kill him because he not only had broken the Sabbath but said also that God was his Father, making himself equal with God.'[10] Anyway, this should not be wholly referred to the Jews, because the evangelist truly said about the Son, that he was 'making himself equal with God.' It was written likewise by the same evangelist: 'Whatever the Father does, the Son also does the same likewise.' And again: 'As the Father raises the dead and gives them life, even so his Son gives life to whom he will.' Likewise: 'As all honour the Son, so they honour the Father.'[11] For equal honour is only shown to equals. Likewise there the Son says to his Father: 'All my things are yours, and yours are mine.' Similarly: 'Philip, whoever sees me, sees my Father also. How say you 'Show us the Father'?[12] He would not have said this unless he was equal with his Father in all ways. Likewise the Lord himself said: 'You believe in God, believe also in me.'[13] And to show

---

[7] Adapted from *Wisdom* 16.21, where *substantia* is in fact the correct reading.

[8] The last three quotes come from *John* 6.32 where the text omits *verum* before *panem* ('true bread'), *John* 6.41 and *Psalms* 78(77), 25.

[9] *John* 10.38, 30.

[10] *John* 5.18. The Vulgate has *magis quaerebant* ('they sought all the more').

[11] *John* 5.19, 21 and 23 (three short quotes).

[12] *John* 17.10 and 14.9.

[13] *John* 14.1.

54 Book Three (A)

thus far the unity of their equality[14] he says: 'No man knows the Son but the Father, neither knows any man the Father save the Son, and he to whomsoever the Son shall reveal him.' And just as the Son reveals the Father to whomsoever he wishes, even so the Father also reveals his Son, as He himself says to Peter, confessing that he was Christ, the Son of a living God: 'Blessed are you, Simon Bar-Jonah, for flesh and blood has not revealed it to you, but my Father which is in Heaven.' And once more the Son says: 'No one comes to the Father, except through me,' and 'No one comes to me, except the Father who has sent me draw him.' From this the equality of the Father and Son is clear, when they attract believers to themselves in turn. He says likewise: 'If you had known me, you should have known my Father also and henceforth you know him and have seen him.'[15]

Section 4: Two Natures in Christ

However, because we profess that there are two natures in the Son, that is, a true God and a true man, having a body and a soul, whatever the Scriptures relate about the excellent power of his sublime nature, we feel should be attributed to his admirable divinity. And whatever is narrated in a more humble manner about him beneath the glory of his heavenly power, we ascribe not to the word of God, but to the human form he took on. With regard to his divinity, therefore, there is what we quoted earlier, when he says: 'I and my Father are one,' and 'Who sees me sees my Father also,' and 'Everything that the Father does the Son does the same likewise,' and the rest as quoted above.[16] But what is recorded about him with regard to being human is this: 'My Father is greater than I am,' and 'I came not to do mine own will, but the will of him that sent me,' and 'Father, if it be possible, let this cup pass from me.' Or when he said from the wilderness, 'My God, my God, why have you forsaken me?' and again the prophet said in the person of the Son, 'You are my God from my mother's belly,' and when he is shown to be 'lower than the angels,' and a great many passages like this, which we have not inserted for the sake of brevity.[17]

---

[14] Rather than *M*'s misleading 'Moreover, to show the unity and the equality.' Beside *adhuc* meaning 'so far,' their unity consists of their equality.

[15] The last five quotes come from *Matthew* 11.27 and 16.17, and *John* 14.6, 6.44 and 14.7.

[16] See above for these quotes, mostly from Saints John and Matthew.

[17] For the last six, see *John* 4.28, 6.38 (2), *Matthew* 27.46 and *Psalms* 22(21).10, 9(8).6.

Therefore, the Son of God was bound by no necessities of the human condition, but by the free power of his divine nature, and he assumed our nature with miraculous piety, in such a way that he did not abandon at all his own nature, which is divine, since divinity neither admits increase nor suffers loss. Wherefore we offer thanks to our same Lord, Jesus Christ, who for the sake of us and our salvation came down from Heaven and redeemed us by his suffering, gave us new life by his death and glorified us by his ascension, who sitting at the right hand of the Father is going to come to judge the living and the dead, to bestow the reward of eternal life on the just and to inflict well-deserved punishments on the impious and the unbelievers.[18]

Section 5: The Birth of the Son

We believe, therefore, that the Father gave birth to his Son eternally and ineffably from himself, that is, from that which he himself is, and that the Son was born not from without, not from nothing, not from another subsistent material, but from God. And he who was born from God is nothing other than what his Father is, and for that reason he is of one substance with him, because the truth of his nativity does not admit a diversity of birth. For if his substance is different from his Father's, he is either not a true Son or, terrible to say, he was born degenerate.[19] For he is the true son, as John says: 'that we are in him that is true, in his Son.' For he is not degenerate, also, because he was born a true God from a true God, as the same evangelist John argues, saying: 'This is the true God and eternal life,' and the Lord himself said in the gospel: 'I am the way, the truth and the life.'[20] Therefore, if he does not receive his substance from elsewhere, he has it from the Father, and if he has it from the Father, he is of one substance with the Father. But if he is not of one substance, therefore he is not of the Father, but from elsewhere, since from where he comes, from there he must have his substance. Everything was created from nothing, but the Son comes from the Father. Let each person decide on one of two choices, either grant the Son substance from the Father or admit that he came to exist out of nothing.

---

[18] This is close to the Nicene Creed.

[19] The *degener* means outside its *genus*, race or family, so not genuine or ignoble.

[20] For the three quotes above, see *I John* 5.20 (2), and *John* 14.6.

56 Book Three (A)

Section 6: An Objection Answered

But perhaps a prophet's witness argues against this: 'Who shall declare his generation?'[21] And why should I not reply: 'Explain to me the manner and quality of divine generation, and announce in human words the mystery of such a great secret, since I have asked from where he was born, not how he was born'?[22] For divine generation is indescribable, not unknowable. For almost to such an extent is it not unknowable, that is, it is not unknown from where He comes, that even his Father protests very often that he gave birth to him and the Son protests that he was born from his Father, and no Christian at all disputes it, as is shown in the gospel, as the Son himself speaks: 'But he who does not believe is condemned already, because he has not believed in the name of the only begotten Son of God.' And John the evangelist says likewise: 'And we beheld his glory, the glory as of the only begotten of the Father.' And so we conclude our declaration with a brief summary.[23]

If he was truly born from the Father, he is of one substance and is his true Son, but if he is not of one substance, he is not a true God either. Or if he is not his true son, he is not a true God either, or if he is a true God, yet he is not from the substance of his Father, then he himself is also unbegotten.[24] But because he is not unbegotten, then his making relies, as some think, on something else, if it is not from his Father's substance. But Heaven forbid such a belief! For we profess a Son sharing one substance with the Father, and we detest the Sabellian heresy, which so confuses the Holy Trinity that it claims that the Father is the same as the Son, and believes that the Holy Spirit is the same, not preserving the three different persons in the unity.[25]

Section 7: Same Substance of Unbegotten and Begotten

But perhaps someone objects: 'As the Father is unbegotten and the Son begotten, it cannot happen that the begotten and the unbegotten have one

---

[21] *Isaiah* 53.8. A question follows with my *cur*, preferable to *cum* in the MSS.

[22] Here *cur* is preferable without a subordinate sentence. *M* translates neither *cum* nor *cur* ('But I did not... ').

[23] The last two quotes are from *John* 3.18 and 1.14.

[24] *M* seems to be confused by this argument, omitting two short sentences.

[25] Sabellius came from the Church in Rome, during the 3rd century, and founded the heretical sect that rejected the independent substance of the Son. Saint Basil suggested that he came from Libya or Pentapolis, but Rome seems more likely.

Arians and Vandals of the 4th-6th Centuries 57

and the same substance. For anyway, if the Son were unbegotten as the Father is unbegotten, then the substance could be more diverse, because each of them coming into existence by himself would not have a substance in common with the other.' But as the unbegotten Father gave birth to the Son from himself, that is, from that which he himself is, if that is something that exists or could be described (or rather because its nature cannot be described at all), it is apparent that there is one substance for both the one giving birth and the one born, as we truly profess that God from God, light from light, is the Son. For the Apostle John bears witness that the Father is the light, as he says: 'That God is light, and in him is no darkness at all.' Likewise he says about the Son: 'And his life was the light of men, and the light shines in the darkness, and the darkness comprehended it not.' And below: 'He was a true light, which lights every man that comes into this world.' This shows that the Father and the Son are of one substance, as the substance of light and brightness, which of course is created from itself and which exists from its own creation, cannot be different.[26]

Finally, in case someone should mention a difference in natural light between the Father and the Son, for that reason the apostle says about the same Son as 'being the brightness of his glory and the express image of his substance.'[27] In this it is shown more clearly that He is coeternal with the Father and inseparable from the Father, and of one substance with him, as the brightness is always coeternal with the light, since the brightness is never separated from the light and the brightness can never be different from the light in its nature and substance. For the brightness of light is the same as the strength of God the Father. And so He is everlasting because of the eternity of his strength and inseparable because of the unity of his brightness.[28]

And this is what we faithfully profess, that the Son was born from the substance of the Father, for which God the Father himself provides the clearest of evidence. To show that He gave birth to his own son from the substance of his own ineffable nature, and to instruct the ignorance of our fragile minds, raising us from things visible to things invisible, He took some words about earthly birth as an example of divine birth, saying:

---

[26] Again the three short quotes are from *I John* 1.5 and *John* 1.4-5, and 9.

[27] *Hebrews* 1.3. The Vulgate uses *substantia*, as in the text above.

[28] *M* gives the Latin for this ending, comparing it with Ambrose *De Fide* 4.9.108. Many similar comparisons can be made between the three defenses, and await a biblical scholar to do justice to them.

'before the daystar I begot you from my womb.'[29] What could His divine nature deign to utter more clearly, what more lucidly? With what proofs, with what examples of things existing could he suggest the propriety of this birth other than show the propriety of the person giving birth by specifying the womb? Not because he is composed of bodily members or is distinguished by some well-shaped limbs, but because we could not otherwise perceive the truth of divine birth with an attentive mind, unless we were challenged by the human wording of a womb, so that there could be no ambiguity any more about his having been born from the substance of God, as it is certain that he came into existence from the womb of his Father.

Section 8: Indivisible Substance of God

Believing, therefore, that God the Father gave birth to the Son from his own substance, without any suffering, we do not say that the substance itself has either been divided in the Son or has suffered a diminution in the Father, through which it could be subject to the imperfection of human suffering.[30] For Heaven forbid that we should imagine or think or believe such things about God! For we faithfully profess that the perfect Father gave birth to the perfect Son, without any diminution of himself, without any derivation and without any weakness of human suffering at all. For if one objects that, if God gave birth from himself, he suffered the vice of being divided, one can say that he found the work hard when he created the universe, and for this reason on the seventh day he rested from all of his work. But he neither sensed any human suffering nor any diminution in giving birth from himself, nor suffered any fatigue in creating the universe.

For so that the freedom from suffering in the divine birth might be shown to us more clearly, we have accepted the Son professing God to be from God and light to be from light. If, therefore, in the production of visible and earthly light, something of this sort is found, as when a light is taken from a light after arising through some manner of birth, and the actual origin of the light that produced another light from itself could neither be diminished, nor suffer any loss at all from the light passed on from itself, how much more rightly and more correctly should one believe, concerning the nature of the divine and ineffable light, that in giving birth to light

---

[29] *Psalms* 110(109) 3.

[30] *passio* comes from *patior* ('I suffer') and regularly has the sense of 'suffering.'

Arians and Vandals of the 4th-6th Centuries 59

from itself, it could not be diminished at all?[31] Wherefore the Son is an equal of his Father, not born within time, but coeternal with the one giving birth, just as the brightness created by a fire is manifestly equal to what created it. Let it suffice to have said as much about the equality of the Father and the Son and about the unity of their substance, as reasonable brevity has allowed.

Section 9: Holy Spirit consubstantial with Father and Son

It remains that we should say something about the Holy Spirit, whom we believe to be consubstantial with the Father and the Son, and coequal and coeternal, and should prove it with evidence. For although this venerable Trinity may be distinct in its persons and names, yet it should not be believed that because of this, there is a difference within itself and its eternity, but the divinity is truly and properly believed to remain from before all time in the Father and the Son and the Holy Spirit, and the Trinity itself cannot be divided by our interpretations, nor itself be turned again into one person and yet be combined. This is our full faith, and this is our belief.

For that reason we do not allow the Trinity to be considered or called 'Gods,' but we confess one God in the three aforesaid persons and names.

For this indescribable divinity did not reveal itself through names and persons, so that it might be shut in or defined, as it were, by words, but so that it might be known to be what it was. It gave to those who believed a partial understanding of itself, so much as the narrowness of the human mind could grasp, as the prophet said: 'If you will not believe, you will not understand.'[32] And thus there is one divine nature in the Trinity and the name of this word signifies one substance, but not one person. To prove this matter to the faithful, the divinity itself was always present as proof of it with many and very frequent testimonies. Therefore, let us be allowed to offer just a few of the many witnesses, for the sake of brevity, since the true proof of its majesty, although it has a plurality of witnesses, does not need a plurality, since a few are sufficient for a believer.

---

[31] His placements of 'not' makes *M*'s version of this period (p. 52) very confusing.
[32] *Isaiah* 7.9. Victor employs the Septuagint's reading, οὐδὲ μὴ συνῆτε, rather than the Vulgate's *non permanebitis* ('you will not be established').

60 Book Three (A)

Section 10: Proof from the Scriptures

First, therefore, from the books of the Old Testament and afterwards from the New Testament also, we shall show that the Father, the Son and the Holy Spirit are of one substance. Thus the book of Genesis begins: 'In the beginning God made the heavens and the earth; but the earth was invisible and unmade, and darkness was over the face of the deep, and the spirit of God moved over the waters.'[33] Then, as the Jews asked who he was, Jesus mentioned his beginning: 'What I told you from the beginning.'[34] And the spirit of God was borne over the waters as the creator, sustaining creation by the strength of his power, so that, about to produce all living things from these waters, he might himself provide his own warmth for the rough shapes of the first creation, and might even then perceive[35] from the appearance of the mystery, the virtue of baptism, through the nature of the water of sanctification, and might give life to the first living bodies. Wherefore David bears witness, by God's favor: 'By the Lord's word were the heavens made firm, and by the spirit of his mouth all their strength.'[36]

See how full his brevity is, and how clearly it refers to the sacrament of unity. Putting 'the Father' in place of 'the Lord' and 'the Son' in the sense of 'the Word,' it named the Holy Spirit from 'the mouth of the Highest.' And in case 'Word' is understood as the product of a voice, He asserts that 'the heavens were made firm through it.' But in case the 'Spirit' is thought to be a breath[37], he showed the plenitude of heavenly virtue in it. For when he said 'strength,' there a person must subsist, and when he said 'all' it signified that they were not separate from the Father and Son, but were consummated in the Holy Spirit, so that the Spirit might not have on his own what is in the Father and the Son, but might have in full what each of the others has.

---

[33] This is a rather free version of the creation as in *Genesis* 1.1-2. The Vulgate reads *creavit Deus ... inanis et vacua, ... super faciem abyssi*i; the text reads *fecit Deus ... invisibilis et incomposita ... super abyssum.*

[34] *John* 8.25.

[35] Here the sense of *perciperet* is more likely 'perceive' than 'receive' as in *M.*

[36] *Psalms* 33(32). 6. The 'virtue' or the usual 'host' suggests the 'army of stars,' with *virtus* suggesting 'strength'.

[37] The text has *status* ('state' or 'condition') but I would suggest reading *flatus* as the letters *s* and *f* were very often confused, and it suits the context far better.

Arians and Vandals of the 4th-6th Centuries

Section 11: Three Persons in one Name

And again, when the Lord was speaking about the calling of all nations, preaching that the Holy Spirit lies within one holy name, he said: 'Go and teach all nations, baptizing them in the name of the Father and of the Son and of the Holy Spirit.' And again, when the apostle preached heavenly words to the Corinthians, he said: 'The grace of our Lord Jesus Christ and the love of God and the fellowship of the Holy Spirit be with you all.'[38]

So that we may confess more openly the unity of substance in this Trinity, we should consider this also, how God, when arranging the creation of the world and of mankind, showed the sacrament of the Trinity when he said: 'Let us make man in our image and after our likeness.'[39] When he says 'our' he shows at any rate that it is not of one person, but when he says 'image' and 'likeness' he suggests equality but implies distinctions between persons, so that in the same work, the understanding of the Trinity is clear, in which neither is plurality lacking nor is likeness causing difference, as the following words show: 'And God said' and 'God made' and 'God blessed.'[40] It is necessary that the author of the whole creation should be one God. An ancient blessing through Moses revealed this reason for faith and approved it, where he is ordered to bless his people with a sacrament consisting of a triple invocation. For God says to Moses: 'So bless my people, and I shall bless them also. The Lord bless you and keep you, the Lord make his face shine upon you and pity you. The Lord lift up his countenance upon you, and give you peace.'[41] The prophet David confirms this, as he says: 'Bless us, God, even our own God, bless us, God, and let all the ends of the earth fear him.' And with a hymn the heavenly powers of the angels venerate this unity of the Trinity, and as their mouths incessantly sing a triple 'Holy, holy, holy, Lord God of hosts,' they exalt his glory to the height of his one dominion.[42]

So that this is more openly forced into the minds of the faithful, we put forward Paul, who knew the mysteries of Heaven. For he says: 'Now there are diversities of gifts, but the same Spirit, and there are differences of administrations, but the same Lord. And there are diversities of

---

[38] These two quotes come from *Matthew* 28.19 and *2 Corinthians* 13.14.

[39] *2 Corinthians* 13.14.

[40] *Genesis* 1.24, 25, 28.

[41] Adapted from *Numbers* 6.23-26.

[42] From *Psalms* 67.5-7(66.7-8), and *Isaiah* 6.3, ending with the Hebrew for 'hosts', *Sabaoth.*

operations, but it is the same God which works all in all.' When he distinguished between the various graces themselves, he certainly showed that the Holy Spirit produced these different divisions according to the quality and merit of the participants, as he made a final point, saying: 'But all these that one and the same Spirit works, dividing to every man severally as he will.'[43] Thus no place is left for ambiguity, but rather it should be clear that the Holy Spirit is both God and author of his own will, as he is shown most clearly to operate all things and bestow the gifts of divine dispensation according to the judgment of his own will. For when a voluntary distribution of grace is recommended, there is no sign of a servile condition. For in created things, servitude should be understood, but in the Trinity, power and freedom should be. And so that we may explain even more clearly than light that the Holy Spirit is of one divinity with the Father and the Son, it is proved by the testimony of John the evangelist. For he says: 'There are three that bear witness in Heaven, the Father, the Word and the Holy Spirit, and these three are one.' Are there, he says, three separated with different equality, or three divided by various grades of differences with a wide separating gap? Rather, he says: 'Three are one.'[44]

Section 12: Their Creation is in Common

But so that the divinity of the Holy Spirit in creating all things is shown still more and more to be one with the Father and the Son, you have the Holy Spirit as a creator in the book of Job, who says: 'It is a Holy Spirit that made me, and a Spirit of the Almighty who teaches me.' And David says: 'Send forth your Spirit and they will be created, and you will renew the face of the earth.'[45] If creation and renewal shall be through the Spirit, without doubt the beginning of creation also was not without the Spirit. And so let us show that after creation the Holy Spirit gives life also, just like the Father and the Son. Indeed the apostle comments on the person of the Father: 'I bear witness in the sight of God, who gives life to all things.' But Christ gives life: 'My sheep hear my voice,' he said, 'and I give unto them eternal life.' But the Holy Spirit gives us new life, as the Lord himself says: 'It is the Spirit that gives life.' Behold, it is clearly shown

---

[43] *1 Corinthians* 12.4-6.

[44] *I Corinthians* 12.11.

[45] From *Job* 33.24 and *Psalms* 104(103).30.

that there is one instance of life being given by the Father and the Son and the Holy Spirit.[46]

Section 13: Foreknowledge

Although no Christian would be unaware that foreknowledge of all things, and a knowledge of hidden things, are in God, it should be shown from a book of Daniel, where he says: 'It is you, God, who knows hidden things, and have foreknowledge of all people, before they are born.' This same prescience is in Christ, as the evangelist states: 'For Jesus knew from the beginning who should betray him, and who they were that believed not in him.' It is clear that he had knowledge of these hidden things, as while speaking, he revealed the hidden thoughts of the Judaeans: 'Why do you think evil in your hearts?[47] Similarly this same Christ clearly showed that the Holy Spirit knew all things in advance, as he said to his apostles: 'When the Spirit of truth shall come, he will teach you all things, and he will show you things to come.' As He is said to announce things to come, it is certain that he has foreknowledge of all things, because he himself searches the depth of God, and knows all things which are in God, as Paul recalls, saying: 'For the Spirit searches out all, even the deep things of God.' And again in the same place: 'Just as no man knows the things of a man, save the spirit of man which is in him, even so no man knows the things of God, but the Spirit of God.'

Section 14: The Power of the Holy Spirit

But to understand the power of the Holy Spirit we must say a few words about some most terrible events. A deceitful disciple had sold a property, as was written in the Acts of the Apostles, and he hid part of the money, but placed the rest at the feet of the apostles, as if it were the whole amount, offending the Holy Spirit, from whom he thought he was concealing the money. But what did Saint Peter say to him at once? 'Ananias, why has Satan filled your heart so as to lie to the Holy Spirit?' and below: 'You have not lied unto men, but unto God.' And he was so

---

[46] The three quotes come from *1Timothy* 6.13 and from *John* 10.27-28 (adapted) and 6.63.

[47] The three quotes are adapted from *Daniel* 2.21-22 and *John* 6.64 and straight from *Matthew* 9.4.

64   Book Three (A)

struck by the power of him to whom he had wanted to lie, that he expired.[48]

How does Saint Peter want the Holy Spirit to be understood in this? It is clear anyway when he says: 'You have not lied unto men, but unto God,' and it is therefore obvious that he who lies to the Holy Spirit is lying to God, and he who believes in the Holy Spirit, believes in God. The Lord shows something like that, in fact something far more forceful, in the gospel, saying: 'All manner of sin and blasphemy shall be forgiven unto men, but the blasphemy against the Holy Spirit shall not be forgiven, neither in this world nor in the world to come.'[49] Behold, with a grim sentence, he says any man's sin is unforgivable if he has blasphemed against the Holy Spirit. Compare with this sentence what is written in the book of Kings: 'If by sinning a man shall sin against a man, they will pray for him; but if he shall sin against God, who will pray for him?'[50] And so if to blaspheme against the Holy Spirit and to sin against God is a similar crime, that is, an unpardonable one, now everyone knows how powerful the Holy Spirit is.

Section 15: The Presence of God everywhere

We learn from the mouth of Jeremiah that God is present everywhere and fulfills everything, as he says: 'Am I a God at hand, and not a God far off? If a man hides himself in secret places, shall I therefore not see him? Do I not fill Heaven and Earth?' But what does the Saviour say in the gospel about his presence everywhere? He says: 'Where two or three are gathered together in my name, there am I too in the midst of them.'[51] As for the Holy Spirit, the prophet says in God's person that he is equally present everywhere: 'May I stand in you, and my Spirit in the midst of you.' And Solomon says: 'The Spirit of the Lord fills the world, is all-embracing and knows what man says.' Likewise David says: 'Whither shall I go from your Spirit, where shall I flee from your presence? If I ascend to the Heavens, you are there, if I descend to Hell you are present. If I take my wings in a straight line and dwell in the uttermost parts of the sea, even there your hand will lead me, your right hand hold me.'[52]

---

[48] For the first half of this chapter, see *Acts* 5.2-5.

[49] Adapted from *Matthew* 12.31-32.

[50] *1 Samuel* 2.25.

[51] *Matthew* 18.20.

[52] The first quote is adapted from *Ezekiel* 36.27, the other two come from *Wisdom* 1.7 and *Psalms* 139(138), 7-10.

Section 16: God lives among his Saints

God lives among his saints according to the promise in which he said: 'I will live among them.' Indeed the Lord Jesus stated this in the gospel: 'Abide in me, and I in you.' And Paul proves it by saying: 'Do you not know that Christ is in you?' And all of this is fulfilled in the dwelling-place of the Spirit, as John recalls, saying: 'We know from this that he is in us, because he has given us of his Spirit.' Likewise Paul also says: 'Do you not know that you are the temple of God and the Spirit of God lives in you?' And he says again: 'Glorify and bear God in your body.' Which God? Of course the Holy Spirit, whose temple we are seen to have.[53]

Section 17: Proof of Father, Son and Holy Spirit

For what the Father rebukes, and the Son rebukes and the Holy Spirit rebukes can be proved in this way. In the forty-ninth psalm we read: 'But unto the wicked, God says: "Why do you declare my statutes, and take my covenant in your mouth?"'[54] And below: "I shall rebuke you and set them in order before your eyes.' David spoke to Christ similarly as he prayed: 'Lord, rebuke me not in your anger,' because he was going to condemn all flesh. But what does the Saviour say about the Holy Spirit in the gospel? He says: 'When the Paraclete has come, he will rebuke the world of sin, and of justice and of judgment.' Foreseeing this, David cried out to the Lord: 'Whither shall I go from your Spirit, or whither shall I flee from your presence?'[55]

Section 18: The Goodness of Father, Son and Holy Spirit

For it is proved in this way that the Father is good and the Son is good and the Holy Spirit is good. The prophet says: 'You are good, Lord, and in your goodness teach me your statutes.' But the only-begotten Son says about himself: 'I am the good shepherd.' Likewise in the psalm about the

---

[53] The six quotes contained in this chapter are from *2 Corinthians* 6. 16, *John* 15.4, *2 Corinthians* 13.5, *I John* 4.13, *I Corinthians* 3.16 and *I Corinthians* 6.20.

[54] *M* omits totally what God said to the wicked: '*Quare tu enarras justitiam meam, et assumis testamentum meum per os tuum*?'

[55] The four quotes in chapter 17 are from *Psalms* 50(49). 16 and 6.1, *John* 16.8 and *Psalms* 139 (138).7.

66 Book Three (A)

Holy Spirit, David says unto the Lord: 'Your Spirit is good. May it lead me into the land of righteousness.'[56]

Section 19: The Dignity of the Holy Spirit

But who could keep quiet about that dignity of the Holy Spirit? For the ancient prophets used to cry out: 'So said the Lord.' When Christ arrived he applied these words to his own person, saying: 'But I say unto you.' What did the new prophets cried out? As the prophet Agabus says in the Acts of the Apostles: 'The Holy Spirit says this.' And Paul said to Timotheus: 'The Spirit speaks expressly.' These words reveal the Trinity's complete lack of difference. And Paul indeed says that God the Father and Christ had called him, and had sent him out: 'Paul,' he said, 'an apostle, not of men nor by man but by Jesus Christ and God the Father.' But in the Acts of the Apostles one reads that he was set apart and sent by the Holy Spirit. For so it was written: 'So spoke the Holy Spirit. "Separate for me Barnabas and Saul for the work whereunto I have called them." 'And a little after he says: 'Sent forth by the Holy Spirit, they departed unto Seleucia.' Likewise in the same book: 'Attend to yourselves and the whole flock, over which the Holy Spirit has made you bishops.'[57]

Section 20: The Common Name of Paraclete

But let no one think that the Holy Spirit is at all contemptible because he is called the 'paraclete.' For the 'paraclete' is an 'advocate,' or rather a 'comforter' in the Latin language,[58] and this title is shared by the Son of God also, as John says: 'These things write I to you so that you sin not; but if any man should sin, we have an advocate with the Father, Jesus Christ the righteous.' For the Lord himself also,[59] when he says to the Apostles: 'The Father will send you another advocate,' without doubt shows himself to be an advocate also, when he says 'another advocate.' But this name of advocate is not alien to the Father also. For it is a name of beneficence, not of nature. Finally Paul writes to the Corinthians as follows: 'Blessed

---

[56] The three quotes from chapter 18 are from *Psalms* 119(118). 68, *John* 10.11 and *Psalms* 143(142).10.

[57] The seven quotations from ch. 19 are from *Matthew* 5.22, *Acts* 21.11,*1Timothy* 4.1, *Galatians* 1.1 and *Acts* 13.2, 13.4 and 20.28.

[58] The Greek παράκλητος was used primarily for the Holy Spirit (as an 'advocate', 'comforter' or 'intercessor').

[59] *M* leaves out the 'also' here and after 'Son of God' above (and often elsewhere).

Arians and Vandals of the 4th-6th Centuries 67

be God, even the Father of our Lord Jesus Christ, the Father of mercies and the God of all comfort, who comforts us.' So since the Father is said to be the 'comforter,' and the Son is the 'comforter' and the Holy Spirit is also the 'comforter,' a single 'omforting' is provided by the Trinity. Just as there is one remission of sins also, as the apostle affirms, saying: 'You are washed, you are sanctified, you are justified in the name of our Lord Jesus Christ and by the Spirit of our God.'[60]

We could have presented still more proofs from the Holy Writ to show clearly that, beside the sacrament of baptism, the Trinity has one glory, operation and power. But because the minds of wise men are full of these examples, we have passed over many for the sake of brevity.[61]

Section 21: Recapitulation

Therefore let us recapitulate our statements. If the Holy Spirit proceeds from the Father, if he sets free, if he is the Lord and sanctifies, if he creates and gives life with the Father and the Son, if he has foreknowledge together with the Father and the Son, if he is everywhere and fills everything, if he lives among the chosen, if he denounces worldly things, if he judges, if he is good and righteous, if men cry out about him that 'the Holy Spirit says these things,' if he has established prophets, if he sends out apostles, if he appoints bishops, if he is a 'comforter,' if he dispenses all things as he wills, if he washes away and justifies, if he kills those who tempt him and if anyone who blasphemes against him has no forgiveness, either in this time or in the future, which is God's preserve anyway; since this is so, why is there any doubt about the fact that he is God, when the magnitude of its works make his nature clear? For, in any case, he is not different from the Father and the Son in majesty, just as he is not different from them in the strength of his works. In vain is his divine name denied, whose power cannot be denied. In vain am I prohibited from worshipping him together with the Father and the Son, when I am obliged to confess him together with the Father and the Son.

If that Spirit confers remission of sins on me with the Father and the Son, and confers sanctification and eternal life, I am excessively ungrateful and

---

[60] The last four quotations are from *1 John* 2.1, *John* 14.16, *2 Corinthians* 1.3-4 and *1 Corinthians* 6.11.

[61] *M*'s version of the final two sentences ('the full understanding of these things is for the wise') distorts the Latin *ex his plenus est sapientium intellectus*. The wise knew plenty of other texts to support the bishop's argument.

68 Book Three (A)

most impious if I do not bestow glory on it with the Father and the Son, and if he is not to be worshipped with the Father and the Son, then he should not be confessed in baptism. And if he is confessed in every way following the word of the Lord and the teachings of the apostles, so that the faith is not half complete, who will be able to prevent me from worshipping him? For if I am ordered to believe in him, I should also pray to him. And so I shall worship the Father, and I shall worship the Son, and I shall worship the Holy Spirit, with one and the same veneration. But if someone thinks this hard, let him hear how David encourages the faithful to worship God, as he says: 'Worship at his footstool.' And if it is sign of religion to worship at his footstool, how much more religious is it if his Spirit is worshipped? The Spirit, that is, which Saint Peter predicted with such great sublimity, saying: 'With the Holy Spirit sent down from Heaven, which thing the angels desired to look at.' If the angels desire to look at him, how much more ought we mortals not to despise him, in case it is said against us as it was said against the Jews: 'You always resist the Holy Spirit as your fathers did.'[62]

Section 22: A Stronger Argument

But if such powerful arguments of this sort do not incline your mind to worshipping the Holy Spirit, accept something still more powerful. For Paul instructed the Church's prophets, among whom at any rate and through whom the Holy Spirit was speaking, as follows: 'If you all prophesy and one comes in that does not believe, or one unlearned, he is convinced by all and is judged by all; and thus the secrets of his heart made manifest, and then falling on his face he will worship God, reporting that God is truly in you.'[63] And the Holy Spirit is certainly in those who prophesy.[64] Therefore if the unbelievers fall on their face and adore the Holy Spirit when terrified, and confess unwillingly, how much more is it right for the believers to worship the Holy Spirit willingly and due to affection? But the Holy Spirit is worshipped not as it were separately, in the manner of the gentiles, just as the Son is not worshipped separately either, because he is on the right hand of the Father, but when we worship the Father, we believe that we are worshipping the Son and the Holy Spirit also, because even when we invoke the Son, we believe that we are

---

[62] The three quotations in chapter 21 are from *Psalms* 98(99)5, *1 Peter* 1.12 and *Acts* 7.51.

[63] *1 Corinthians* 14.24-25.

[64] For *prophetant M* rightly prefers the plural on p. xix, yet wrongly translates it as 'the Holy Spirit who prophesies' here. The prophets of the Church are inspired.

invoking the Father, and when we invoke the Father we are confident that the Son hears us, as the Lord himself said: 'Whatever you shall ask the Father in my name, that will I do, that the Father may be glorified in the Son.'[65]   And if we worship the Holy Spirit, the one of whom he is the Spirit is worshipped anyway.

But nobody is ignorant of this, that nothing can be added to divine majesty, nor can anything be taken away from it, through human supplication, but each person, following what his will proposes, either acquires glory for himself by worshipping faithfully, or he acquires eternal shame by resisting obstinately.   For arrogance and contempt certainly condemn him, but by paying due honour he awaits the fruit of his devotion.   But why would the faithful not honour the Trinity honestly, confident that they are dependent upon it, by the name through which they boast that they are reborn, and whose servants they are proud to be called? For just as they are called men of God from the name of God the Father, as Elijah was said to be 'a man of God' and Moses was called 'a man of God,' even so we are called Christians after Christ, and so also we are called spiritual, after the Spirit.   Therefore if someone is called a man of God, and he is not Christian, he is as nothing.   If he were called Christian and was not spiritual, he should not have much trust in his salvation.

Section 23: The Confession of Baptism

Therefore, let us have complete faith in the Trinity, in accordance with the confession of baptism that brings salvation, let us have a single pious devotion.   Let us give no thought to different powers, in the manner of the gentiles, or be suspicious of a created being in regard to the deity of the Trinity.   But do not let the stumbling blocks of the Jews move us, as they deny the Son of God and do not worship the Holy Spirit, but rather let us worship and magnify the perfect Trinity, and as we say with our mouths in the mysteries, so let us hold in our minds, 'Holy, Holy, Holy, Lord God of hosts.'   Saying 'Holy' three times we confess one omnipotence, since there is one religion, one glorification of the Trinity, so that we may hear from the apostle, just as the Corinthians heard: 'The grace of the Lord Jesus Christ and the love of God and the communion of the Holy Spirit be with you all.'[66]   This is our faith as confirmed by the evangelical and apostolic traditions and authority, and founded in the society of all the

---

[65] *John* 14.13.

[66] *2 Corinthians* 13.14.

70 Book Three (A)

Catholic churches in the world, in which we trust and hope that through the grace of almighty God we may survive until the end of this life.'

So ended the booklet, sent on April 20th,[67] through Januarius of Zattara and Villaticus of Casa Mediana, bishops of Numidia, and Boniface of Foratiana and Boniface of Gratiana, bishops of Byzacena.[68]

---

[67] *a d xii cal. Mai.* in the Latin text (*alii xvii,* the 16th).

[68] In the *Notitia*, Villaticus, of Casa Mediana, is mentioned among Numidia's clergy, and Boniface of Foratiana, among those of the province of Byzacena, but neither Januarius (bishop of Zattara, mod. Kef Bezioun) nor the other Boniface (bishop of Gratiana) was included. These four bishops had the unenviable task of presenting the work to the king, rather than the archbishop (or Victor of Vita).

BOOK THREE (B)

SAINT AMBROSE [C. 333-397]

DE FIDE ORTHODOXA CONTRA ARIANOS, ALIAS DE FILII DIVINITATE ET CONSUBSTANTIALITATE TRACTATUS ('TRACT CONCERNING THE DEFENCE OF THE CATHOLIC FAITH AGAINST THE ARIANS, THAT IS, CONCERNING THE DIVINITY AND CONSUBSTANTIALITY OF THE SON')

Preface

The *De Fide Orthodoxa* is considered by almost all scholars to have been written by Saint Ambrose, and this seems most likely when it is compared with the similar tract in Vita's History of the Vandals and their Arian priests. There is no mention at all of the Vandals in this text, and the Nicaean synod seems to be a recent event, pointing to a pre-400 origin. The Latin text used for this English translation is in Migne's collection, *CC Series Latina* volume xiv columns 580-598. It is included in the appendix to *Opera S. Ambrosii*. The text makes mostly judicious use of earlier editions, but there are some typographical errors in it and a few false readings. These are *primogentius* for *primogenitus* (*bis*) in col. 583, *lumen ex lunine* for *lumine*, and *ispsius* for *ipsius*, *opportere* for *oportet* in col. 587, *qui nisit* for *qui misit* in col. 588, *idetatis* for *dietatis* (rare) and *quem* for *cum* in col. 589, *virtulus* for *vitulus* in col. 590, *metuentes* for *metuent* in col. 592, *credi* for *creari* in col. 593, *ut Dominum* for *ut in Dominum* and *rubo* for *rubro* in 594. But the Latin is almost always grammatical, and there are several long and well-organized periods.

72 Book Three (B)

Ambrosius' rhetorical training is very evident, as can be seen from the opening, in col. 580, that ends with a very neat, rhyming chiasmus: *spiritu offensum, intelligibilem auditu*. Above this is one of many powerful antitheses with rhyme and harsh *s, t and m* sound effects: *et simplicitatem sensus mei ostenderem, et scrupulum legentibus amputarem*. The final *clausula* would have delighted Cicero. There are many very neat antitheses throughout, but his fondness for parataxis is rather overdone at times.

There is quite a large body of biblical quotations, and in many places the author expands and repeats the quotation, to reinforce his argument. Far the most popular texts were John's gospel (with 21 quotes) and I Corinthians (with ten quotes). There are none from Matthew, which is surprising, and only one from Mark and one from Luke. For the Greek Scriptures, others are from Acts (one), Romans (one), Ephesians (one), Colossians (three) and II Timothy (one), 40 in all. In the Hebraic Scriptures, Exodus has seven and Psalms six (very low by comparison), Isaiah four, Wisdom and Genesis three, Jeremiah two and just one in Proverbs, Joel, Baruch, Sirach and Numbers, 30 in all. Most seem to be quoted from memory, with minor changes in the best-known ones, but several are very freely adapted. As with the other texts, I have used the Vulgate as a check, and a modernized version of the King James Bible for my English, as far as it matches the Latin. A close comparison with Victor of Vita's similar work is left for a theologian. So too is a new biography of Saint Ambrose. A final bibliography describes recent works.

Confession of Faith

We believe in God, the Father Almighty, Maker of all things visible and invisible, and in Jesus Christ, his only Son our Lord, a son born of a father, that is, of the substance of the Father, God from God, Light from Light, True God from True God, born not made, of one substance with the Father, which the Greeks call ὁμοούσιον, through whom all things were made, whether that which is in the sky, whether that which is on earth, who for us men and for our salvation came down from Heaven and became flesh and was made man, and suffered death and rose on the third day and ascended to Heaven. From thence he shall come to judge the quick and the dead, and we believe in the Holy Spirit. And the Catholic and Apostolic Church anathematizes those who say: 'He was when he was not, and before he was born he was not, and is a changeable or transferable Son of God.' Amen.

Prologue

Led by my love of the Catholic faith, I had long ago composed a small work against the Arians, and when I had given it to a friend to read, as he liked it, he believed that it should be published. I asked him this especially, to withhold the author's name for the moment, and read it to learned and prudent men, so that if what seemed better or worse expressed in it had aroused anyone, it could have been emended with the advice of a lot more people. For there is nobody who could assume for himself the summit of heavenly learning so arrogantly, as to think that he clearly retains an understanding of all the mysteries, although the Apostle Paul says:

'Who therefore thinks he knows anything, does not yet know how he ought to know,' and 'now we see through a glass darkly, but then face to face.'[1]

But if, however, all that was written in it should seem to all to be certainly in accord with the true faith, then he would not deny it to those seeking it. And it is quite clear that he did just this. And because the subject matter has been considered by the judgment of the whole Church as worthy as much for a Catholic's confession as for a response to heresy, many wanted to read it and describe it. But there was no lack of those who, either for a study of doctrine or for a labor of love, would reconsider what we have said more carefully. And they would say that some material was superfluous or ambiguous, and that some people could interpret what I said differently. And so I rearranged the text itself in this little book, with clearer wording, so that I might both show the simplicity of my feelings and remove difficulty for any readers.

For this is what they say can be criticized, that when we derived the Word of God from the person of the Son, we thought we could understand this Word just like the grammarians describe the mouth's air, odious with its breath, but intelligible with its sound. But we know the wisdom that comes not from this world, that is destroyed, but from God, which suggests that the Word of God is God, when He says:

---

[1] *I Corinthian*s 8.2 and 13.12.

74   Book Three (B)

'In the beginning was the Word, and the Word was with God, and the Word was God. All things were made by Him, and without him nothing was made.'[2]

For this reason, I admit that I am amazed that this could be so understood, as if we denied the proper person of the Word, which is the Son. Nobody gives a name only as far as its meaning goes, as he admits truly that it is in its person more often. For how have we confessed either the true Son or the true Father, if we have not truly preserved the peculiar nature of the persons as much of the Father as of the Son? But because we have said the word of one God, we are thought to have denied his persons. And from this, what we proposed seemed truthful. We named the Father and the Son in such a way that we assigned one God with these persons and names. Furthermore, again with Father and Son, although two names are given, yet they are only one in reason and substance, and when I set forth the Father and the Son, I assign unity of birth.

It has been thought that all of this could be understood, as though those words have been allotted exactly in the same way that one person has a family name and a surname, although this suspicion could not be admitted from the words given above or below. For how have I said that the Son of God was not born otherwise than properly from the Father, whole from whole, complete from complete, perfect from perfect and consummated goodness? How could I put forward the Father himself and his Son himself, and in this way address one person with two names? For indeed, when I condemned this sect, that is the Sabellian one,[3] in the same little book, would I have also distinguished between their persons according to their names? For nobody can say for one person 'they are one' or assign unity of birth, unless it is to persons.

And what Catholics do not know that the Father is truly the Son, the Son truly a Son, and the Holy Spirit truly a Holy Spirit? As the Lord himself says to his disciples: 'Go and baptize all nations in the name of the Father, and Son, and Holy Spirit.'[4]

We profess this perfect Trinity, that is made of one substance, consisting of unity. For we do not make a division in God according to the condition of human bodies, but according to the power of divine nature, which is not

---

[2] *John* 1.1, 3.
[3] See the note above on Sabellius.
[4] Adapted from *Mark* 28.19.

Arians and Vandals of the 4th-6th Centuries

75

in material things, and we believe that the persons truly consist in names, and we testify to the unity of divinity. Nor do we say that the Son of God is an extension of some sort from the Father, as some have thought, nor a word without matter, since we hear the sound, as it were, of a voice. But we believe that the three names are three persons of one essence, of one majesty and power. And so we confess one God, because the oneness of majesty prevents gods being addressed with a plural word.

Finally we name the Father and Son in a Catholic manner, but we cannot and should not say that they are two gods. Not because the Son of God is not a God, rather a true God from a true God, but because we do not know other than that the Son of God comes from the one Father himself, in the same way we say there is one God. For the prophets handed this down, and the Apostles likewise, and the Lord himself, when he says:

'My Father and I are one.'[5]

Here the 'one' refers to the oneness of his divine nature, as I said, and he assigns 'are' to the two persons. But the apostle also says:

'There is but one God, the Father, of whom are all things, and we in him; and one Lord Jesus Christ, by whom are all things, and we by him. But there is not in all men that knowledge.'[6]

And so, with these words of explanation, that caused doubt not for me, as I know what I said, but for others, I think any reason for a wrong interpretation has been removed. For the profession of faith is clear and the person agrees with the words, and a single divinity has been assigned. Or if there is something in the words that still seems ambiguous to readers, the words should be applied to their good sense, because it is not simplicity of words, but the obstinacy of an evil mind that smells of sin. But when our good sense agrees with truth, words too should be totally sincere with good reason. Let the academic disputer withdraw from Christian simplicity.

---

[5] *John* 10.30.
[6] *I Corinthians* 8.6 and 7.

76   Book Three (B)

Chapter 1

'We know that many really serious heresies pour forth from a great many people, and like poison, the strength of their cancer spreads deep into the heart. But they can neither be overcome with ease, nor avoided easily, yet every heartfelt resolution is betrayed by their first proposition. But indeed, those who are in many ways the same as we are, can easily corrupt minds that are innocent and devoted to God alone, with their fraudulent friendliness, while they defend the virus of their evils through our goodness. For nothing can be more dangerous than these heretics, who charge vigorously through everything, and with one word, as if with a drop of poison, infect that pure and simple faith in the Lord, and from that, the apostolic tradition.

Therefore, we must take very strong care in case something of this sort creeps into our senses or into our ears, without being noticed, because nothing compels one to die as much as violating a faith with the pretence of a faith. For just as gypsum mixed with water looks falsely like milk in its colour, even so here a hostile tradition is supplied through a similar sort of confession. For this reason, not the similarity of the confession, but the sense of the mind should be considered, whereby confession itself is confirmed.

Finally, if you pay attention more diligently and more carefully, as to why they wanted the name of substance removed from the evangelical and apostolic faith, and from the tradition of the Fathers, without doubt you approve of the Arian heresy, summed up in a thin abridgment, introduced with the removal of this name. Nor indeed do I affirm that this conclusion was reached with suspicion or conjecture, nor do I stand as an academic disputer, as they imagine, to twist simple senses with subtle words, but rather to expose to the light of learning twisted and small works composed with tenuous argument, so that when known and discovered, the iniquity can be more easily avoided by people.

For indeed what case or what reason exists that pains should be taken for the removal of what has been handed down, that should be taught to all the churches and be believed by them all? Should we remove what our apostolic Fathers laid down with Catholic reasoning, when purified by the Holy Spirit, against all the heresies, and especially the Arian one, as if it were some barrier to truth, where pestiferous doctrines would obstruct every opening? And it requires great effort to deal with these who are

Arians and Vandals of the 4th-6th Centuries 77

addicted to the record of the Arian disgrace, unless it is to claim falsely that the Son of God is mutable and convertible, seeing that he does not consist of his Father's own substance. Could they now hand over and recommend to the churches forthwith, freely and without care and without hesitation, that his beginning was instantaneous and his birth came from nothing, and his name came from another person, as they have always taught, due to which they have often been condemned also.

Chapter 2

Do you see, therefore, that they have placed everything in their tract, not with evangelical faith, but with cunning malice, so as to lead astray all simple minds. It should now be as much suspect as quite obvious to all that they have placed God apart from God, just as Arius was accustomed to hand down that Christ was made from God, not born from God. If he was born, he is of one substance, if he was made, he is not a true son, and if not a true son, he is not a true God either; or if he is a true God, and he is not from the Father, then there are two who each have their own wishes and different realms. Or if they are one only in concord and fellowship, he is not a God true in substance also, as I have already said.

So he will be God, as Moses was to Pharaoh, in power, not in birth. The Son also will have to be believed, just as was said to the people through Isaiah:

'I have given birth to sons and have raised them high,' and again elsewhere: 'You are Gods, all of you are children of the most High.'

But he too will be considered as first-born, just as God called Israel also his 'firstborn son.' Moreover, let him be thought firstborn of all creation, as if the firstborn in the order of things made. For through him they should assign some sort of series in the creation of all the things in the world.[7]

Finally they have removed ὁμοούσιον, that is the word for being of 'one substance,' but use ὁμοιούσιον, as 'of a similar substance,'[8] for their

---

[7] For Moses see *Exodus* 7.1, for the prophet Isaiah see *Isaiah* 1.2 and for elsewhere, see *Psalms* 82(81). 6. The final quote comes from *Exodus* 4.22.

[8] The two Greek words are 'consubstantial' and 'of a similar substance' in English. The second word appeared in a gloss (Liddell & Scott) but Ambrose may have coined it originally. The two words became extremely common thereafter.

78 Book Three (B)

Maker, although one may be similarity, the other the truth. For man too was made in the image and similitude of God, but he is not a God anyway, nor should a man be believed to have existed who is God. They want a Son similar to God, in such a way that they say he is similar, other than coming from one holy and blessed substance of the Father. And if he is not from the substance of his Father, he is ἐξ οὐχ ὄντων, that is, 'from nothing in existence,' as the same Arius handed down. For by removing that which is the Father, from wherever the Son may have come, it is necessary that he had his beginning from nothing and his birth was instantaneous; for there is nothing without a beginning, except for God alone.

And from where is the Son, as the Lord himself says: 'I and my Father are one.' And he said that so as to show the names of two persons for the majesty of one deity, just as the prophet also said through the voice of God: 'My heart uttered a good word, I tell my works to the king.' Do you see, then, that this good Word is the Son of God, and we believe that he was born in no other way than from his Father's breast, and, to put it so, from the womb of God's heart. And in the same way he calls that king, who is himself the King of kings, the Lord God, to whom all divine works submit, who said: 'All things that the Father has are mine.'[9] On this the evangelist also says:

> 'In the beginning was the Word, and the Word was God. All things were made by him, and without him nothing was made that was made.'

And so, what was in the beginning should be believed to have existed always, but not to have come from anywhere else other than from that which does not have a beginning, that is, from the heart of the Father, as he said 'my heart uttered a good Word.' For he did not say: 'In the beginning the Word was made,' but he said 'in the beginning was the Word.' Whatever beginning you want to assign for the Word, you will have it prejudged, because he said, 'it was in the beginning.'[10]

Do not let us say that there are two beginnings, from the diversity of things, but that the Son as Word is always with his Father and has been born from his Father. And in the same way he whose origin has no beginning, must be believed to be eternally with the Father, since neither can the Father ever be named without the Son, nor can the Son be called

---

[9] These three quotes come from *John* 10.30, *Psalms* 45(44).2 and *John* 16.15.
[10] Again see *John* 1.1 and 3. See below also.

upon without the Father. And through this he is always the Son, because his Father exists always. And he said: 'And the Word was God.' What is God is eternal, in the case that it was not eternal, it could not be a true God, just as with the name of Sophia, because following the apostle, he himself is the 'Wisdom of the Father.' And he said: 'I came forth from the mouth of the Highest.'[11]

And so it is not otherwise than from the Father, because he is always with the Father. And for that reason he is called the wisdom of God, so that it is believed that the Father is never without wisdom, that is, without his Son. This is that ineffable wisdom, which is described 'in the beginning of the way of God,'[12] by Solomon, either formed or born or created. But he says that it was born in such a way that it shows wisdom had always been with God. For what beginning will you give to God, so that you can vouch for the beginning of wisdom itself? For God did not form his wisdom in that way, as if he had once been without wisdom. But when he says the 'beginning of his way,' he shows the beginning of the movement of some work, so that the wisdom of God has this beginning which has proceeded from God to create all things, as much celestial as terrestrial, not how it began to be in God. Wisdom was created, therefore, or rather born, not for itself, as it was eternal, but for what needed to be born from it, so that, because its greatness and quality could not be known, its virtue and power might be known from the outcome of its works, as we would fear more what we value from things created, when we wonder at creation.

But if you should say that wisdom was created in the same way as you understand the Son as the creation of God, the apostle opposes you, condemning those who worship a creation, saying:

> 'Because of this God gave them up to desire, to impurity in their hearts, to affect their bodies with abuse among themselves, who changed the truth of God into a lie, and worshipped and served the creation rather than the Creator, who is God, blessed for evermore.'[13]

This is, I say, that wisdom of God, which says: 'I came forth from the mouth of the Highest,' the founder and producer of the universe, that is the Son of God, through whom were all things, and in whom are all things, because, as the apostle said:

---

[11] Wisdom of God' comes from *I Corinthians* 1.24, 'I came... ' from *Sirach* 24.3.
[12] *Proverbs* 8.22.
[13] *Romans* 1.24-25.

80 Book Three (B)

'In him were all things created in Heaven and on earth, visible and invisible, whether they be thrones or dominions or virtues or principalities or powers, all things were created through him and for him. And he is before all things, and all things consist in him.'[14]

On this Solomon also says: 'She who is one can do all things, and renews everything while herself enduring; and passes into holy souls through nations.'

Confirming this the apostle says that 'Christ may dwell in a person's heart,' so that he through whom all things were made from the beginning, shall bring salvation to all things at the end.[15]

Chapter 3

But you say to me that they prefer to worship ὁμοούσιον (*homoousion*), that is the name of one substance, rather than the Creator, observing the same as the apostle said:

> 'That at the name of Jesus every knee should bow, of things in Heaven, and things on earth, and things under the earth. And that every tongue should confess.'

And Moses said: 'Let all the angels of God adore him,' and David: 'All kings will fall down before him.' This would not be said in the Scriptures if it were not for the fact that the Son himself, as the Word, is the maker of all things.[16]

But you say that consubstantiality (ὁμοούσιον) ought not to be mentioned, because it is not contained in the Scriptures. And I ask you, Sir, as you prohibit this, if it should not be named, is it because it was not written, or because it should not be believed like that? If it is to be believed, then why is it not to be proclaimed? As the apostle says:

---

[14] *Colossians* 1.16-17, followed by *Wisdom* 7.27. 'She' is 'Wisdom.' The virtues are an addition.

[15] Adapted from *Ephesians* 3.17.

[16] *Philippians* 2.10-11, continuing 'Jesus Christ is Lord,' plus the comments of Moses in *Deuteronomy* 32.43 and of David in *Psalms* 72(71)11.

Arians and Vandals of the 4th-6th Centuries   81

'For with the heart, man believes unto righteousness and with the mouth confession is made unto salvation.'[17]

Or if it should not be named because of the fact that it should not be believed in the same way, an assertion of the Arian heresy has prevailed, that denies the common substance of Father and Son for that reason, because it supposes a Son of God, now from nothing, and now from the Father, but with a different substance, when it wants and how it wants and from where it wants it done, provided it pretends that He came into existence from elsewhere, and not from the Father's substance, although the Arian says He was born, but only as far this statement, that he realizes everything born was made, from the fact that we too should be named as born from God, as it is certain we are a creation.

Or if you are not an Arian, and you recognize that the true Son was born from a true Father and not made, why do you not say that He is one substance with the Father? You are afraid in vain, Sir, to admit what you believe. And you believe in vain, if you do not have this belief, and you are rightly branded as a heretic, although you have changed the statement whereby you are thought to have prohibited the Son of God being named as creation. But when it adds: 'Like one of these that has been made,' you show quite openly that you were not unwilling for him to be called a creation because of this, as if he should not be understood as created, but you do not want him created in this way, like one of these that has been created, but created nevertheless. For you say he has been created differently, namely a perfect creation, through whom all things have been created. Provided you understand that He himself was created, although not in the same way as the rest.

But so that I may return to that ὁμοούσιον which you say is not found in the holy Scriptures, in that sense of being of 'one substance,' imagine for a moment that this is so, that wherever substance is read, the matter of God, not God himself, should be accepted. Although there is another word that has not been written, that is God from God, Light from Light. What do you say to this? Either stay with me totally, or leave me totally. For if you are afraid to say the word of a single substance, for the reason that it has not been written, you ought to be afraid of saying God from God continually, and Light from Light.

---

[17] *Romans* 10.10.

82   Book Three (B)

But I declare that God from God and Light from Light and the Word of one substance are contained in the sacred Scriptures. For since the Son himself of God, who is God, says in his gospel: 'I came forth from the Father,'[18] we justly and rightly profess God from God, because we know that from God the Father, the Son of God was born as a true God from a true God. But not with that birth whereby we have been called 'Gods,' or whereby Moses was said to be 'a God to Pharoah,[19] but because he is a true God, born from a true Father. He should be described truly and confidently as God from God, like Light from Light.

You certainly discuss with me what has not been written, but you do not agree with me at all over it. And because it was written about the Father: 'God is Light,' and about the Son: 'He was the true Light that lights every man that comes into this world,' and that 'Light shines in darkness,' that is Christ in our time, and 'the darkness comprehended it not.' Those men, of course, whose hearts have been blinded by the darkness of ignorance, have not acknowledged Christ as the true God and the true Son of God. But the Lord himself says:

> 'I am the Light of the world; he who follows me will not walk in darkness, but will have the Light of life.'

Therefore, since the Father is the Light and the Son is Light, it is rightly 'Light from Light.'[20] But you so assert 'Light from Light' as though from the Father, who is a true Light, but made differently, as it is not from the substance itself of the Father, but like some other sort of Light, although made from God, but very different from him who made it. And for that reason you say 'Light out of Light,' not 'Light from Light.' Therefore, when I said this before, although you do not understand it with me, yet pronounce those words in whatever way you like, as they have not been written down. Or do you not pronounce equally with me the word of 'one substance,' which you do not think is contained in the Scriptures? Unless it is because you had there a means of concealing your malignant thoughts with hidden deception, in each case, to express this with me with the sound of your voice, and yet widely separate any understanding of what was said.

---

[18] *Romans* 10.10 again.
[19] From *Psalms* 82(81).6 and *Exodus* 7.1.
[20] *John* 1.9, and 5, and 8.12.

Just as those heretics who deny the resurrection of the flesh, to deceive the souls of the simple-minded, speak, alas, to these who do not rise again in the flesh. But if you should discuss with them why they said this, although you know they deny totally the resurrection of the flesh, they will say to you:

'Alas, it will happen to him anyway, who has not been baptized in the flesh, that his soul, while in his body, after the death of his sins, when his crimes are buried through baptism, may yet rise up again to the same sins.'

For they defend the resurrection of a single soul in the flesh, through the grace of a life-giving bath, but exclude the salvation of the flesh itself. And these through a true confession will seduce the minds of innocents with hidden fraud. And as a deadly drink mixed with the sweetness of honey usually kills the drinker as the sweetness deceives him, even so this evil also, through the pleasure to men's ears, infects the senses of those listening, as some heresy contaminates them with the contagion of a vice that clings to them.

Chapter 4

Finally they could even now name ὁμοούσιον correctly,[21] just as they name the rest, provided they had a way of subverting it with a foolish sense, to be understood differently. But when they saw that they were trapped with this word, they did not want any mention at all to be made of it, in case they either believed it by acknowledging it, or believing it, seemed to be confessing it, excusing with a subtle mind, saying that either it would not have been written, or God should not be mentioned in substance, in case he was believed to be corporeal. They say:

'For God indeed brings it about that there is substance, but not so that God himself is considered to partake in substance, for indeed all substance receives what is its opposite, and God in fact, who can admit nothing different, ought not to be called a substance.'

I would pardon you, if you were saying this simply, or if you wanted to know its reason, or if you came to this enquiry ignorantly, or if you were not the actual person who always defended the Son of God, over the existence of either another substance or of none. But when you yourself

---

[21] As we have seen, this word is regularly used (in Greek) as an ideal definition for the Trinity, but it is not found in Scriptures.

84 Book Three (B)

are the same person who has often been convicted over this and has often confessed and has often denied it, you have been condemned more often by changing in a different way. Even now you disturb everything, as you stir things up with violence, ambition and power. How do you think I can pardon you as you reconsider the same issues so frequently? But so that this perversity does not appear to have been condemned as more prejudged than examined properly, let me respond to you briefly over this opposition.

So you prohibit substance from being named in God, as if all that substance is said to be, it should be considered the actual matter of one species. Do you not know that the heavens consist of one sort of matter, the earth of another, and that there is a great difference between heavenly things themselves and earthly things? For angels have received their substances in one way, and the individual virtues of their constitutions in another way, as the apostle said:

> 'There is one glory of the sun, another glory of the moon, and another glory of the stars.'

Thus also in this world, as there are different species of things, so also there are different bodies of living things, and in everything a substance of each species, as the apostle said: 'All flesh is not the same flesh.'[22]

If, therefore, those things that were made by God have diverse qualities for their substances, do you think that in God there is such a quality as is found in one of these things that is made so as to include contrary qualities? Heaven forbid! For what is the substance of God? Just what God is, simple, singular, pure, mixed with no matter, clear, good, perfect, blessed, whole, totally sacred. Or do you think there is something empty and vacuous that is God? For this is a blasphemous comment, that he be thought vacuous, through whom all things were made, who brought forth all things with the Word, settled all with reason, perfected all with virtue, by whose nod and command the universe is governed, whom all things serve.

And you do well to read what is written about God: 'I am that I am' and 'Who is has sent me,' and the Lord our Saviour himself said: 'This is the life eternal, that they might know you the only true God, and Jesus Christ, whom you have sent.'

---

[22] Paul's quotes are from *I Corinthians* 15.44 and 15.39.

Arians and Vandals of the 4th-6th Centuries 85

And so God is his own essence in substance, knowing whom is eternal life, and he also is so great that his name cannot be said. Then he is properly valued when he is said to be beyond value, whether you wish it or not.[23]

Therefore, just what it is, that is the substance of that matter, is defended to be so; but as has already been said, its greatness and its nature cannot be conceived by the mind nor estimated by the senses, nor defined by the spirit, provided what is believed to exist is agreed to exist. So that from that itself which is God, from there is the Son, so that he is a true Son, and a true Father in the Son, and Son in the Father. This will be ὁμοούσιον, that is, of one substance with the Father, as the Lord himself said: 'I am in the Father, and the Father in me,' and, 'I and my Father are one,' and, 'I came forth from the Father,' and, 'He who has seen me, has seen the Father.'[24]

Not undeservedly so, because the Son of God was born from God his Father, and for that reason, from their unity of substance and majesty of godliness, they are one, as Jeremiah also prophesied: 'Who shall stand in the substance of the Lord shall also see the Word of the Lord.' And again, 'If they had stood in my substance, and if they had heard my words, I would have turned them away from their very evil ways.' And from Solomon: 'My substance is my delight.'[25]

Chapter 5

Since, therefore, you understand this unity of substance in the Father and Son through the authority not only of the prophets but also of the evangelists, how can you say that ὁμοούσιον is not found in the Scriptures, as if ὁμοούσιον were any different from what He says: 'I came forth from my Father,' and 'I and my Father are one,' or the fact that the prophets openly suggested the substance of God?

But this is the reason for the name, that you believe in the unity of substance in the Father and the Son, although you cannot define the matter

---

[23] The two quotations above are from *Exodus* 3.14 and *John* 17.3.
[24] The four quotations are from *John* 14.10, 10.30. 16.28 and 14.9.
[25] The quotations are from *Jeremiah* 23.18 and 22 and *Wisdom* 16.21. Besides a very free adaptation of the Vulgate in all three, *consilium* is used in the first two, not *substantia* (found in *Wisdom*, however).

86   Book Three (B)

itself, which is indescribable, so that you may say 'light from light' or 'word from word,' or 'spirit from spirit,' or 'Lord from Lord,' and whatever you say about it, yet you should believe that the Father and Son are of one essence. And you should understand the Son from the very fact that he is the Father. For if you were to make a comparison with it from these things that are visible, you would show no understanding by the very dissimilitude of the things, but would bring in an argumentative altercation, as was described by his voice: 'To whom will you liken me?'[26] And therefore, let it be sufficient for God to be believed, to whom nothing can be likened, since he himself is thought not to have been revealed, although he wanted himself to be believed.

Finally, if you might wish to confer on God what you admit to me, with some similarity, I do not know whether you could define more clearly what you may achieve. As for instance when you say 'light from light,' if you are forced to explain that with a precise analysis, I ask you, in what way do you believe in 'light from light'? Do you bring forward two Gods, as it were, with this example, like a lamp, as it were, from a lamp, or a sun, as it were, from a sun, or either two lamps or two suns? Or do you assign 'light from light' to the splendour of that lamp's light, or the sun's clarity shining from that sun, as you would assimilate the Father's figure into a source of light, but show the Son as the splendour of clarity? As the prophet would say on this: 'With you is the fountain of life, and in your light we shall see light,' or, as Solomon says:

> 'There is brightness of eternal light, and a mirror of God's majesty without stain, and an image of that goodness.'

And the apostle predicted here that our Saviour was the image of the invisible God, for the reason that the image of the sun is its light, which proceeds from the same light.[27]

But it would take a long time to describe the powerful replies that could be made to this, creating conflict that the apostle prohibits.[28] For indeed it may be agreed that that light which is God cannot be judged, understood and defined, and nothing from what is in this world could be compared truly with his divine majesty, as nothing from all those things that are seen

---

[26] *Isaiah* 46.5.

[27] The two quotes above come from *Psalms* 36(35).9 and *Wisdom* 7.26. For the 'image of the invisible God' see *Colossians* 1.15. See Vita's defense above, ch. 8.

[28] See *II Timothy* 2.24; teaching gentleness and patience.

Arians and Vandals of the 4th-6th Centuries   87

or described, considering what God is, can be judged with a worthy comparison, as he is too great for our intellects and senses.

For that reason, he forewarned that you should believe in the substance of the divine, and know the true Son from a true Father, but you ought not to enquire into the nature of His matter, because you could not know his quality or his greatness. For this the prophets, this the Apostles proclaimed.

Chapter 6

Finally, for our comprehension, for our strength, for our faith, let us consider what God is, and let us see whether anything could be compared with him. Certainly this is He, and even when he is being named, he cannot be named. When He is judged, he cannot be judged, when he is compared, he cannot be compared, when he is defined, he grows greater by his very definition. He opens the sky with his hand and closes with his fist all the vanity of the world. Nothing knows him totally, and knows him by fearing him. This world serves his name and virtue, and the momentary vicissitude itself of succeeding elements testifies to him. See, therefore, if there can be anything with which the Father could be compared, and the Son, because the Son has the same nature as the Father; for he himself would not say that he was one with the Father unless he knew that he had the same nature as his Father.

There is a 'reason,' that is called λόγος (logos) among the Greeks, and it distinguishes persons and names between the Father and the Son, because the Son himself is also called 'reason.' But this reason is addressed with many names, now as a word, now virtue, now wisdom, now right hand, now arm, now a pearl, now a treasure, now nets, now a plough, now a fountain, now a rock, now a square stone, now a lamb, now human, now a calf, now an eagle, now a lion, now a path, now the truth and now life itself. So, since God is everything in all things, so that through these words of divine disposition the mysteries may be known, he would not appear properly defined as the Son's majesty.

For what is the Son, from that which is the Father? Another, who is just the same. For he is called the 'Word' for this reason, because it proceeds from his divine mouth, and his Father neither ordered nor did anything without it. He is called 'virtue,' because he is truly from God and is always with God, and all of his Father's power is vested in him. He is

88 Book Three (B)

called 'wisdom,' because coming from the heart of his Father he opened up the secrets of the heavens for the true believers. He is called 'right hand,' because through him all the divine works reach completion. He is called 'arm,' because he holds all things. He is called 'pearl,' since nothing is thought more precious than him. He is called 'treasure-house,' since it is known that all the resources and riches of the heavenly kingdoms are contained in him. He is called 'nets,' because through him and in him from the sea of these times a diverse multitude of people congregate in the Church like fish, through the water of baptism, where a difference is recognized between the good and the evil. He is called 'plough,' because hard hearts are subjected to the sign of his cross, for them to be prepared for a necessary seeding. He is called 'fountain of water,' because from him thirsty hearts are irrigated with the grace of heavenly water. He is called 'rock,' because to true believers he provides fortitude, to the incredulous, hardness. He is called 'square stone,' because he joined together both walls of the New and Old Testament on his own and as mediator, containing them within him. He is called 'lamb,' so that the innocence and passion of Christ might be shown. He is called 'human,' because he has deigned to be born of the flesh for the sake of us humans. He is called 'calf,' because he put up with suffering for our salvation. He is called 'eagle,' because after his venerable resurrection, he flies to his Father's seat like the king of the birds. He is called 'lion,' because he is the king of kings, who has diminished death and the devil with the power of his virtue. He is the 'way,' because he ascended through it, 'truth,' because he knows no lie, and 'life,' because he himself gives life to the universe.

Do you see, therefore, that through these words, the significations of the divine dispositions and works have been made clear, and yet God himself has not been properly defined? And so God the Father is immense, eternal, incomprehensible and inestimable. And his Son is our God and Lord, just as great as his Father, but from no other place than his Father; as he said: 'Because I came forth from my Father,' that is Light from Light.[29]

Chapter 7

But in case a heretic should take some opportunity from this, when I set up two names, or two persons, that is, of the Father and Son, as if I were speaking of two Gods (as they create two from diversity), we so name the

---

[29] For this quote from *John* 16.20, see the beginning of Chapter 5.

Arians and Vandals of the 4th-6th Centuries 89

Father and Son that we attest just one God in these names and persons. Let the philosophers see, let their heretical disciples see, who are varied by a diversity of powers. As the apostle said:

> 'But to us there is but one God, the Father, of whom are all things, and we in him, and one Lord Jesus Christ, God and Son of God, by whom are all things, and we by him.'[30]

For what else is understood by 'through two' except the substance of two divided through their parts, and a nature of doing and ordering, unconnected with the names themselves, as much free-will as a divided command? Furthermore, although the Father and Son are believed to be two persons, yet they are one in reason and substance. For the society of unequal persons is offensive for the better one, and the other untrue God is harmful for him who is the true God. But when I put forward Father and Son, I assign them unity of birth, and if I divide that in persons, yet those same names again consign differences of person to their unity, by a natural legal agreement.

From this, the Son is as great as the Father shall appear to be, whole from whole, complete from complete, perfect from perfect and with consummate virtue, as the apostle says: 'In whom dwells all the fullness of the Godhead bodily.'

For Jeremiah also, the most acceptable of the prophets, aware of this unity of godliness in the Father and the Son, says:

> 'This is our God, and no other will be esteemed by him; he found every way of prudence, and gave it to his boy Jacob and his beloved Israel. After this he was seen on earth and conversed with humans.'

And Isaiah made this very prediction, saying:

> 'The Lord God said this:' The labor of Egypt and the merchandise of Ethiopia and of the Sabaeans, men of stature, will pass over unto you, will be your slaves, and will walk behind you with their ankles in chains, and will pray to you, saying: 'surely God is in you, there is none else, for you are God.'[31]

---

[30] *I Corinthians* 8.6.

[31] For these three quotes, see *Colossians* 2.9, *Baruch* 3.36-38, with some variants and likewise in *Isaiah* 45.14.

90   Book Three (B)

In case you think that I said this with the arrogance with which Sabellius is said to have spoken, who professes the Father himself and the Son himself, we do not restrict it all to one sentence, so that we are caught out by the fraud of other heretics. But because in the very name of the persons an undivided authority is recognized, and the Son is named not by his birth but personally by his Father, we therefore ascribe all that is the Son to the Father, and all that is the Father to the Son. Nothing of the Father will not be seen which will be judged to be of the Son, nor of the Son, which is defended as of the Father, because the unity of majesty does not allow Gods to be addressed in the plural. Since indeed it is agreed that Father and Son are of one substance, from that each of the two has been called a single God.

Before all things, they should fear this, that if the Father and the Son are not one, the falsified birth would lead to ill will towards the Creator. For this pleased the heretics, that that almighty, invisible and immense God should degenerate in the Son, not only in power but in a changed condition, as if the Father could not produce from himself such a person as He himself is. Therefore, we defend the true Son from a true Father, who always was and is of one substance with his Father. And this is what the Greeks call ὁμοούσιον, that is, another oneself with one, so that who hear the name should become persons, and words should not separate a substance.

Chapter 8

But so that I may expose every mystery of the Arian heresy, I shall briefly explain why they do not want the Son created from the Father's substance.[32] For they argue:

> 'Since God the Father is almighty, invisible, unchangeable, immutable, perfect, always the same and eternal, yet the Son was visible, since he was seen often by the Fathers, and he was changeable and mutable, as he revealed himself to each person with varied figures, and if he had been of the substance of his Father, they say, it could never have come about that he was visible and mutable before the assumption of the flesh, but rather, he would have remained in equality with the Father, of whose substance he was. For one should believe that what is from the Father cannot be seen, nor be changed nor be altered.'

---

[32] The text's *credi* ('believed') with *de* ('from') must be a slip for *creari* ('created').

Added to their case was that when He entered into Mary and filled the Virgin's womb, he was born from her certainly different from how he had come there. From this, they say, the corrupt substance now changes its state, loses its order and at once has to be formed by changing itself from God into man, from spirit into flesh. And anyway any transfer is a destruction of the pristine state. And through this they say:

> 'If the Son had been of the Father's substance, now the Father too would seem lesser by the transfer or end of his own substance.'

And therefore they preferred to believe that the Son came from another substance, which could be converted and be changed and be seen, because one could not believe this about the substance of the Father.

This is the cause of their error, this is the origin of the Arian heresy, while they do not understand God's virtue, and do not acknowledge the disposition of such a great sacrament, so that they compare God with human conditions. One must first reply to them that the Son of God was not seen in such a way in his place, as he was God, but as man he could receive from God. Then with various figures He was not mutable and changeable himself, but this was a mark of God's power, that when He deigned to reveal himself to individuals, as he wished, he changed his clothing, not his substance. Nor would he lose his peculiar quality, but would exhibit a due measure of majesty according to the merit of the person who sees him. But He himself, as is always the case, would still remain the same in the special nature of his substance, as has been written: 'You will change them and they shall be changed; but you are the same yourself, and your years shall have no end.'[33]

For there are many things, out of what we see in this world, that are changed from one form to another, so that they cease to be what they were, and become what they were not before, as when clay is molded into a human shape, it now ceases to be clay, or when fish or birds come out of the water, it is no longer water thereby, because it is something else. Like when a potter's clay is made solid as a brick, or a stone, when it is boiled and reduced to lime, like sand changed into glass, and so on; it would take a long time to count them all. But there is a great difference, you foolish heretic, between those that were made and Him who has made all things according to his will. What have been made are subject to the conditions

---

[33] *Psalms* 102(101). 26-7. The imagery describes Creation's garments growing old.

92   Book Three (B)

imposed on them, but He who has made them possesses his own will and proper right. Nor can He be changed into something other than he is, forced by anyone else; but He shows himself as he wishes, and to whom he wishes. For if angels have often been seen in the shape of human beings, and yet they are no other than what they know they are, and do not change their substance when they take on the shape of a human body, how much more is this true of our Lord himself, who made all things, and who granted the angels to have this power by his own instruction.

To this is added the fact that we approve of the Son of God, as has just been said, being seen thus by the Fathers, although not totally, due to the fact that he is a God. But His arrangements for future matters, which had to be completed during each of their times, would be seen in Him through his likeness. For who could see the Son of God, before he assumed visible material, as it pleased him, and deigned to dress himself as a human? Although Abraham saw him, yet he saw him in the form of a human body, by which, of course, it was shown that He would come for mankind at the latest times.[34]

He appeared to Jacob also, in one place as an angel, in another also as a human being.[35] And He revealed himself as an angel to indicate that he was announcing a great counsel, but in human shape, with whom Jacob is even described as having wrestled, to show especially an image of the future struggle that He would have with Israel, when he had come as a human. But to trust in the Lord, with whom he was wrestling with such a great fight in the figure of a man, he received the name of Israel, that is man seeing God. As he said: 'I have seen God face to face, and my life is preserved.'

And he had seen the figure of a human anyway, which God the Son of God had put on.

He appeared to Moses in red, in the flame of a fire, to show light to the believers and judgment to the disbelievers, because Christ is salvation for those who believe in him, and punishment for the disbelievers, as the apostle says:

---

[34] See *Genesis* 18.1 for the Lord's appearance before the 99 yr old Abraham.
[35] For Jacob's ladder, with God at the top, see *Genesis* 28. 12-13, and for the stranger wrestling with him, see *Genesis* 32.24-30.

Arians and Vandals of the 4th-6th Centuries 93

'To some we are the savor of life unto life, for others the savor of death unto death.'[36]

He went before the people of Israel in a column of cloud through the day, and in a column of fire through the night, as if in charge of the journey, so that he might reveal the grace of baptism through the cloud and the gift of the Holy Spirit through the fire, because Paul the apostle wrote about the Fathers baptized in the cloud and the Acts of the Apostles declare the Spirit to be like a fire.[37]

Do you see, therefore, heretic, the characters of the Holy Scriptures foreshown to the Fathers in honour of God, but not God himself, as has been properly revealed? Finally, when Moses was praying that he might see the face of God totally, what did God say to him at once? He said: 'You will not be able to see my face, for no man shall see my face and live.'[38]

From the fact that a look is denied, clearness is implied, which of course is as great as it is believable, and is shown to be invisible. So Moses, who considered, revealed and expressed the situation of the sky and the orders of the earth and the changing elements and finally the trappings of the whole world, to whom the Lord himself bore witness, saying:

> 'There will be nobody from my prophets like my servant Moses, to whom I have spoken face to face, mouth to mouth.'

And yet he was not able to see God clearly. Indeed, he was rightly worthy of any prophesy, but not to such an extent that he could look at God, for the fact that he was only a human being.[39]

And we defend all of these words of the Son, anyway, as we know He spoke with Moses on Mount Sinai, after arriving from his Father to carry out and explain various things, because it was appropriate for them all from the beginning to be both ordained and explained and remain through Him, as this special reason was manifest for the Son being used. And yet

---

[36] For Moses and the flaming bush see *Exodus* 3.2 and for two different savors see *II Corinthians* 2.16 (reversed in the text).

[37] For the columns see *Exodus* 13.21-2, for Paul's comment *I Corinthians* 10.1-2, and for the fiery spirit, *Acts* 2.3.

[38] *Exodus* 33.20.

[39] The quotation came from *Numbers* 12.7-8.

94   Book Three (B)

so seen, He was accepted, so that he might be seen, assuming the placement of some visible material, as I have said, with his invisibility intact, of course, which his intervening majesty kept away from the sight of everyone. For He was not revealed to human sight in such a way that the whole deity appeared, but like a mirror, when it encloses a person's face, captured in its light, like a full image.[40] Even so, as the splendour of His majesty goes before him, within this it seemed that He gave a proper display of an image of truth, but not of God himself.

But even when He deigned to put on human form, he did not inflict a stain for eternity, turning spirit into flesh, but so as to provide the immortality and eternity of heavenly life, by putting on human form. For although the apostle says that He laid aside his glory, by taking on the form of a slave, we do not accept his laying aside of his glory, anyway, so that the same Spirit would become other that what He was, but so that he might put aside meanwhile the honour of his majesty, and take on a human body, to become the salvation of all races by accepting it. For as when the sun is covered by a cloud, its brightness is reduced, but not blotted out. And that Light, which spreads throughout the world, spreads over all things with its bright splendour, and is shaded by the quite small obstacle of a cloud, but not removed. So too than human shape that Lord Jesus, our Saviour, that is God and the Son of God, put on; but He did not take away God in it, but hid it.[41]

Finally, when on the mountain He had removed himself just a little outside his human body, the apostles were almost blinded by the brightness of his light and fell to the ground, as they were human, their lives at risk, if the merciful Lord had not helped them by again by checking the honour of his majesty, following that sentence: 'No one saw God and lived.' So, therefore, the brightness of the sun, when it does not shine right into our eyes, is safe for itself; since what is not seen is due to our weakness, when the obscurity of clouds has covered our eyes. And so He proves that he was not concealed by his loss of proper brightness, but by the benefit of human flesh, as I have said, for the sake of which the Son of God put up with being the son of man.

---

[40] The mirror suggests a very Platonic argument.
[41] The sole use of the verb *intercapio* ('I take away') used by Ambrose is credited to Priscian (over 100 years later) in Lewis and Short.

For the Virgin certainly conceived from the Spirit of God, and what she conceived, this she bore, that is, a God associated with her human body, as I have already said, as He himself stated:

'That which is born of the flesh is flesh, and that which is born of the spirit is spirit.'

This is because God is spirit, and He was born from God. As the angel also said to the Virgin Mary:

'The Holy Ghost will come upon you, and the power of the Highest will overshadow you; therefore that holy thing which will be born from you, shall be called the Son of God.'[42]

You see, therefore, that the Spirit itself, that is, the Son of God, came to the Virgin, and that from her the Son of God and man came forth. But the Son of God was not altered by that covering of flesh, but was the same in man as he had been before the world with his Father, through whom all things were made, and without whom was nothing made, as the evangelist says: 'The world was made by him, and the world knew him not.'

But is it foolish to believe that He may free one who was lost, so that he might free men? He was oppressed so as to be born, and crossed into death so as to receive immortality. Heaven forbid, you heretic, that the Catholics should ever accept your wicked thoughts; for we believe that He is immutable and unchangeable. We believe in the Word and the Spirit, that is the Son of God, who when he put on a human form did not alter his state, did not lose his rank, did not change his substance, but lit up the uncleanness of that same body with the eternal light of his brightness, so that the light of the Holy Spirit might reach us through the path of his body, and the grace of eternal life might abound.

Although we believe that He suffered and was buried, yet that human suffered, whom the Son of God had taken on, had put on and carried. But because whatever that human was suffering was referred entirely to the Creator, for that reason it is judged to be the death and passion of the Lord; for it is certain that what is of God is immortal, what is fleeting is of man.

Also on the third day it was not God who was born again as man, but man rather reborn as a God. He ascended into Heaven, offered to his Father

---

[42] From *John* 3.6 and *Luke* 1.35.

96 Book Three (B)

that human as a very welcome gift, and sat at the right hand of the Father, following what was written: 'The Lord said unto my Lord: Sit at my right hand.'[43]

He sent us the Holy Spirit from his own proper substance itself, as protector, sanctifier and guide into eternal life, as was written in the voice of God:

'Upon my servants and my handmaids will I pour out my spirit,' and again: 'The spirit will come forth from me,' and our Lord and Saviour said: 'He shall take of mine.'

From Him anyway, because he is the Son, as he is Son also of that which is his Father.[44]

Afterwards He is going to come at an appointed time and will judge the living and the dead, to reward the believers but punish the disbelievers. Whose kingdom is eternal, immortal, without a beginning or an ending, for whom there is honour and glory, for ever and ever.

Conclusion

I beg you who read this in God's name not to twist simple thoughts into ambiguous ones, nor treat it other than as it was said. For we trust in the Father, the true Father, and believe in the Son of God, the true Son of God, and in the Holy Spirit, the truly Holy Spirit, confessing three persons of one substance and of one godliness. But we condemn the sect of Sabellius and of Photinus and also of Arius, and any others there may be, that appear contrary to the rule of truth. But we embrace the creed of the Nicaean Synod with every effort of our minds, serving it with total faith, for we know that this creed is opposed to all the heresies with invincible truth.'[45]

---

[43] *Psalms* 110(109).1.

[44] The three quotes are from *Joel* 2.29, *Isaiah* 57.16 and *John* 16.15.

[45] The Nicaean Council was held in 325, convoked by the Emperor Constantine, mainly to deal with Arianism, the first such worldwide Council for the Christian bishops.

BOOK FOUR

VICTOR OF VITA

Chapter 1: False Accusations by the Arians

When this poor book of mine was being read, the light of truth was brought before them, but they could in no way put up with it with their blind eyes. In their madness they roared at us with their voices and were furious that we claimed the name of true Catholics for ourselves. And they at once made false suggestions to the king about us, saying that we had caused an uproar, trying to avoid the hearing. At the same time, aroused by anger and believing the lies, Huneric hastened to do what he wanted to do.

He had already written a decree, and he sent his own men secretly with that decree through the different provinces, while their bishops were kept in Carthage. In a single day he closed the churches throughout Africa, and donated the entire property of the Catholic bishops and of their churches as a gift to his own bishops. And 'not knowing also what he was saying, or about what he affirmed,'[1] they did not blush to apply against us that law which our Christian emperors had long since given against those and other heretics,[2] for the honour of the Catholic Church, adding many items about themselves, as pleased the tyrant's power. For this is the form of the law issued and published:

Chapter 2: The Edict of King Huneric against Catholics

Hunerix, king of the Vandals and Alans, informs all the peoples subject to our reign:

---

[1] Based on *I Tim* 1.7.
[2] Huneric misused his imperial decrees, in fact directed on behalf of Catholics against the Donatist heretics, as Augustine had shown on several occasions (tract. 6 *In Joannem* 25; book 2 *Contra Petilianum* 58). See *M* n.2, p. 64.

98   Book Four

'It is well known that it is the part of triumphal majesty and royal virtue to turn back evil counsels against their authors. For whoever finds something depraved, must blame himself for what happens to him. In this matter Our Clemency has followed the will of divine justice, and while it judges all persons according to what their deeds have deserved, whether good or perhaps contrary to that, at the same time it also results in rewards. And so, being provoked by those who have rejected the precept of our father of famous memory, and who thought that they should resist Our Clemency, we have adopted a severe judgment. For by our authority we made it known to all peoples that in every land allotted to the Vandals, the consubstantial priests should not conduct any services, nor claim any of the sacraments for themselves, which cause greater pollution.

When we saw that this was neglected and we found most saying that they retained the only true rule of faith, it is certain that they were all warned afterwards, with a nine month space of time allotted, that on the first of February in the eighth year of our reign they should meet without any fear of a new debate, in case something might be added to their proposals.[3] And while they came together here in the city of Carthage, after a delay of a prescribed period of time, we are known to have granted them yet another delay of several days. And while they got themselves ready for the debate, on the first day it seemed to them that our venerable bishops had proposed that they should give proper proof of their consubstantiality (ὁμοούσιον), using Holy Writ, as they had been warned; or certainly that they condemn what was excised by a thousand or more bishops from all over the world in the Councils of Rimini or at Seleucia.[4] But they were in no way willing to do so, and having aroused the people, they turned everything into discord. Nay rather, on the second day also, when we asked them to reply concerning that same faith, as had been proposed, they seemed to have added this to their past temerity, that by disturbing everything with seditious shouting, they made it impossible for any debate to begin.[5]

With their provocation, we decided that their churches be closed, but we add this proviso, that they should be closed as long as they were unwilling

---

[3] *M* was wrong to cut out *novaeque*. The connective is necessary and the 'new' is explained by the added proposals. The 'fear of' qualifies the two gens (*novaeque contentionis*). The calends denote the 1st, not the 25th Feb., as in *M*'s version.

[4] These Arian councils of Rimini (Ariminium) and Seleuca were summoned by the Emperor Constantius in 359.

[5] A difficult passage. *M*'s version for the last 5 lines is very confused (pp 65-6).

Arians and Vandals of the 4th-6th Centuries 99

to enter the proposed debate. They refused to do so, with an obstinacy that they seem to have acquired from some evil advice.[6] And so it is most necessary and very just to turn against these men what the contents of their own laws show, those matters which, when they had been led into error, emperors of various times had reason then to promulgate.

The composition of these laws is seen to contain the following:

1. No church should be open to anyone except for the bishops of its own disposition.
2. No bishop should be allowed to be maintained or to have meals together, or to hold meetings.[7]
3. No bishop should possess completely[8] or construct any churches either in cities or in any very small places. Taken over, they should be subject to the laws of the imperial treasury.
4. But also, the patrimonies of the bishops too, associated with churches of their faith, should be handed over to the Arian bishops.
5. Such bishops should not be given the freedom to travel to any place, but should be banished from all cities and other places.
6. They should not have any opportunity at all for baptizing, nor for a chance of religious debate.[9]
7. They should have no right of ordaining either bishops or priests or others who happened to belong to the clergy.
8. A severe penalty was laid down for those who allowed themselves to accept honours of this sort. They should be punished as well as those ordaining, with a fine of ten pounds of gold each, and with the postscript that they should have no place nor hearing for a supplication.
9. But even if they had shown special merit, they should not prevail at all.
10. If they persisted with this pernicious behavior, they would be removed from their own soil and sent abroad in exile, subject to a fitting punishment.[10]

The emperors just mentioned were similarly savage towards these people also, saying that they had no right at all to give donations or make wills or

---

[6] In Migne's text the positive *voluerunt* is read, a misprint for *noluerunt*.

[7] *M* omitted *ali* ('to be nurtured' or 'maintained') and *convictus* are 'meals,' not 'assemblies' (*conventus*).

[8] The advb *penitus*, omitted by *M*, underlines the once total power of the bishop.

[9] The *aut forte* cannot mean 'in case they should happen' as in *M* (p. 66).

[10] With Migne's *sub persecutione*, more apposite than *sub prosecutione* in other MSS and *M*; a 'suitable guard' would be too considerate, and unparalleled.

100   Book Four

inherit even what was left by others, either under the name of a bequest to a third party, or by a legacy, or by special grants, or by an abandonment in a deemed cause of death, or by any sort of codicil or by any other possible writings, so much so that even those who served as guards in their palaces should be subjected to very heavy condemnation, in accordance with their dignity, so that, stripped of all privilege of rank, they should incur infamy. And persons of this sort would know that they themselves were subject to general prosecution. Also a penalty of thirty pounds of silver was laid down for the officials of various judges, and if it so happened that those persisting in error were fined five times, then they were to be convicted finally and subjected to beatings and exiled.

Then they had commanded that all the books of the priests whom they were persecuting should be handed over to the flames. And we order this to be done to books like this, through which wickedness has persuaded them to adopt the error of that heresy. For as has been said, the emperors had ordered that these laws should be observed in accordance with each of those persons, so that each of the illustrious class would pay fifty pounds of gold, each of the high class forty pounds of gold, the senators thirty pounds of gold, the commoners twenty pounds of gold, the priests thirty pounds of gold, the municipal senators five pounds of gold, the merchants five pounds of gold, the common people five pounds of gold and the itinerant monks ten pounds of silver.[11]

And if any of them should happen to continue supporting this heresy, all of their goods would be confiscated and they would be punished with exile. They were ordered to afflict the magistrates of the cities and also the managers and renters of properties with such a penalty, that if perchance they chose to hide such men and not publicize their names at all, nor make them appear when bound for trial, they themselves would be held for punishment. And for the tenants of the royal estates this fine was proposed, that they would be forced to pay as much to the exchequer as a penalty, as they would contribute to the royal palace. They decided that this should be generally observed with all renters or owners of properties who believed they should continue to support that superstition. Also if any judges would not crack down on this heresy most vigorously, they

---

[11] Victor uses usual homonyms for high ranks, *v.i.* (*viri illustres*) for the most senior magistrates, followed by *v.s* (*viri spectabiles*) for the next most senior, and then senators (*v.c.*, *viri clarissimi*), a usual title for a consul. The *decuriones* were 'municipal senators' and *circumcelliones* most probably 'itinerant monks' not attached to a monastery. See *CV* p. 147, and *M* note 6, p 67.

would be punished with the penalty of proscription and with the shedding of their blood. But three in number of the chief officials would be punished, while the others would be condemned and fined twenty pounds of gold.

Therefore, all supporters of the consubstantial faith[12] must be bound by these constitutions, all those who have clearly supported and are still supporting the substance of this wicked heresy. And we decree that they abstain from all the wrongdoings mentioned above, or they will be facing prosecution through the high officials of all the cities, as will any judges who neglect the orders above, and are shown not to have inflicted grim punishments on the deviants. And so we command all of those who are implicated in the errors of the consubstantial faith mentioned above, which has been condemned by an entire Council consisting of so many priests, to abstain from all the aforesaid practices and agreements, as they will know that they are permitted to uphold none of them. But let a similar penalty await and bind them all, unless they have converted to the true religion that we venerate and worship, before June the first in the eighth year of our reign.[13] And Our Piety has decided on the prearranged day, for the reason that pardon should not be denied to those renouncing their error, and suitable punishments should force obstinate minds to comply. But let those who shall remain in the same error, whether members of our palace guard or perhaps in charge with various titles and interests, be forced to accept the infliction of the fines described above in accordance with their ranks, and what anyone happens to earn by deception over such matters will have no validity. Our promulgation has ordered this to be observed even in the case of private persons, of whatever grade and status, as was seen expressed in the laws mentioned above that such people should be subject to fitting penalties. But if provincial judges refuse to carry out what has been enacted, we have decided that they should be bound by a superior court with the penalty prescribed for such men.

But we have decided with this decree that all the churches and all the clergy of the aforesaid heresy, established in whatsoever lands and regions are possessed by the rule of our empire, through the grace of God, together with the goods that pertain to them, should benefit the true worshippers of the divine majesty, that is, our priests. Nor should they hesitate to provide

---

[12] The Greek technical term ὁμοούσιον is used several times in this text as it was in book 3, although this is the only derogatory use of it, in the king's mouth.

[13] This was four months after the Synod began on February 1st.

102   Book Four

more alms for the poor, as has been justly collected by our sacrosanct bishops. And so we order all men to pay attention to this law, which flows from a fountain of justice, so that nobody can pretend that he knows nothing of this precept. We pray that you are in good health.'

Given on the 25th February, in Carthage.

Chapter 3: Savagery towards Catholic bishops

After these deadly edicts, laced with toxic poison, he ordered all the bishops who had assembled in Carthage, whose churches, homes and fortune he had already seized, to be stripped of possessions in the hostelries where they stayed, and when stripped, to be driven outside the city's walls. No animal, no slave, no change at all of the clothes they had brought with them, was sent out with them. He added to this that nobody should grant any one of them hospitality or provide him with sustenance. And those who had attempted to do so out of pity, were to be cremated in a fire, together with all their household.

Even then the bishops thrown out acted wisely, not leaving the place despite being beggars. Because if they were to go away, they would not only be recalled most violently, but the Vandals would also falsely claim, as they had lied before, that the bishops had fled from the debate; especially because when they turned back, they would no longer have any support from their churches or occupied homes. And so while the bishops lay groaning all around the walls in the open air, it came about that the evil king had ridden out to the swimming pool, and all the bishops chose to come up to him, saying:

'For what reason are we afflicted like this? For what crimes maybe[14] committed by us do we suffer this? If we were brought together for a debate, why are we being stripped of our goods, why are we being moved away, why dispersed, and deprived of our churches and houses, why do we suffer from hunger and nakedness, wallowing in the midst of dunghills?'[15]

---

[14] The *'forte'* is an interesting concession from the scared bishops (omitted by *M*).
[15] As with human excrement in ch 2.10 above, animal droppings (horses especially) made parts of any large city and areas around it most unsavory for pedestrians. Motorcars saved London from becoming a gigantic 'dung-heap.'

He stared at them with fierce eyes, and before he had heard all their complaints he ordered the horses with their riders to gallop over them, so that with such violence they might not only be crushed but even be killed. Then many of them were trampled to death, and especially the elderly and infirm.[16]

Chapter 4: Deceived by Trickery

Then those men of God were ordered to meet the king at a certain place called the Temple of Memory, and they hurried there, not knowing that a trap had been set for them.

When they had come there, a rolled papyrus was shown to them and read out to them with that cunning worthy of a serpent: 'Our Lordship, King Huneric, although he grieves that you have been contemptuous and are still slow to obey his wish for you to join the religion to which he belongs, yet now has had a good idea for you. If you will swear to do what that sheet contains, he will send you back to your churches and homes.'

All the bishops replied to this:

'We always say, and have said, and shall go on saying that we are Christian bishops, and hold the one true, apostolic faith.'

After this confession of faith, there was a short silence. Then those who had been appointed by the king hurried to extract an oath from the bishops. But then the blessed men, Bishops Hortulanus and Florentianus, spoke on behalf of all the bishops and to them all: [17]

'Are we irrational animals, ready to swear easily and rashly without knowing what the roll contains?'

Those men sent by the king were then quick to reveal the purport of the writing, which had been coloured with words of this sort. For a succession of deceits contained the following:

---

[16] The picture of the king at his private swimming pool close to the city walls, with his smart courtiers around him on smart horses, is well depicted. They had to shield him from the mob of dusty, gesticulating and complaining bishops.

[17] In the *Notitia Africana,* Hortulanus (or Ortulanus) was the bishop of Benefum in the province of Byzacena and Florentianus was bishop of Milidi in Numidia.

104   Book Four

'Swear that, after the death of our Lordship the king, you want his son Hilderic to succeed him, and that none of you will send letters to countries overseas. For if you swear an oath over this, he will restore you to your churches.'

Then their pious simplicity made many swear the oath, even though it was contrary to divine prohibition, in case the people of God might say later on that their churches had not been restored through the fault of their bishops, who were unwilling to swear the oath.

Other bishops also with shrewder minds suspected a crafty trap, and were totally unwilling to swear, saying that evangelical authority had prohibited it, as the Lord himself said:

'Swear not at all.'[18]

The king's servants said to them:

'Let those who are ready to swear move to one side.'

As they separated, scribes wrote down what each bishop said and from what city he had been taken. It was done similarly for those who did not sign at all. And at once each group was handed over to custody.

Chapter 5: Forced into Exile

But afterwards the fraud that was concealed became fully apparent. To those who swore this was said:

'Because you were willing to swear contrary to the command of the gospel, the king has ordered that you never see your cities or your churches, but be banished, and accept that you become peasant farmers with some fields to cultivate. But this is on the condition that you sing no psalms, make no prayers, nor hold a book in your hands to read, nor baptize anyone nor ordain nor presume to reconcile anyone.'

Similarly they said to those who did not swear:

---

[18] As in *Matthew* 5.33-36: 'not by heaven, nor by the earth, nor by your head.' It is possible that Victor knew about the Catholic bishops' attitude to the succession, but not very likely. See *CV* pp 294-5.

'Because you do not wish for the reign of our Lordship's son, that is why you were unwilling to swear the oath. For that reason, you have been ordered to go to the island of Corsica as exiles, to cut down timber for the ships of our Lordship.'[19]

---

[19] The timber from Corsica is of interest. Pope Gregory the Great himself each year supplied the shipyards in Alexandria, through its patriarch, Eulogius, with timber from the papal estates in Calabria. The Arian and Gothic kings had large fleets, also in need of plenty of good timber. Pope Gregory used this timber to repair churches in Rome as well (see my article in *Med et Human* 29, 2003, 1-25).

BOOK FIVE

Chapter 1: General Persecution

And so that foul beast,[1] as he thirsted for the blood of innocents, before the bishops had yet been sent into exile, went on to send out simultaneously most cruel torturers through all the provinces of the land of Africa, and no home or place was free of wailing and mourning, as they spared neither age nor either sex, except for those who succumbed to their will. They destroyed some with clubs, others with hanging and yet others on pyres. But they tortured women, especially noble ones, totally naked and in full public view, contrary to the laws of nature.

I shall succinctly and briefly mention one of them, our Dionysia. When they saw that she was not only braver but also a more beautiful woman than the others, they first attempted to strip her and to attack her with their clubs. When she was suffering this onslaught she said this without care, thanks to the Lord:

'Torture me however you like, but do not expose my private parts.'

They were all the more furious, and stripping off all her clothes, they set her on a higher place, making her a spectacle for all. But as they struck her with canes, and as small streams of blood now poured out all over her body, she spoke with a free voice:

'Servants of the devil, what you reckon to be a reproach for me is in fact my glory.'

And because she was filled with a knowledge of Holy Writ and was beset by the tortures applied to her, she herself was now a martyr and she

---

[1] The *bestia* torturing noble women needs a 'foul' to give it its true force. Migne notes that Lactantius used it for the early persecutors, like Nero and Diocletian. The wild beasts in the Roman games specialized in butchering Christian martyrs, but for Victor here, it might be based on the Beast from the sea in *Revelation* 13.

Arians and Vandals of the 4th-6th Centuries 107

comforted others facing martyrdom. And with her saintly example she freed almost all of her homeland. And when she saw that her only son, still of tender years and a delicate boy, was a little afraid due to his fear of punishment, she chastised him with wounding glances and upbraided him with a mother's authority, and thus comforted him[2] and made him much braver than his mother. And as he stood amid cruel beatings she spoke as follows:

'Remember, my son, that we have been baptized in the name of the Trinity, in our mother, the Catholic Church. Let us not lose the garment of our salvation, so that our host when he comes finds a wedding garment, and says to his disciples:

'Cast him into outer darkness, where there shall be weeping of eyes and gnashing of teeth.'[3]

'That punishment, my son, is to be feared that never ends, that life is to be desired that lasts forever.'

And so with such words she gave strength to her son, and quickly made him a martyr. For the admirable young man, who was called Majoricus, gave up his spirit in the defense of his confession, and completed his palm-strewn course. And she embraced her sacrifice, offering thanks to the Lord as loudly as she could, joyful in her future hope. And she chose to bury him in her own home, so that whenever she poured out prayers to the Trinity over his grave, she might be confident that she would never be separated from her son.

It would take a long time to describe how many people in that city were acquired for God through that woman, as we have described above. For her sister also, called Dativa, was called, and Leontia, daughter of the holy Bishop Germanus and the venerable doctor Aemilius, a relative of Dativa, also a religious man Tertius, famous for his confession of the Trinity, and Boniface of Sibida. Let he who can, describe in due order how much all of these endured, and with what tortures their bodies were torn apart.[4]

---

[2] The 'thus comforted him' is missing in *M*'s translation. Her son's tenderness and delicate limbs made it a more harrowing experience. Despite her beatings, she lived on to bury him and pray over his grave, for years to come, it seems.

[3] *Matthew* 22.13.

[4] The venerable Bishop Germanus had been beaten to death with cudgels, in book 2, chapter 16. His see was in Byzacena, in the town Peradamium, according to the

Chapter 2: Suffering of Servus[5]

Who could describe the punishments that were endured on behalf of Christ by Servus also, a citizen of fair sized city of Tuburbo,[6] and a magnanimous, noble man? After the blows of countless clubs he was lifted up by mass of pulleys,[7] and while he hung before the whole city,[8] they raised him much higher, and then with a quick blow the ropes of hemp were again slackened and with the weight of his body he fell on to the flint-stones on the street below, hitting the flagstones like a rock. But he was more often dragged along, and grazed by very sharp stones, and as his skin separated, you could see flaps of his body hanging from his flanks and back and stomach.

He had already suffered not greatly different torments in the time of Geiseric, to avoid revealing the secrets of a certain friend of his. How much more now, when he was protecting the sacraments of his faith? And if he faithfully showed his trust without reward for a human, how much did he owe to God who would return a reward for his true faith?

Chapter 3: Bravery of Victoria

But in the city of Culusi I cannot report what was done there, as it is impossible for anyone to reckon the number of martyrs and even of confessors. And there a certain matron, called Victoria, lived up to her name. For while she was being burnt alive in full view of the commoners, continually hanging over the fire, she was asked as follows by her already corrupted husband in the presence of their children:

Notitia. These victims appear as martyrs in the Latin martyrology for December 6th. The indirect question (*sint*) was missed by *M*.

[5] The editors are divided between Servus, *servi* and Majorus. 'Greater' (*maioris*) is rather odd, and a slave is most unlikely with *nobilis*. The early martyrologies included this Servus, which seems to be the right reading. Three of the bishops on the *Notitia* are called Servus and two clerics in Gregory's letters, Servusdei.

[6] The city (mod. Henchir Kasbat) was in the Proconsular province, and its bishop was Benenatus.

[7] The word *frequens* normally means 'crowded' or 'in great numbers' rather than 'frequent,' wrongly agreeing here with *elevatus*, instead of *trochleis*, as in *M* p. 73.

[8] The pulleys and ropes would not have been moved 'throughout the city for the whole day' as in *M* (*totam per orbem* (sic!)), but firmly located in the main square, as in Migne's (*tota prae urbe*) 'before the whole city/citizens.'

Arians and Vandals of the 4th-6th Centuries 109

'Why do you suffer this, my wife? If you despise me, at least pity these sweet young children to whom you gave birth, you impious woman! Why do you forget your womb, why count as nothing those whom you bore with groans? Where is our contract of conjugal love? Where the bonds of the union that written tablets made between us long ago with a just law? Consider your children, I beg you, and your husband, and hasten to fulfill the order of the king's command, so that you may save yourself from still imminent tortures and at the same time may be given back both to me and to our children also.'

But she heard neither the weeping of her children nor the flattery of the serpent, as she raised her love up from the earth, to a far greater height, and despised the world below with its desires.[9]

When those who were torturing her could now see that she was as good as dead from the continual suspension, which had torn her shoulders out of their sockets, they at once took her down, totally lifeless. But she reported afterwards that some virgin had stood before her and had touched each of her limbs, and thereupon she had been restored to good health.

Chapter 4: Faith of the martyr Victorian[10]

But I do not know how I may extol Victorian, a citizen of the city of Hadrumentum, who was the proconsul of Carthage at that time. Words fail me! Nobody in the regions of Africa was richer than he was, and he was also considered most loyal in the retinue of the impious king, over matters regularly entrusted to him. The king sent him a friendly order, saying that he would consider him above all of his retainers if he gave ready assent to his edict. But that man of God gave a reply like this to those sent to him, with great faith:

'I am secure in Christ my God and Lord.[11] Tell this to the king. Let him raise me over fires, force me on beasts, torture me with all sorts of

---

[9] Victoria's husband seems to have been a lawyer, who was now cooperating with the king. The pointed 'snake' was normally reserved for Eve and her descendants. Her recovery from being hung so long over a fire was certainly miraculous.

[10] Victorian seems to have been a senior adviser and confidant to the king and was well rewarded as one of Africa's highest officials. With the two brothers in ch. 5, his martyrdom was celebrated on March 25th. Hadrumentum. now Sousse, was one of Africa's largest cities then, and capital of the province of Byzacena.

[11] For the formula, see *M* p. 75, note 12.

110   Book Five

torments. If I give in, then in vain have I been baptized in the Catholic Church. For if this present life was the only one, and we could not hope for another eternal life, which is sure to come, I still would not do so, to obtain a small amount of temporal glory, and prove ungrateful to Him who bestowed his faith on me, my Creator.'

The tyrant was greatly stirred up at this, and human speech could not express over how long and with what great punishments the king afflicted him. But rejoicing in the Lord, he ended his life happily as he received a crown of martyrdom.

Chapter 5: Two Brothers, Confessors

Who could describe the martyrs' battles also waged in the city of Thambaia? There two blood brothers of the city of Aqua Regia,[12] both of them secure in the Lord, swore in turn to ask the torturers to torment them with one penalty and an equal punishment. And when they were first strung up, and were hanging there for the whole day with weighty stones tied to their feet, one of them asked them to let him down, to give him a respite. But the other brother was afraid he would deny his faith, and he cried out to him from where he was hanging:

'Don't do this, don't do it! That was not what we swore to Christ. I shall accuse you when we come before his terrible throne. For we have sworn over His Body and Blood to suffer together for his sake.'

Saying those and many other words, he comforted his brother for the agony of his suffering. And his brother cried out, speaking with a loud voice:

'Bring us Christians to any punishments you want, and crush us with cruel pains. What my brother is going to do, this shall I do also.'

That sequel shows with what fiery plates they were now roasted, with what claws they were scoured and by what torments they were twisted, as those torturers cast them out of their sight saying:

'The whole population is imitating those two, so that no one at all is being converted to our religion.'

---

[12] For these two towns, see the *Notitia,* under the fathers of Byzacena.

And they said this particularly as no bruises, nor marks at all of their punishments, could be seen on their bodies.[13]

Chapter 6: Amazing Faith of people of Typasita. A great Miracle.

However, let us quickly introduce for the glory of God what took place in Tipasa,[14] a city of greater Mauritania. When they had seen an Arian consecrated as bishop of their city, previously a notary of Cyril, so as to destroy their souls, the whole city fled at the same time to nearby Spain, escaping on boats. Very few were left behind, who had not found access to any shipping.[15] The bishop of the Arians began to force them to become Arians, at first with flattery and afterwards with threats. But remaining steadfast in the Lord they not only derided the madness of the bishop's attempts to persuade them, but also began to celebrate the divine mysteries in public, congregating in one of their homes. Discovering this, the bishop secretly sent a report on this to Carthage, hostile to them.

When this had notified the king, he was furious, and sent a Count ordering him to bring together all of the provincials into the middle of the forum, and to cut off their tongues to the root, and their right hands. When this had been done, with the help of the Holy Spirit they spoke, and are still speaking just as they used to speak before. But if anyone doubts this, let him now go to Constantinople, and there he will find one of them, the sub-deacon Reparatus,[16] who is delivering eloquent sermons without any impediment. For that reason he is considered extremely venerable in the palace of the emperor, Zeno, and is venerated especially by the queen, with amazing devotion.

---

[13] Most of these episodes of torture end unexpectedly with a miracle that somewhat undercuts the self-sacrifice, and it may have been used by Victor to give some relief to the otherwise unending horrors for the Christian reader.

[14] Modern Tifech.

[15] The availability of boats is at issue, not their ability to sail them, as in *M*.

[16] Another account of this tongue-less eloquence, but on a far larger scale, can be seen in ch. 50 of the *Chronicon*. Reparatus had previously been bishop of Typasensis, according to the *Notitia,* and lost his See to the Arian bishop, but he prospered as a sub-deacon in the palace in Constantinople. Zeno was emperor of the East from 474 to 491, and it is possible that contact with Reparatus stirred him into sending Uranius to help the Catholic Church, but without success. It took a Byzantine army under Belisarius to remove the Vandals, not diplomacy. For other versions of the tongues episode, see *M* pp 76-77, note 15.

Chapter 7: Vandals' savagery to their own people

But who could describe with appropriate speech or gather together all the different types of penalties that the Vandals themselves inflicted even on their own people? If a writer tries to recount one by one what things were also done in Carthage itself, even without ornate speech, he will not even be able to give the actual names of the tortures. But what is placed in full view today shows this clearly. For you can see some without hands, others without eyes, others with no feet and others shorn of noses and ears, and you can see others with shoulder-blades torn from their sockets by too much hanging, and heads that used to be held high, now sunken between shoulders, as they had tortured them, hung up continually in high buildings, the ropes jerked with a tug of their hands, that kept them hanging, swinging to and fro through the empty air. Sometimes the ropes snapped, and from that high altitude where they were hung, they crashed down with a heavy blow, and many lost the top part of their brains and their eyes. Others at once gave up their spirit as their bones were shattered, and others breathed their last a little later.

But if anyone thinks that this is a fable, he should question Uranius, the emissary of Zeno, as these deeds were done especially in his presence, for the reason, of course, that on coming to Carthage, he boasted that he had come to defend the Catholic churches. And so that the tyrant might show him that he was afraid of nobody, he placed more and crueler torturers in those squares and streets where the emissaries were accustomed to walk on their way to the palace, as they climbed up to it and then climbed down. This led of course to shame for the Empire itself, and a blot on our now decaying age.[17]

Chapter 8: Constancy of an Exiled Matron

And so, at this time the wife of a certain steward of the king, called Dagila, a lady who had already been a confessor of Christ many times in the days of Geiseric, a noble and delicate matron, was also totally weakened by whips and clubs, and was relegated to an arid and trackless exile, where no one could perhaps go to give her some comfort. She was happy to leave behind her husband, together with their children.

---

[17] The Empire under Zeno was thus insulted (*respublica* had lost its early sense).

It is said that afterwards an offer was made to her for her to move to a less savage desert, where if she wanted to, she could enjoy the support of friends. But she believed it a great joy for her to be where no human affection would comfort her, and so she begged that it should not be done.

Chapter 9: Struggles of Clergy in Carthage. Muritta's splendid deed

Then also, with Bishop Eugenius now still held in exile, all the clergy of the church of Carthage were afflicted by slaughter and starvation, that is, about five hundred or more. Among them very many were child readers, who rejoiced in the Lord, as they were sent far away to a cruel exile.[18] But I should not keep quiet about the greater freedom of speech shown then by the deacon Muritta than by the others, when clergy were being killed[19] in the middle of the city. There was a man called Elpidofor who was excessively cruel and fierce, and had been given the task of tearing the limbs off the confessors of Christ with violent tortures. This man had formerly been baptized before me in the church of Faustus, where the venerable deacon Muritta had taken him up from the bowl of the font, reborn. But afterwards he gave up his religion and showed such ferocity against the Church of God, that he had been found to surpass all others in carrying out persecution. Need I say more? While the priests were first being called up according to rank, to be torn apart by tortures, after the archdeacon, Salutaris, the above-mentioned Muritta was prepared for torture,[20] as he was the second in rank among the deacons, as while Elpidifor was sitting and shouting at him, the honourable old man was getting ready to be stretched on the rack. But before undressing, he held up those linen cloths with which he had wrapped Elpidifor previously when lifting him out of the font.[21] He was carrying the linen cloths secretly, and by chance nobody knew about it. At the same time he waved

---

[18] Young boys were quite often made 'lectors', as in the case of young Gregory, who later became bishop of Agrigento. See also *M* p. 78. n. 18. His version wrongly suggests that 500 clergy were exiled. The clergy were tortured, as ch. 9 shows, but it was the boys who were at once exiled.

[19] The context and normal use of *caedere* suggest deaths here, not just beating (so *M*). The next sentence in *M* has 'also' not in the text, an unusual reversal.

[20] Rather than *M*'s 'punishments were imposed on Muritta,' and 'rank' is clearer than 'order.'

[21] Before torture, victims were normally undressed, to shame them. It cannot be 'they began to stretch' (*M*) but 'he was getting ready to be stretched.' He could thus produce the linen cloths, presumably hidden under his cassock.

114   Book Five

them in the air and held them out for all to see, as he rose to speak with these words - and it is said that he moved the whole city to weeping and tears:

'These are the linen cloths, Elpidifor, minister of heresy, that will accuse you when the majesty of the Judge shall come.[22] I shall keep them most carefully, as proof of your perdition, to sink you in the bottomless pit of brimstone. These cloths were once wrapped around you, wretched man, as you rose immaculate from the font, and they will follow you more ardently, most miserable man, when you begin to occupy the flames of Hell. For you 'clothed yourself with cursing like as with a garment,'[23] tearing and throwing away the sacrament of true baptism and faith. What are you going to do, wretched man, when the Father's servants have begun to call together those invited to his royal banquet? Then when you are finally called, the king will look at you, devoid of your nuptial gown, and with terrible indignation he will say to you: 'Friend, how have you come in here not having a wedding garment?'[24]

I do not see what I gave to you, I do not recognize what I bestowed on you. You have lost the cloak of military service, which I wove over ten months to protect your virginal limbs,[25] and drawing the sign of the Cross, I washed you clean in the water, and adorned you with the purple of my blood. I do not see the decoration of the sign of the Cross, I do not see the branding mark of the Trinity.[26] Such a man will not be able to take part in my banquets. 'Bind him hand and foot'[27] with ropes, because he has wanted to separate himself voluntarily from his one-time Catholic brothers. He himself 'spreads out ropes tied together to be a snare', with which he has bound himself also. And he has prevented others from coming to that dinner table. 'He has placed a stumbling-block alongside the path'[28] for many, and now I have cast him out of my dinner table for perpetual shame and everlasting disgrace.'

---

[22] This shows that the writer's highly emotive language still depicted a proper Christian baptism, with the linen cloths and the holy water.

[23] From *Psalms* 109[108].18

[24] Adapted from *Matthew* 22.12. See below for the sequel.

[25] *M*'s 'on the loom of virgin limbs' (from the variant *tela*) is far-fetched, whereas 'to protect your virginal limbs' well suits the young boy (with Migne's *tutela*).

[26] For the use then of *character* see *M* p. 79, n. 21.

[27] The king orders the guest without a wedding garment to be bound and cast into outer darkness.

[28] For the snare and stumbling-block, see *Psalms* 140.5[139.6].

Arians and Vandals of the 4th-6th Centuries 115

As Muritta said these and other things, Elpidifor was struck dumb, roasted by the fire of conscience before the eternal conflagration.

Chapter 10: Clergy forced into Exile

And so, as they all braced their backs for beatings, they were quick to go into exile.[29] And when they were still set on their journey along a very long road, at the suggestion of the Arian bishops, unmerciful and violent men were chosen to take away from them cruelly what might perhaps help them, donated to them for sustenance by Christians who commiserated with them.[30] But then each one of them sang out perhaps more gladly:

"Naked came I out of my mother's womb." Naked also should I go into exile, because the Lord knows how to provide food for the hungry and how to clothe them in the wilderness.'[31]

For two Vandals, who had quite often confessed their faith under Geiseric, accompanied by their mother, spurned all their riches and set out for exile with the same clerics. But at the suggestion of a certain traitorous man, called Theucarius, formerly a reader, said that those whom he knew had strong voices, suitable for the melodies of songs, should be separated from the mass of confessors traveling, that is from the clerics of the church of Carthage. These included twelve young boys as designated by him, whom he had himself had as his pupils when he was a Catholic. And at his suggestion, they were at once sent off at top speed by that man,[32] as the boys twelve in number were recalled from the journey by the force of barbaric fury. They were segregated from the flock of holy people in body, but not in spirit, and fearful of ruin, with sighs and tears they grasped the knees of their companions with their hands, to avoid being dragged away. But the violent heretics separated them with menacing swords and called them back to Carthage.

---

[29] Those who have somehow survived the tortures and killings are very keen to escape, along 'a very long road,' suggesting the deserts south of Carthage, unlike the young lectors above, sent 'far away' overseas.

[30] *M* is misleading here. For *miseratio*, 'commiseration', not 'kindness,' is the sense, and *profuturum* was omitted ('which would help them').

[31] See *Job* 1.21. It continues: 'And naked I shall return thither.'

[32] *M* reads the variant *veredi* ('of a post-horse'), translating 'they were sent away on fast post horses.' If so, better *veredorum*, but an unlikely error, and how would a dozen such horses be available? Migne's *viro* makes good sense, and is needed, stressing the sinister role of the treacherous Theucarius.

116   Book Five

But while they were dealt with at first with flattery, suitable for such an age, they were found to be older than their years, and 'lest they sleep the sleep of death,'[33] they lit a lamp of evangelical light for themselves. The Arians were greatly indignant over this and were embarrassed at being defeated by young boys. Enraged thereby, they ordered them to be again subjected to cudgels. For they had struck the boys already just a few days before, with various whips. Wounds were cut into wounds and pain renewed broke out again. But it turned out, with the Lord's comfort, that the pain did not overcome even their younger age, and their courage grew greater, strengthened by their faith.

Now Carthage worships them with amazing affection, and sees this choir of twelve boys as the twelve apostles. They live together and eat together and sing psalms side by side, as they rejoice together in the Lord.[34]

During those days also, two merchants of that city, both called Frumentius, were crowned with a splendid martyrdom. Then as well seven brothers, not by nature but by grace, living together in a monastery, completed the struggle of their confession and arrived at the unfading crown, that is, the abbot, Liberatus, the deacon, Boniface, the sub-deacons Servus and Rusticus and the monks, Rogatus, Septimus and Maximus.[35]

Chapter 11: Antony's savagery towards the holy Eugenius

For at that time the Arian bishops, priests and other clergy were raging more cruelly than the king and the Vandals were. For, to persecute the Catholics, they were hurrying everywhere with their clerics, girt with swords. For example, a certain bishop called Antony, even crueler than the rest, carried out such wicked and unbelievable acts against our people that they cannot be narrated. He lived in a city very near to the desert, which was close to the province of Tripolitania. Like an insatiable beast, he was thirsty for the blood of Catholics and hurried here and there roaring, to seize them. For the unholy Huneric, knowing the ferocious

---

[33] *Psalms* 13.3[12.4]. *M* accepts the *non* in some mss, but an initial attempt to flatter them makes better sense than his 'They were not treated with kindly acts' - not the sense of *blanditiis* ('flattery,' 'fawning,' a derogatory word).

[34] This suggests a triumphant end a few years later for the brutalized choirboys.

[35] *M* (p.81) notes that the martyrdoms of these seven priests were described in a work possibly written by this Victor. It is likely that local martyrologies would have been used by the historian where available.

nature of Antony, wanted the holy Eugenius to be banished to those same parts of the desert.[36]

When Antony had taken him into custody, he surrounded the bishop with an extra close guard, allowing nobody to go inside to him. What is more, he planned to put him to death with various punishments involving plots and pain. But holy Eugenius bewailed the troubles of our persecution, and wore out his old body with the roughness of goat's-hair cloth, and slept on the bare earth. Soaking his bed with showers of holy tears,[37] he finally felt the grim disease of paralysis. When this was announced, the Arian felt joyful and quickly went to the cell of this outstanding man of God.[38] And as he noticed the true bishop uttering stammering words, under the pressure of his suffering, he decided to put him to death, as he did not want him to survive.

He ordered vinegar to be sought, the most bitter and the sharpest there was. And when it had been brought to him, the Arian forced it into the throat of the venerable old man, as he refused and gagged. For if the Lord of all, who had come to the state of needing a drink, was unwilling to drink when he had tasted it,[39] how much more would that servant and faithful confessor be unwilling, if heretical madness had not forced it in him? And from that vinegar especially, the bishop's disease was increased with his noxious suffering. But afterwards he was cured, with the merciful help of Christ's pity.

Chapter 12: On the Holy Habetdeum

The facts themselves make clear how much trouble that Arian could cause for another of our bishops, Habetdeum, who was similarly relegated to the city of Thamalluma where Antony was living. For when Antony was afflicting him with various persecutions and was unable to make him an Arian, and saw that the soldier of Christ was always constant in his confession, he made a promise to his men, saying:

---

[36] Again the roaring 'beast' is persecuting the Christians; in the *Notitia,* Eugenius is said to have been exiled to Tamallen or Tamallum, where Habetdeum was exiled, either in outback Byzacena or in Mauritania Sitifensis.

[37] See *Psalms* 6.6: 'I water my couch with my tears.' *M* rightly deleted the tautology of *sacci sui* ('his sackcloth'), but I read *sacris* to explain the error.

[38] Migne's *eximii* ('outstanding') is more apt than the variant *exilii* adopted by *M.*

[39] See *Mark* 27.34,48 for the vinegar in Christ's passion.

118   Book Five

'If I fail to make him join our religion, may Antony cease to exist.'[40]

But when he was found to have failed in his promise, with the suggestion of the Devil he thought of something else. He bound the bishop's feet and hands and tied him tightly with huge chains, and blocked his mouth to stop him from crying out, and then sprinkled the water of rebaptism, as he thought, on his body, as if he could bind his conscience as well as his body, or as if He who hears the groans of those in fetters, and lays open the secrets of the heart, was not there to help him; or as if the false water could overcome the intent of such resolution, that the man of God had already sent to Heaven as his messenger, marked out by his tears. Antony at once took the chains off the man and, as if quite happy, he spoke to him with such words:

'Look now, brother Habetdeum, you have become a Christian of our faith. What more will you be able to do, other than consent to the king's wishes?'[41]

Habetdeum replied:

'Impious Antony, that is a deadly damnation, when a voluntary assent is obtained by force. I held fast to my faith, and confessing with frequent statements, I cried out, defending my present and past belief. But even after you had bound me with chains and had blocked the entrance to my mouth, in the strong room of my heart I described the violence done to me, and with the angels' signatures I sent a report to my Emperor for him to read.'

Chapter 13: Violent acts by the Arians

That violence of the tyrants was indeed generally inflicted. For the Vandals had been sent everywhere for this reason, so as to bring Catholics traveling on their journeys to be killed by their Arian priests.[42] But when they had annihilated them with the sword of deceitful water, they handed them a token witnessed by words of perdition, to avoid being dragged off elsewhere with a similar violence. For it was illegal for either merchants

---

[40] Here the subj. *sit* is needed for the sense; the condition refers to the future.
[41] *M*'s version is far from the Latin ('what could you have done, if you were in agreement with the will of the king?'). The tenses and conditional are wrong.
[42] This passage is misleading in *M*: 'people traveling along their roads to their priests so that they would be slaughtered.' The *sacerdotibus* (abl.) are the agent.

Arians and Vandals of the 4th-6th Centuries   119

or private citizens to travel anywhere, unless the wretches displayed their moral death as described by this token of their mark.

Christ had already shown this through his revelation to his servant John long before, when he said:

'No one will be allowed to buy or sell anything, unless he has the mark of the beast on his forehead and on his hand.'[43]

For their bishops and their priests also kept on circulating villages and towns during the hours of night, with a band of armed men, and they so despised the doorposts that they forced their way in, to steal men's souls, bearing water and a sword. And when they found people at home, they sprinkled some of them who happened to be asleep in their beds with a shower of fire and lightning. At the same time with devilish screams they called them their Christians, so that they revealed the parody of their heresy rather than any true religion. In this, those less capable and dull witted thought that the sacrilege of this pollution had been implemented in them, but the wiser ones rejoiced that no harm had been done to them, as it had been forced on them when unwilling and asleep. For many at that time also threw ashes on their heads, some covering themselves with gloomy goats-hair shirts because of what was done, and some coated themselves with stinking mud, and they cut up the linen cloths violently placed on them, throwing them into latrines and stinking holes with their faithful hands.[44]

Chapter 14: Woman's egregious deed

Such was the violence when, in my sight, the son of a nobleman living in Carthage, who was about seven years old, was separated from his parents at the command of Cyril. His mother, forgetting her matronly modesty, let her hair hang down[45] as she ran after his abductors all over the city, while

---

[43] Taken from *Revelation* 13.16-17.

[44] For the great significance of these *linteamina* ('baptismal cloths'), see Muritta describing those of Elpidifor in chapter 9 above.

[45] In ancient Rome and in this time, upper-class women only let their hair hang down when in mourning (or in a brothel). A public display was exceptional.

120   Book Five

the poor infant cried out as best he could: 'I'm a Christian, I'm a Christian, by Saint Stephen I'm a Christian!'[46]

As he declared the Trinity with this triple cry, they closed his mouth, and drowned the innocent infant in the abyss of their sin.

The same thing is proved to have happened to the children of the venerable doctor, Liberatus. For when he was ordered by the king's command to be sent into exile with his wife and children, the impious Arians decided to separate the poor young children from their parents, so that they could use their pious affection to destroy their parent's resolution. And so the tender pledges of their children were torn away from their parents. And although Liberatus was ready to shed tears, he was rebuked by the authority of his wife, and as they set out on their journey, his tears dried up at once. And his wife said to him:

'Look, are you going to lose your soul because of your children. Liberatus? Count them as never having been born. For Christ will also claim them totally. Do you not see them crying out, and saying: "we are Christians"'?

But what this woman did in the sight of the judges cannot be passed over in silence. For she and her husband were held in prison under guard, although not together, to the extent that they could not see each other at all. And an order came to the woman, saying:

'Now give up your stubbornness. Look, your husband has obeyed the king's command and has become a Christian of our faith.'

And she said: 'Let me see him, and I shall do what God wants.'

And so she was led out of the prison, and found her husband standing with a great crowd before the tribunals. She thought that her enemies' lies were true,[47] and stretched out her hand to grasp the edge of his clothing nearest to his throat, and as they all watched, she started to throttle him, saying:

---

[46] Migne omits Saint Stephen in his text, found in five mss and adopted by *M*. As the note points out, Stephen was very popular at that time in North Africa due to his miracles in Palestine, alluded to by Saint Augustine in his *De Civitate Dei.*

[47] The *finxerant* in Migne makes perfect sense, unlike the *fecerant* ('had done') in *M* (p. xix), although *M* then translates 'what the enemies had made up.'

'Traitor, reprobate, unworthy of the grace and mercy of God, why have you been willing to find momentary glory and eternal death? What good will gold do for you? What good will silver do? Will they ever free you from the furnace of Hell?'

She said a lot of other things. And her husband replied to her:

'What's the matter with you, woman? What are you thinking of?[48] Whatever could you have been hearing about me? I remain a Catholic in the name of Christ, and I shall never be able to give up what I believe.'

Then the heretics, conscious of their lie now they had been detected, could not gloss over their deceit at all.

Chapter 15: Confessors' Deaths in the Deserts

I briefly mentioned above the violence of their savagery. This terrified a great many Christians, and so both men and women hid themselves, some of them in caves and others in desert areas, without anybody knowing where they were. And there, without a steady supply of food, they were overcome by hunger and cold and gasped their last breaths, full of contrition and affliction. But among these distressing afflictions, they carried with them the security of an inviolate faith. For in this way Cresconius, a priest of the town of Mizeita,[49] was found dead in a cave on Mount Ziquense, with his corpse already beginning to decompose.

Chapter 16: Holy Habetdeum

We have already spoken about the holy Habetdeum.[50] Afterwards he went to Carthage and decided to approach the wicked king, to make his conscience clear also to all men, as he had always kept it as an intimate friend of the Trinity. And Antony could not stop him, because of his sense

---

[48] *M* misses two common idiomatic verb usages, with his 'Why are you suffering?' and 'What does it look like?'
[49] Modern Aîn Babouch. See *CVV*, p. 47. In early martyrologies, 23rd March is given as the feast day of Cresconius.
[50] In chapter 12 above, where he preserves his faith despite two attacks on it by the Arian priest Antony.

122   Book Five

of shame.[51] And Habetdeum offered the most unholy king a supplication in words similar to these:

'What do you get from those already expelled? Why do you fight every day with those whom you have banished? You have taken away their wealth, and have deprived them of their churches and country and homes. Only their souls remain, which you strive to capture. "O the times! O the morality! The whole world knows this, and He who avenges sees it."[52]If you say it is a faith that you hold, why do you disturb the members of the true faith with such great persecutions? What do you get from our exile, what from the poor of this world, whose lives are always in Christ? At least permit those whom you have sent away from the face of all people to enjoy the company of beasts.'

When the bishop of God had said this and similar things, the wicked tyrant is said to have given him this order:

'Go to our bishops, and follow what they tell you to do, because they are known to have the complete power in this matter.'

But not even this business could recall Antony from his madness, knowing rather that he could please the king's rule much more because of this. But Bishop Habetdeum rejoiced in the goodness of his conscience, and chose to return to his place of exile.

Chapter 17: Serious Famine

At that time an incredible famine arose, and began to devastate the whole of Africa with a depopulation in one go. No rain appeared then, not a single drop fell from the sky. Nor was it to no purpose, but was due to the true and just judgment of God, that where the water of a muddy

---

[51] His shame was over the way his lies to Liberatus' wife had been exposed. *M* wrongly translates: 'he was not a diffident man,' applied to Habetdeum (despite the reflexive *suam*).

[52] Cicero used this well-known exclamation three times before exclaiming how the times were really out of joint, most notably at the start of his first speech against the revolutionary nobleman, Catiline. But his greatest speeches were against the debauched Antony, and led to Cicero's murder. In the original, the Senate knows, and Consul sees it being done. *M* rightly has God avenging it here.

Arians and Vandals of the 4th-6th Centuries 123

whirlpool[53] was bubbling with fiery sulphur, as the Arian persecution continued, the rain of heavenly indulgence that had always fallen in abundance was now being denied. The appearance of the whole land remained pale yellow. The vine was not protected from the summer heat by the shade of its leafy branches, and the scattered seeds did not turn the tops of the sods green, while the olive, always green and covered with healthy leaves, did not have its usual panoply of beauty. The branches of fruit trees, married to the earth, produced no flower buds, nor the usual return of fruit afterwards.

Everything was gloomy and grim, and the disaster had shattered the whole of Africa like a plague. The earth had not produced the greenness of germinating grass at all, either for men or for beasts of burden. The basins of rivers once flowing fast with headlong impetus had long since dried up, and the bursting veins of springs had been dried out likewise.

All the sheep and the oxen, and the beasts of the field,[54] as well as the forest animals, were destroyed by starvation, and could not be seen anywhere at all. And where there happened to be a grassy bank located in a still moist valley, it had begun to produce the pallid colour of new hay, rather than the greenness of grass, and then at once a burning, fiery blast of air swept in and dried it all out with its baking heat, as a dusty storm desiccated everything beneath its arid air, overshadowing the whole place.[55]

At that time there was no commercial activity, no plough pulled along by oxen turned over the sods of earth, or tilled them, since there were no oxen to pull, and not a single plough had remained.[56] But amid all these evils,[57] some of the country dwellers had died, and afterwards those who happened to survive were already waiting for burial. And because, with

---

[53] For the 'muddy whirlpool' (*caenosi gurgitis*') of Hades, see Juvenal *Sat* 3.266, and for the *sulphuris ... ignis* of lightning ('fiery sulphur') see Lucretius 6.221-2.

[54] From *Psalms* 8.7.

[55] A striking picture of an unexpected dust storm, like those that sometimes cover whole cities along the southern coast of Australia, with its similar climate.

[56] See Virgil *Georgics* 3.515-566 and Lucretius *De Rerum Natura* 6.1138-1286 for two very dramatic plagues clearly used by Victor of Vita. At that time a Classical education was not unusual among the upper class in North Africa and Spain. The variant *castra* ('camp') used by *M* ('villages') had rightly been rejected by Migne. For the dramatic effect of abandoned, decaying ploughs, see Virgil *Gics* 1.494-5.

[57] The opening sentence was left out by *M*.

124   Book Five

the disagreeable pressure of the famine, there was none of the usual trade, as we have said, and due cultivation was not being given to the earth, throngs of the living and funeral processions of young men, old men, adolescents, male and female, and also of young boys and girls, were being spread about in every direction, wherever they could go and however they could, touring towns and villages and isolated cities. For 'turning aside like a deceitful and crooked bow,' and 'angering God at the waters of strife,' 'they suffered hunger like dogs,' not that they might eat bread, but to feel the hostility of the Trinity that they had denied.[58]

Some spread through the fields, others sought secret places in the woods, looking for the old roots of plants or for other off-scourings. Some of them[59] collapsed on their front doorsteps as they tried to leave their homes, and fell in large numbers, overcome by famine. Indeed, the streets and lanes were filled with the corpses of dead people, exhaling foul smells, which were killing those still alive as they walked about in every area. There was no shortage each day of funerals everywhere for the dead, and none had the courage to look after a merciful burial. For there were not enough people alive to bury them, as the famine raged, and they themselves were going to die after a while. Individuals sought to turn their freedom and that of their children into permanent servitude, but could find no takers.[60] Mountains and hills, streets of cities, roadways and paths provided a single grave for all those people everywhere, for their unremitting starvation had denied them sustenance.[61]

But the Vandals themselves, who had been enriched before by the frequent spoils from the many provinces, and at first by the retention of the riches of Africa, were now tormented by a greater shortage of food. And the more they thought themselves superior by their accumulation of slaves, the more badly they fared when weakened by the torture of hunger. No man kept his son, or his wife, or his personal servant, but each went out not where he wanted but where he could, and either collapsed at once, or

---

[58] These three quotations were adapted from *Psalms* 78(77).57,106(105).32 and 59(58).6 and 14.

[59] Not 'in large numbers' as in *M. Non-nulli* ('not none') is usual for 'some.'

[60] This reflects a tradition going back to early Roman times of free but usually bankrupt and destitute people selling themselves into slavery in wealthy homes.

[61] Pope Gregory twice refers to a plague in North Africa, in *Ep* 9.232 sent in Aug. 599 to Sicily, Africa was 'being devastated by disease' and in *Ep* 10.20 sent in Aug. 600 to Dominic, bishop of Carthage, the plague continues unabated. *M* notes that Dutch archaeologists have found signs of plague in 5th century Africa (p. 88).

Arians and Vandals of the 4th-6th Centuries 125

never returned at all. Then also an unlucky multitude was forced to congregate in the city of Carthage itself. And as those still living corpses flooded inside in waves, and the king he saw the grim results of the deaths being brought in there, he ordered them all to be driven out of the city at once, in case infection from those dying might provide a common grave for his army also.[62]

And so he ordered individuals to return to their own provinces and homes. But there were none who could return, while each bore the look of death on his face. And for that reason a greater destruction of those re-baptized could perhaps have resulted, because while the Arians promised the completion of one's present life, that did not come to pass, and the first death that followed re-baptism came before a second death.[63] The devastating famine claimed dominion for itself so much so that in most places, certainly once populated, with the death of their occupants and with deep silence, and only the ruins left standing, all was at rest.[64]

Chapter 18: Morality of the Barbarians

But why do I now continue with what I cannot explain? For if they were still alive today and were allowed to talk about such things, the flow of Ciceronian eloquence would dry up and Sallust would remain totally tongue-tied. And to pass over others as being unworthy to give such a great account, neither Eusebius of Caesarea, should he arise as suitable for this work, nor his translator Rufinus, decorated with the garlands of Greek and Latin eloquence, nor even, to keep it brief, Ambrosius, nor Jerome, nor our Augustine himself, would be sufficient.

'Hear this, all you people; give ear, all you inhabitants of the world, you of lowly birth or high estate, rich and poor together.'[65]

---

[62] The *exercitui eius* in Migne is an unlikely scribal error for *suis sibi*, in Lorichius and translated by *M*. Armies often brought home plagues in ancient times, but here it is the backbone of the small Vandal occupation, not to be put at risk.

[63] *M* prefers *primam secunda* ('a second death came before the first') to *prima secundam* in Migne, yet translates correctly 'a first death came before a second.'

[64] This chilling picture suggests the end of the World. The contagion certainly depicts a plague in North Africa, as the basic hygiene collapsed, as in 600, when archbishop Dominic was one of its victims, like Pope Pelagius in Rome's in 590.

[65] See *Psalms* 49(48).1-2. For supporters of barbarians see *M* n. 31, p. 89.

126 Book Five

Some of you, who love barbarians and sometimes praise them, to your own condemnation, now consider their name and understand their morality. Could they have been called by any other proper name, except to be called 'barbarians,' possessing a name that suggests ferocity, anyway, and cruelty and terror? With whatever great gifts you pamper them, with whatever great compliance you portray them, they know nothing else to do other than envy the Romans. And as far as their wish is concerned, they always desire to overshadow the splendour and nobility of the Roman name, and do not want any of the Romans at all to survive. And where they are known to spare their subjects[66] so far, they only spare them for use as their slaves; for they have never loved any of the Romans. If their barbarian ferocity tried to discuss with us matters of faith, then Arian heretics would dispute rationally also. But when do they make sense, as they separate God the Son and Saviour from God the Father?'[67]

Why did they need deceits and false accusations? Why did they want to subvert everything with their raging fury, like the tempest of a storm? If disputation was necessary for the bishops, why were the hangings, why the fires, why the hooks at the same time and the crosses? Why did the serpentine offspring of the Arians devise such types of tortures against innocent men, the sort that even Mezentius[68] did not discover? Furious greed and cruel avarice fought against innocence, so as to destroy men's souls and plunder their fortunes. If a debate was desired, why did they steal others' properties, not only of priests but of all the laymen also? But they were delighted, of course, at being despoiled, and accepted the robbery of their possessions with joy![69]

---

[66] Taken from the *parcere subiectis et debellare superbos* that ends Anchises' warning to Rome, in Virgil *Aen* 6.853.

[67] Their theological dispute can never be resolved rationally, with the Vandals' extreme form of barbarity, and separation of the inseparable.

[68] Mezentius, king of Etruria, infamous for his impiety and cruel tortures (see *Aen* 8.483-8), was primarily damned for his merciless opposition to Aeneas when the Trojan hero invaded Italy, in Virgil's ambivalent epic. A very neat chiasmus follows, one of many such devices that suggest rhetorical training for Victor in his youth, together with the acquisition of a sound knowledge of the Classics. This type of education was available to Pope Gregory as a young man. See also Pierre Riché *Education et Culture*, pp 255-262. The last few chapters are clearly rhetorical in content and style, but with biblical quotations to prove his case.

[69] The acceptance is clearly ironical, as my addition of 'of course' makes clear.

Chapter 19: Lamentation for Africa

Be present now, I beg you, people of every age, every sex and every condition. Be present, I beseech you, all the mass of those called Catholics throughout the world who have been carried in a mother's womb,[70] you who alone know how to bestow a brotherly affection and have learnt from your master Paul how to 'rejoice with those rejoicing and weep with those weeping.'[71] Let them come together at the house of our pain, and let us pour forth rivers of tears from our eyes together, since our cause and faith are as one. I do not want any heretic to meet me to console me, who perhaps is longing 'to add to the pain of my wounds'[72] and daily 'take joy in my misfortunes.'[73]I do not want, I do not seek a stranger's affection, but a brother's. I do not want one of those 'sons of strangers whose mouths have spoken vanity and their right hand is a right hand of iniquity.'[74] For 'the sons of strangers have ever lied to me, those who have grown old and have limped from their paths.'[75] Those men 'say to me daily: "Where is your God? " '[76] while that people ordained by the precious blood of the Lamb is afflicted. Amid their insults I 'prepared for the whips,'[77] I do not stop singing to the Lord as he beats me. 'Take your whips away from me,' for 'I have been laid low,' not 'by the strength of your hand'[78] but by the persecution of the Arian heresy.

And so let all those come forward now who are to travel along the narrow path with me, and because of 'the words on the lips of God follow hard pathways,' 'let them see if there is grief like my grief, since I have been gathered like grapes in the day of the Lord's fury.'[79]'All my enemies have opened their mouth against me; they have hissed and gnashed their teeth; they have said: "We shall swallow her up. Behold, this is the day we looked for. We have found it, we have seen it. "' 'Be present, angels of my God, who have never failed in your established ministry for those who

---

[70] This is loosely modeled on *Isaiah* 46.3.

[71] See *Romans* 12.15.

[72] *Psalms* 69(68),27

[73] *Psalms* 35(34).2, 6.

[74] *Psalms* 144(143),8

[75] *Psalms* 17.46 (Vulgate).

[76] *Psalms* 42.3(41.4).

[77] Psalms 37.11 (Vulgate).

[78] *Psalms* 39.10(38.12).

[79] Adapted from *Psalms* 17(16).4 and *Lamentations* 1.12. The grape gathering is passive, not active (*M* has 'I am a gatherer of grapes').

128   Book Five

shall be heirs of eternal salvation,'[80] and look at the whole of Africa, once supported by rows of such great churches, but now stripped of all of them. Adorned by such great ranks of priests, Africa now lies stripped of them and abject. Its priests and elders perished in deserts and islands, 'and in searching for food to eat, they have found none.'[81]

Consider and see that 'Jerusalem, the city of our God, has become vile, as if polluted by a menstrual woman amid its adversaries.' 'The enemy has put his hand on all her desirable things, for she has seen that the heathen invaded and entered into her sanctuary, whom you commanded that they should not enter into your church,' and 'Her pathways mourn, since nobody assembles on the holy day. All her beauty and delight have left her face.' Her virgins and her young men learnt to walk along a rough path, and brought up in the cloisters of monasteries, they went into captivity under the Moors, while 'the stones of her sanctuary are scattered, not only at the top of every street,' but in squalid parts of mines too. Tell our God, her protector, confident in your supplication, 'that she is in distress, and her bowels are troubled' by her weeping, because 'she dwells among the heathen and finds no rest' and 'she has none to comfort her.' She sought to find from the Fathers of the East 'someone to share her sadness, and there was nobody. She sought consolation, and found it not, as she ate gall in her food and drank vinegar in her thirst,' imitating the passion of her spouse and God, 'who who suffered on her behalf so that she followed in His steps.'[82]

Chapter 20: The Author invokes the Saints

Pray for us, most holy patriarchs, from the stock of whose family she was born who now labors on this Earth. Pray, holy prophets, as you know her affliction, about which you sang before with a prophetic proclamation. Apostles, be her supporters, to add her to your flock, as you ran through the whole world like the swiftest of horses, while the Lord ascended above you. Especially you, Saint Peter, why do you not speak on behalf of the sheep and lambs recommended to you with great care and concern by the

---

[80] Close to *Lamentations* 2.16, and see *Hebrews* 1.14 for the second quote.

[81] *Lamentations* 1.19.

[82] After 'Consider' the first six quotes are adapted from *Lamentations*, 1.11 & 1.17 (where the text has Sion for Jerusalem), 1.10, 1.4 and 6, 14.1, 1.20 and 1.2-3. The last two quotes are from *Psalms* 69.20-21 (68.21-2) and *I Peter* 2.21. Victor's quotes, mainly from *Psalms* and *Lamentations*, are very neatly adapted to the plight of his fellow Catholics.

great Lord whom we share? And you, Saint Paul, the teacher of the gentiles, who taught the gospel of God 'from Jerusalem to Illyria,'[83] realize what the Vandals and Arians are doing now, while your children groan and lament as captives. You, the brother of Peter, and no different in suffering, glorious Andrew,[84] who are recognized as manly as you fought in a manly way, consider the groan of the African people, and do not let it displease you, but intervene on our behalf before God. Lament together on our behalf, all of you holy apostles. But we know we are unworthy of your prayers on our behalf. For those things that happened were not due to us as a test, like saints, but to evil-doers as punishments. But pray now even for your wicked sons, as Christ also prayed even for his Jewish enemies. Let what has been justly inflicted on us be sufficient for our castigation, and let a pardon be requested for our delinquency just now. Let it be said to the Angel of destruction: 'It is enough; stay now thy hand.'[85] Who does not know that the sins of our shameful acts has procured these ills, as we 'kept not the covenant of God and refused to walk in his law?'[86] But we request you on our knees, do not spurn your wretched sinners, through Him who raised your humble fishermen to the apostolic crown.

Chapter 21: Huneric's Reign[87]

The most criminal Huneric kept control of the kingdom for seven years and ten months, consummating it with the death he deserved. For putrefied and bubbling with worms, it seemed not his body, but bits of his body that were buried. Just as that one-time king who broke the given law was buried as an ass, even so Huneric perished quickly with a similar death.[88]

---

[83] For Peter, see *John* 21.15-16, for Paul, *Romans* 15.19.

[84] This passage from 'You the brother' to 'before God' comes from Migne's text (see p. 258, n. d), but mss and editors had omitted it, and *M*.

[85] *Luke23.34* & *II Samuel* 24.16. The angel was not 'persecuting' (*M*).

[86] *Psalms* 78(77).10.

[87] *CVV* p.16 and *M* p. xvi wrongly saw this as a later addition. See below.

[88] As in *Jeremiah* 22.19, where the prophet predicts Joakim:'will be buried putrefied with an ass's burial and cast forth beyond the gates of Jerusalem'). For an inapposite interpolation of Donatists and Nicasius (or *ut Arius* as conjectured by Courtois), see *M* p. 93. As a prophetic picture of Huneric's death, it is an ideal ending to the history. But the Donatist interpolation should have been consigned to the notes.

B. VICTOR OF TONNENA

CHRONICLE

Preface

This translation is based on the edition of Victor's *Chronicon* by Carmen C. de Hartmann. Her text is readily available and preferable to those in Migne and MGH, but her mediaeval spellings would confuse most modern readers, rightly modernized by Migne.[1]

There has been some uncertainty over the identity of the author of the *Chronicon*, although he suffered the same sort of early life as the young Bishop Gregory of Agrigento.[2] For as an equally young bishop of Tonnena, he was first imprisoned and beaten, in the Balearic Islands it seems, and again in Alexandria, and was then carted off to Constantinople in 564, with five other bishops, to be imprisoned in its local monasteries, until ready to accept the Catholic Church's position on the divisive Three Chapters issue, that figures so repeatedly in his *Chronicon*, and caused such trouble for Popes and Emperors. Victor reappears in North Africa as the reinstated bishop of Tonnena in the letters of Pope Gregory, dated September 601 (*Letters* 12.3, 8 and 9), sent about 37 years after his departure to Constantinople. How long he had been back in Africa before the Pope's letters is unclear. But by then he was supporting the Catholic position and was quite ready to condemn the Three Chapters, in line with the repeated condemnations by the new Pope, Gregory the Great. In his final years, Victor became a very senior bishop, it seems, the Primate of

---

[1] in the *C C Series Latina* clxxiii A, Brepols, 2001, its title *Victoris Tunnunensis Chronicon cum reliquis ex Consularibus Caesar -augustanis et Iohannis Biclarensis Chronicon*, the historical commentaries on the last two works having been edited by Roger Collins. The overlong 150 pp introduction is mainly concerned with the manuscripts' evidence. There is no translation of the text.
[2] See my annotated English version of his life in *A Translation of Abbot Leontius' Life of Saint Gregory, Bishop of Agrigento*, Mellen, New York, 2004.

Numidia, described as 'the Primate among you' in *Letter* 12.8, one of fourteen sent to the Pope's friend, Columbus, the bishop of Numidia. If he was 33 years old as a headstrong young bishop in 564,[3] he would be nearly seventy by 601, old, but that age was reached by several bishops in Pope Gregory's letters,[4] and by many of the first ecclesiastical victims of the Vandals in North Africa. The best known of these, Saint Augustine, was in charge of the defense of Hippo Regius against a Vandal siege when he died, aged seventy-seven. The Pope's only letter to Victor is letter 12.9, sent in March 602, in which he asks him to join with Bishop Columbus and the papal Secretary, Hilary, to investigate the serious charges of brutal treatment of his clergy and of sinful simony brought against Paulinus, the bishop of Tegisis. Nothing more is heard of Paulinus or of this Victor in the Pope's later letters.

On pp 93-102 of her Introduction, Hartmann gives a brief biography of Victor, and rightly accepts Mommsen's *Tonnonensis* (but adds 'o Tunnonensis'), and his *in insulis Balearicis* rather than the unknown *Valeriacis*, and she ends by suggesting a date for his death after 568 and perhaps as late as 575, to finalize his manuscript. But she made no mention of the bishop of Tonnena, also called Victor, who received a letter from Pope Gregory in 602. There is no certain date for Victor's death, but if 575 or later is possible for the completion of his chronicle, a return to his church and a later honorific office are certainly equally possible. The alternative is that another Victor became bishop of Tonnena very soon after the death of the chronicler, which is possible but is a most unlikely coincidence.[5]

Hartmann's text is mostly judicious in its choice of variants, but there seems to be no point in *nichil* for *nihil, tocius* for *totius, vite sue, prelio, prefuit* for *vitae suae, proelio, praefuit, damptnauit* for *damnavit,*

---

[3] Pope Gregory was very happy to consecrate Gregory in Rome, as the new Bishop of Agrigento, when the Sicilian was barely thirty one years old.

[4] The elderly and frail (or deranged) bishops included Januarius of Sardinia (*Ep* 14.2), Ecclesius of Chiusi (*Ep* 14.15), Castor of Rimini (*Ep* 2.25) and John of Prima Justiniana (*Ep* 13.6). The Pope wanted to keep them in their sees until death.

[5] Note that 'Victor' was the second most frequent name for Bishops in the North African Church. In the *Notitia* that follows Victor of Vita's history of the Vandals' occupation of North Africa, there are 26 clergy called Felix, 22 Victor and 19 Donatus. No other names reach double figures. In the letters of Pope Gregory, 23 bishops were called John, 9 Felix, 8 Peter and 6 Theodore, 4 Victor and 1 Donatus.

132   B. Victor of Tonnena

Vuandali, Gotti/Gothi etc. Such variations often on the same page would
be unlikely from any scholarly bishop's pen.

Covering the years 444 to 566 AD

Up to this point Prosper, a most religious man, has described all the
previous years in due order, and we have added the following to it.[6]

1. And so under the consuls Theodosius for the eighteenth time, and
Albinus, Domnus[7] succeeded John as bishop of the Church of Antioch.
[444]

2. Aetius and Symmachus were consuls. [446]

3. Calliopus and Ardabures were consuls [447], as Eutyches appeared,[8] the
priest and abbot of a monastery in Constantinople, who established a
heresy under his name. For indeed this man asserted that our Lord Jesus
Christ was so born from his mother forever a Virgin that he argued there
was nothing in him of human nature. He was invited to a Synodal
assembly, called together in Constantinople,[9] over which the holy bishop
of that city, Flavian, presided, and because the priest was unwilling to
confess that Christ had two natures after his birth from the Virgin and that

---

[6] Saint Prosper of Aquitaine (c.390-c.463) was a secretary to Pope Leo I, and his
poems and holy writings included a *Chronicle*, which followed Eusebius and
Jerome up to 378, and proved most valuable between 425 and 455, his mature
years, especially for the history of dogma. For '*huc usque ... subiecimus*' see
Migne, who after a heading of '*Continuans ubi Prosper desinit,*' has '*A xviii
consulatu Theodosii Junioris, Victor episcopus Tununensis Ecclesiae Africae
historiam prosequitur, ubi Prosper reliquit.*' ('Victor, the bishop of Tonnena,
continues the history of the African Church, from the eighteenth consulship of
Theodosius the Younger, where Prosper left off.') For Victor's account of his
rebellious youth, see under the years 555, 556 and 564 below. As mentioned
above, this translation is based on the text of Carmen Cardelle de Hartmann,
Brepols, 2001; Migne's text appeared in his *Patrologiae Cursus Completus* vol.
68, Paris, 1866, pp 941-962.
[7] *Domnus* seems preferable to the far more normal *Diaconus* in Migne.
[8] The *apparuit* in P seems preferable to *paruit* ('obeyed' normally) of U, adopted
in the text of Hartmann.
[9] The locative *Constantinopoli* is required (as in Migne) rather than the accusative
used by Hartmann.

Christ was consubstantial[10] with us through the flesh, he was condemned, together with his error. And Leo, the holy bishop of Rome, confirmed this condemnation with his apostolic authority.

4. For this, with the Emperor Theodosius presiding, together with the Bishops Leo of Rome, Dioscorus of Alexandria, Domnus of Antioch, Juvenal of Jerusalem and Flavius of Constantinople, and with Posthumianus and Zeno as consuls, [448] a second General Synod met in Ephesus, at which Dioscorus of Alexandria usurped the presidency and absolved Eutyches by imperial favor after he had been legitimately condemned. With unholy authority, he condemned the critics of Eutyches for teaching the two natures of Christ, namely Bishops Flavian of Constantinople, Eusebius of Dorylaeum,[11] Theodoret of Cyrus, Ibas of Edessa and the rest of the others, although contradicted by the legates of the Apostolic See. With the monks' sedition and military violence he forced the whole Synod to give him their support.

4a. During these days the Goths fought a battle against the Huns, on the plains of the Catalauni,[12] and during it their king, Theodored, was slain, and the Goths were victorious, led in battle by King Thurismund. Attila, king of the Huns, was nowhere to be seen.[13]

5. Asturius and Protogenes were consuls.[14] [449]. Attila, the king of the Huns, after he was defeated in battle by the generals of the Emperor Valentinian and forced to flee, regained his strength and made for Italy, without support, and the Roman State countered his evil plans with a peace treaty. And this Attila received a legation from Pope Leo and not only stopped laying waste to the State, but even retreated across the Danube, once he was granted peace.[15]

---

[10] Cotelerius and Hartmann rightly read *consubstantialem* rather than the text's *substantialem*. Medieval scribes very often missed the abbreviation for *con-*.

[11] H accepts P's *Durelei*, but the Phrygian city *Dorylaeum* in both Cicero and Pliny is preferable. Some MSS wrongly read Cyprus for Cyrus.

[12] A tribe near Châlons-sur-Marne, in Gallia Belgica. *Cathalaunicis* in H is wrong.

[13] From Isidore *Goth*. 25. In Migne, these excerpts are also included in the notes.

[14] H prefers *Austurio* (in U), but keeps *Protogene* in P, rather than U's *Protegene*.

[15] The perfect in P is preferable to U's *recedit*, after *quievit*.

134   B. Victor of Tonnena

6. Valentinian was consul for the seventh time, and Albinus was consul.[16] [450] The Emperor Theodosius died in Constantinople, in the sixty-second year of his life.

7. Chrysaphius became emperor, but since he mistreated the followers of Eutyches, he was slain. And Marcian was made emperor (47th) of the Romans with the consensus of the whole State.[17]

8. Marcian the 47th emperor ruled the Romans for five years and six months. And right from the start of his reign he sought peace for his Churches, and with his imperial authority he denounced the Synod that took place in Chalcedon.

9. After Flavian, Anatole took over the Church of Constantinople.

10. In the consulship of the Emperor Marcian, on the twenty-fourth of September [451], the Bishops Leo of Rome, Dioscorus of Alexandria, Maximus of Antioch, Juvenal of Jerusalem and Anatole of Constantinople, called together a general Synod in Chalcedon, [452] at which the second Synod of bishops at Ephesus was rejected as anathematized. Eutyches was condemned together with his patron Dioscorus, bishop of Alexandria, and Nestorius. And the Catholic bishops, unjustly condemned by the same Dioscorus in the aforesaid Synod at Ephesus, were duly released, and the faith of the Holy Fathers who met at the Holy Synods of Nicaea, Constantinople and Ephesus, was explained. And so, when these matters had been determined and strengthened with the signatures of the whole Synod, Eusebius was restored to his own Church of Dorylaeum, Theodoret to his in Cyrus and Ibas to his in Edessa, and those whom the heretical Dioscorus had put in their place were driven out. All things were arranged concerning the status of the Church, and received a settled ending.[18]

10a. After Theodored, his son Thurismund ruled the kingdom of the Goths for six years.[19]

---

[16] For *Attieno* in MGH and M, *Albino* in U being read by H.

[17] Chrysaphius in P and Migne, is preferable to *Crisafius* in U, and in H's text. On this section, see Prosper *Chron.* 1 p. 482, 1367.

[18] The settled ending was not to last for long, before the Three Chapters schism was again dragging the Church apart. The writer's personal involvement as a young bishop in this schism explains his keenness to follow every development in the very divisive controversy.

[19] See Vasaeus *ad a.*452.

Arians and Vandals of the 4th-6th Centuries   135

11. Opilio and Vincomalus were consuls. [453] Dioscorus was sent away in exile to Gangra, and Proterius took over the bishopric of the Church of Alexandria.[20]

12. At that time Attila died. While his sons fought over his crown, the Huns were devastated and then diminished in number.[21]

13. Aelius and Studius were consuls. [454] The patrician Aetius, after first being struck by the hand of the Emperor Valentinian inside the palace, then died a cruel death from the swords of those standing around him. The prefect Boethius was killed anyway.[22]

14. Valentinian was consul the eighth time, and Anthemius consul. [455] The Emperor Valentinian perished in Rome on the Field of Mars, through the treachery of the patrician Maximus and prefect Heraclius, and the same Maximus from his consulship and patrician status took over the throne, for seventy-seven days.[23] But then the hidden evil was fully revealed, as he soon took in marriage the widow of Valentinian, the Empress, not letting her mourn her husband's death. But worse things followed these evil deeds. While he was fearful over the arrival of Geiseric, the king of the Vandals freely allowed all those who wanted to leave Rome to do so, but before he could begin the flight that he planned, he was killed, and cut up limb by limb and thrown into the river Tiber.

15. Aelius and Studius were consuls and prefects. On the third day after the death of Maximus, Geiseric, the king of the Vandals, entered the city of Rome and for fourteen days he stripped it of all its wealth, and took away with him from there the daughters and wife of Valentinian and many thousand captives. But he abstained from burning, torture and the sword, due to the intervention of Pope Leo. And on the seventy-fifth day of this captivity Avitus, a total simpleton, took over the rule of Gaul.

---

[20] Gangra was a town in Bithynia, modern Turkey (Çankiri).

[21] This, and similar comments were appended to Migne's text by some scribe, taken from Isidore, Theodorus or Vasaeus. Scaliger rightly argued that these excerpts were well worth including. Here as often elsewhere H follows a manuscript (U here) with *Ugni*, although another (P here) has *Hunni*. It occurs on the same page. The author would not be so inconsistent.

[22] Was this Boethius a grand father of Anicius, who supported an over ambitious Aëtius, consul thrice, an outstanding general, who got too close to the throne, as protector of Placidia and Valentinian III?

[23] As in U; Migne has LXVII as in P.

136   B. Victor of Tonnena

16. John and Varanes were consuls. [456] The patrician Ricimerus defeated Avitus, and sparing His Innocence, he made him bishop of Placentia.

17. Constantine and Rufus were consuls. [457] Marcian, the emperor of the East, died in Constantinople, and in his place Leo was made emperor.

18. Leo, 48th emperor of the Romans, ruled for sixteen years.

19. Alexandria and Egypt were weakened by the heresy of Dioscorus, and did not accept the decrees of the Synod of Chalcedon. Timotheus, whose first name was Aelurus,[24] had organized a conspiracy with some supporters of Dioscorus, and had killed Proterius, the bishop who had taken over from Dioscorus and who observed the decrees of the Synod of Chalcedon. This was on the 25th of March, on the sixth day of the last week of Lent, on the day on which our Lord and Saviour was crucified by the Jews. For then comes the Passion of our Lord, when it is celebrated on the 27th of March. And so, once Proterius was dead, the aforesaid Timotheus, also called Aelurus, who opposed the Synod of Chalcedon, usurped his episcopacy and his Church.

19a. During these times, Theoderic, brother of Thurismund, ruled over the Goths for nine years.

20. The Emperor Leo was consul. [459] Majoranus took over the rule of Rome.
21. Timotheus, usurper of the Church of Alexandria, attacked the defenders of the Synod of Chalcedon

21a During this time the Goths fought a battle against the Suebi on the plain of Paramus, by the river Orbe, and in this battle the Goths were victorious.[25]

22. Patricius and Recimerus[26] were consuls. [459] Juvenal, the bishop of Jerusalem, was armed with a letter from Leo, the bishop of Rome, against the heresy of Eutyches and of Dioscorus.

---

[24] Rather than the *Heluro* in P and the *Illuro* in U, Migne follows P, with *Aerulo,* in brackets. Proper names from medieval times were then a permanent source of uncertainty for scribes, and fare little better today.
[25] Added from Theod. AN.E 371. For the Suebi (or Suevi), see 21a above.
[26] Migne has *Ricimero*, as in P-E.

Arians and Vandals of the 4th-6th Centuries   137

23. Magnus and Apollonius were consuls. [460] Bishop Timotheus, who had killed Bishop Proterius, was forcibly removed from the See of the Church of Alexandria by the command of Pope Leo, and was sent into exile on the Chersonese. And after five months, another Timotheus, with a first name Salafiarius, and a defender of the Synod of Chalcedon, was ordained bishop of that Church of Alexandria.

23a During these days the Emperor Majorinus came to Saragossa.[27]

24. Dagalaifus[28] and Severinus [were consuls][461]

25. The Emperor Leo II [462] and Severus [were consuls][29]

26. Vivianus, a most famous man, and Basilius were consuls. [463] For the Church of Carthage, after Capreolus, Quodvultdeus, and after Quodvultdeus and Deogratias, Eugenius, were consecrated bishops.[30]
26a While they were consuls, the Emperor Majorinus was killed by Ricimerus.

27. Majorinus died in Rome and Severus took over the empire on the 7th July.

28. Olybrius and Rusticus were consuls. [464] Geiseric, king of the Vandals, after bringing disasters to many provinces, and after despoiling and killing the Christian people in Africa, died in the fortieth year of his reign.[31] After him his son Huneric was king for seven years and five months. His father Geiseric had handed over to this Huneric for marriage a daughter of Valentinian, whom he had abducted from Rome as a captive.

---

[27] Added in MGH. The city of Caesaraugusta in Spain became Saragossa (on the river Ebro). As Vasaeus read *ad a*. 461: 'Majorinus, emperor of the East, came to Saragossa in Spain to obtain a fleet there and approach the Vandals in war, but through his own men's betrayal the Vandals found out about his plan, and he returned to Italy with his hopes frustrated, and was killed by the patrician Ricimerus.'
[28] For *Gadalaifo* in the MSS. The usual *coss.* was omitted, as in 25.
[29] See the neat solution to the problem of the two years of consuls in Hartmann's text and *apparatus* (p.10).
[30] H. rightly added the *post Quodvultdeus* in U and *atque Deogratias* in P-S.
[31] He reigned for 37 years; the XL in most mss is better than XI in Isidore and H.

138 B. Victor of Tonnena

29. Herminerichus and Basiliscus were consuls.[32] [465] Alexander took over the bishopric of the Church of Antioch. After Juvenal, Anastasius became bishop of the Church of Jerusalem.

30. The Emperor Leo was consul for the third time. [466] Huneric, king of the Vandals, aroused by Arian fury, persecuted the Catholics throughout Africa more than his father. He destroyed the Churches of the Christians and sent Catholic priests into exile.

30a During these days Theodoric, king of the Goths, was killed by his men with a sword, and his brother Euric was made king of the Goths and reigned for sixteen years.[33]

31. Puseus and John were consuls. [467] A sign appeared in the sky for ten days from a cloud that looked like a pillar.[34]

32. Anthemius took over the rule of Rome.

33. Leo was consul for the fourth time and Anthemius for the second time. [468] The Emperor Leo was moved by the supplications of the Egyptians that a Synod be held to judge the acts of the Synod of Chalcedon, and wrote to each of the Church's protectors to find out their individual beliefs. He received very similar letters from each one as if in agreement that it was in no way possible, but that the acts of the Synod of Chalcedon remained more and more firm in their perpetuity, and what are called in Greek the ἐγκύκλια ('encyclicals') still remain.

34. Zeno and Martian were consuls. [469] Hilary succeeded Leo as the bishop of the Church of Rome.

35. Jordan and Severus were consuls.[35] [470] The Emperor Leo appointed Patritius, Aspar's son, as his Caesar.[36]

---

[32] *Herminerichus* for *Hermia* in Migne (with *Herminericho* in brackets).

[33] See Isidore *Vand.* 78.

[34] The MSS are divided between *Puseo* and *Buseo*. The pillar of cloud would remind them of the one that saved Moses at the Red Sea, as God looked 'through the pillar of fire and cloud' and smote the Egyptians (*Exodus* 14.19-24).

[35] As in MGH, for the *Johanne* in the MSS and H.

[36] Thus denoting his succession to the throne, as with Zeno's son in 37.

Arians and Vandals of the 4th-6th Centuries 139

36. The Emperor Leo for the fifth time and Probinus were consuls. [471] Aspar and his two sons, Patritius Caesar and Ardaburius, were killed in Constantinople at the command of the Emperor Leo.

37. Leo was consul for the sixth time and Probinus [for the second time]. [473] The Emperor Leo made his grandson, the child of Zeno and of the daughter of his wife, his Caesar, and ruled for two years.

37a During their consulships, Arelatum and Massilia were occupied by the Goths.[37]

38. After Hilary, Simplicius was ordained bishop of the Church of Rome, and after Simplicius, Felix.[38] Gennadius succeeded Anatole as the bishop of Constantinople, and Acacius succeeded Gennadius. Martyrius was ordained bishop of the Church of Antioch after Alexander, and Julian was ordained after Martyrius. But Martyrius was ordained bishop of the Church of Constantinople after Anastasius.

39. In the time of these consuls, Olybrius came to Rome and although Anthemius was ruling, he took over the throne, through the support of the patrician Ricimerus.[39] When he found this out, Anthemius turned to flight, but was killed, and after the specified days Herculanus, the son of Orestes, seized the throne, but was killed together with his father, and his grandson assumed the throne.

40. Emperor Leo the Younger was the new consul. [474] Emperor Leo the Elder died in Constantinople.

41. Zeno was crowned by his own son, the Emperor Leo, in the Septimus, contrary to custom.

42. After the consulship of Emperor Leo the Younger, Zeno, the 49th emperor of the Romans [475], reigned for seventeen years, seeking to kill his own son the Emperor Leo, and take over his empire. His wife, the Empress Ariadne, put another young boy to death in his place (as he looked like him), and secretly tonsured that Emperor Leo and made him a

---

[37] From Isidore *Goth*. 34. The French towns today are called Arles and Marseilles.
[38] These were three Bishops of Rome (Popes), Saint Hilary (461-468), Saint Simplicius (468 -483) and Saint Felix II (483-492).
[39] Consul in 459, Ricimerus had later assassinated the Emperor Majoranus in 464.

140   B. Victor of Tonnena

cleric in a Church in Constantinople. And this Leo lived until the time of the Emperor Justinian.

43. In the same consulship, Basiliscus seized Constantinople's throne with his son Mark, most tyrannically.

44. The Emperor Zeno fled to Isauria where he had been born, and his Empress Ariadne followed him, traveling by ship heedless of the danger of winter.

45. With these two as consuls, the tyrant Basiliscus passed a law, and ordered the Synod of Chalcedon to be condemned, and the second Synod of Ephesus to be absolved and accepted.

46. Bishop Timotheus, called Aelurus, both the successor to and murderer of Proterius, returned from his exile in the Chersonese, and put to flight the other Bishop Timotheus, called Salafatiarius, a defender of the Synod of Chalcedon, and again invaded the Church of Alexandria.

47. Basiliscus the tyrant and Armatus were consuls. [476] The Emperor Zeno, in the twentieth month, had an army given to him and returned to Constantinople from Isauria, and resumed his rule. He sent Basiliscus with his children and wife into exile to Sasima in Cappadocia, and he ended his life there in a miserable way.

48. Among these events, because no consul was appointed and the tyrant Basiliscus had retired from his consulship, Armatus remained consul for the present year. [477]

49. After the consulship of Armatus, a most distinguished man [478], Timotheus, called Aelurus, died, the critic of the Synod of Chalcedon and murderer of the Bishop Proterius. And the other Timotheus, called Salafatiarius, a defender of the Synod of Chalcedon, resumed his bishopric of the Church of Alexandria. And so Sallustius succeeded Martyrius as bishop of the Church of Jerusalem. But Peter called Fullus was ordained bishop of the Church of Antioch, following Julian, who had succeeded Martyrius.

50. The Emperor Zeno was consul. [479] Huneric, king of the Vandals, spreading persecution excessively throughout the whole of Africa, in Tubunnis, Macri Nippis and other parts of the desert, now consigned to

Arians and Vandals of the 4th-6th Centuries 141

exile in much harsher places not only the Catholic priests and clergy of every order, but also monks and laymen, about four thousand in all, and he made them confess their faith and be martyrs, and cut the tongues off those who confessed.[40] The Royal City bears witness to the fact that these confessors of the faith spoke perfectly right up to their deaths, even with their tongues cut off. Then Laetus, the bishop of the Church of Nepte, was crowned with martyrdom on September 23rd.[41] The archbishop of the Church of Carthage, Eugenius, after his dreadful exile in the desert, was considered famous for his very many afflictions and punishments.

51. And so this Huneric, amid the countless, impious murders inflicted by him on the Catholics, in the eighth year of his reign, as all of his internal organs dissolved, ended his life in misery, as his Arian father had done.[42]

52. And Guntamundus succeeded him and reigned for twelve years, and he recalled our flock from exile straightaway.

53. After the third consulship of Zeno [480], Timotheus, called Salafatiarius died, a defender of the Synod of Chalcedon. And in his place, John Tabennesiota, priest and steward and a defender of the Synod of Chalcedon, was consecrated as bishop of the Church of Alexandria. But Peter, who had been consecrated bishop by the heretics, while Timotheus, called Salafatiarius, was still alive, ejected this bishop, as ordered by the Emperor Zeno, and took over the Church of Chalcedon. And he at once condemned the Synod of Chalcedon from his pulpit in the presence of the people, with the support of the Emperor Zeno. He removed the names of Proterius and Salafatiarius from the Church records, writing in the names of Dioscorus and Hellurus, who had killed Proterius, and he threw the body of the aforesaid Timotheus Salafatiarius out of the Church and consigned it to a deserted place outside the city.

---

[40] Rather than this mass of tongueless speakers arriving in Constantinople, Victor of Vita (chapter 6) chose to pick just one, Reparatus, a priest of Tipasita, and now a sub-deacon there, whose eloquent sermons without any impediment had greatly impressed the Empress herself.

[41] See ch. 118 below and ch. 18 in bk 2 of Victor of Vita's history of the Vandals for Laetus' successful attempt to obtain Justinian's help against the Vandals and Arians, and Huneric's use of him as a grim warning to the uncooperative Bishops, by burning him publicly in Carthage on a pyre.

[42] For a full version of this summary of the very extensive damage inflicted on the Catholic Church by the Vandals and their Arian bishops, see the vivid account of it above by the eyewitness, Victor, Bishop of Vita.

142   B. Victor of Tonnena

54. Tricundius, a most famous man, was consul. [482] The Emperor Zeno was misled by Eutychius' heretical brew, when Peter, bishop of Alexandria and Peter, bishop of Antioch condemned the Synod of Chalcedon. He associated with the bishop of Constantinople, Acacius, promoted by Zeno through Henoticus, and was polluted by sharing Mass with them, and with them withdrew from the Catholic faith.

55. After the consulship of Tricundius, a most famous man, [483] the tyrant Leontius, with the support of the patrician Hyllus, took over control in Isauria, with a tyrannical rule.

56. Theodoritus, a most famous man, was consul, [484] Felix, bishop of the Church of Rome, wrote to the monks and clergy living throughout the East, Egypt and Bithynia, telling them to shun Peter, bishop of Alexandria, a critic of the Synod of Chalcedon, and those contaminated by him, as heretics.

57. After the consulship of Theodoritus, a most famous man, [485] the bishops of the East, except for a few, were corrupted through Henoticus, with the support of Zeno, and by the complicity of Peter, bishop of Alexander, Peter, bishop of Antioch, and Acacius, bishop of Constantinople, and they rejected the Synod of Chalcedon.

57a During these days King Euric died, and his son Alaric was crowned king in his place, and reigned for 23 years.[43]

58. Longinus, a most famous man, was consul. [486] Acacius, bishop of Constantinople, was warned in a letter from Felix, the head of the Roman Church, to abstain from communion and association with those who condemned the Synod of Chalcedon, but he subjected Felix' legates to custody.

59. After the consulship of Longinus, a most famous man, [487] Acacius of Constantinople, Peter of Alexandria and Peter of Antioch, bishops hostile to the Synod of Chalcedon, were condemned by Pope Felix and by a Synod held in Italy. And that condemnation was applied to Acacius, after legates had been sent to Constantinople, through monks of the monasteries of Basanus and Dius in Achoimeton.

---

[43] See Isidore *Goth.* 36 and Vasaeus *ad a.* 483.

Arians and Vandals of the 4th-6th Centuries 143

60. After the second consulship of Longinus, a most famous man, [488] the body of Saint Barnabas the apostle was found on Cyprus, and the gospel written in Matthew's hand, was revealed by that Longinus.[44]

61. The tyrant Leontius and patrician Hyllus were captured, when their castle was betrayed, and they perished with most despicable deaths.[45]

62. Peter of Antioch died, facing condemnation, consecrating Calendio in his place. But the eastern bishops, as if unaware of this, consecrated John, called Codonatus, as the bishop of that Church, and the heretical Peter was his successor.[46]

63. Eusebius, a most famous man, was consul. [489] Acacius, the bishop of Constantinople, died while facing condemnation, and then Flavitas was consecrated bishop in his place. But he also died during the third month of his promotion, and Euphemius, who upheld the decrees of Chalcedon, succeeded him in the bishopric.[47]

64. After the third consulship of Longinus, a most famous man [490], Peter, the usurper of the Church of Alexandria, died facing condemnation. Anastasius took over his bishopric and his heresy.

64a When he was consul, Theuderic, king of the Ostrogoths, came from Thrace and Pannonia into Italy.[48]

65. Calendio, bishop of Antioch, gathered the remains of his predecessor, Eustochius, bishop and confessor, from Philippopolis[49] in Macedonia, and brought them to Antioch with the greatest of honour.

66. At this time, the hermit Annianus with his prayers cured those with gout above the river Euphrates. Auxentius put devils to flight. Daniel, Anastasius, Vindemiolus, Manasse, Severus and certain others through different parts of the desert achieved fame with their various virtues and prescience.

---

[44] For these two extraordinary discoveries, see Isidore *Chron.* p 474, 388.

[45] Presumably this is the patrician Hyllus mentioned in the year 483.

[46] Codonatus, from Theodosius' Ἀκοιμήτων, rather than *Aquimitensium* in U & H.

[47] *Flavitas* was adopted by H from U and P-S, but P's *Flavianus* is equally likely.

[48] See Vasaeus ad a. 490.

[49] Rather than the meaningless *Philippis populi* in Migne's text, with *Philippopoli* in brackets.

144 B. Victor of Tonnena

67. Olybrius, a most famous man, was consul. [491] The Emperor Zeno died in Constantinople in the forty-second year of his life. Ariadne, the Empress and widow of Zeno, designated Anastasius as emperor. He came from Silentiae in Illyria, his father was called Dyrrachenus and his mother Ariana. But as the Pope already knew from far off about his faith, or rather his lack of faith, he was forced, with pressure from Euphemius, the bishop of Constantinople, to promise in writing not to do anything injurious against the Apostolic Faith and the Synod of Chalcedon. Bishop Euphemius received his handwritten assurance and deposited it in the Church's archives.

68. Anastasius, Rome's fiftieth emperor, ruled for twenty-seven years. And on becoming emperor he used violence to recover his handwritten assurance from Bishop Euphemius, and his savagery towards the bishops who were defending the Synod of Chalcedon was atrocious. Peter, the bishop of Antioch, was one among those who died. The heretics had consecrated him during the time of Emperor Zeno, while Calendio, who defended the Synod of Chalcedon, was still alive, and he changed his mind for the worse, so that Calendio was in fact led from evil deeds to worse ones, and Palladius was consecrated in his place.

69. Anastasius and Rufus were consuls. [492] Gelasius succeeded Felix as Vicar of the Roman Church and Anastasius succeeded Gelasius.[50] But the heretical Athanasius was in charge of the Church of Alexandria, and Palladius had been made bishop of the Church of Antioch while Calendio was still alive, and Sallustius was bishop of Jerusalem.

70. Euphemius, bishop of Constantinople, having foreseen the trickery of the Emperor Anastasius, called together a Synod, and it confirmed the decrees of the Synod of Chalcedon.

70a While the tyrant Odeacer was consul, he was slain by King Theodore.[51]

71. Asterius and Praesidius were consuls. [494] John, bishop of Alexandria, coming from the Church of Rome, begged the Emperor Anastasius to restore him to his throne, for the sake of their old friendship.

---

[50] Saint Felix II 483-492, Saint Gelasius I 492-496, Anastasius II 496-498.
[51] Omitted by P-E and Migne.

Arians and Vandals of the 4th-6th Centuries   145

But as he did not obtain this for the defense of the Synod of Chalcedon, he secretly returned to Rome from where he had come.
71a During their consulships, the Goths invaded Spain.

72. Victor, a most famous man, was consul [495] when the war flared up in Isauria and the two tyrants Athenodorus and Longinus were killed.[52]

73. When Athenasius had died in Alexandria, he was succeeded by John, called Hemnla. When he passed away, after a few days another John, called Niceta, succeeded him as bishop.

74. Paul, a most famous man, was consul. [496] The Emperor Anastasius followed the Synod of the heretics, and confirmed Zeno's man Henoticus, and deposed Euphemius, the bishop of Constantinople, who had defended the Synod of Chalcedon, and sent him into exile in Euchaita, appointing Macedonius in his place.[53]

74a During these consulships Burdimelus assumed the Spanish throne.[54]

75. Emperor Anastasius was consul for the second time. [497] Macedonius, bishop of Constantinople, held a Synod and condemned both those who accepted the decrees of the Synod of Chalcedon, and those who defended the views of Nestorius and Eutyches.

75a During these consulships the Goths accepted a resting place within the Spains, and Burdemalus was handed over by his men and sent to Tolosa, where he was placed on a bronze bull and cremated over a fire.

76. At the death of Anastasius, the Roman bishop, Symmachus succeeded him, and on the other side, Laurentius, no longer willing to be content with the bishopric of the city of Nuceria, was ordained and promoted by the priests meeting together for a Synod held at Rome.[55]

---

[52] As in the MSS, but H may be right in reading Mommsen's *Viatore*, a rarer name and likely to have been normalized. Victor was an extremely common name.

[53] Another bishop is exiled to Galacia (mod. Turkey); but to Euchaita, rather than to the Euchaida (in the text). For Italian bishops found guilty of heresy, Northern Spain was much more usual at that time.

[54] See Vasaeus *ad a.* 497, and for 75a, *ad. a.* 498.

[55] Reading *episcopatu,* as was proposed by Migne; otherwise an *ut* would be necessary with *episcopus* after *contentus.*

146   B. Victor of Tonnena

77. Palladius of Antioch died; Flavian was ordained bishop in his place. John called Niceta was still in charge of the Church of Alexandria, but in Jerusalem Elias took over the bishopric after Sallustius.

78. Guntamund, the king of the Vandals, died in Carthage, and Thrasamund ruled for twenty-seven years and four months. And this king, filled with Arian madness, attacked the Catholics. He closed the Catholic churches, and sent one hundred and twenty bishops into exile in Sardinia, taken from the whole of the African Church.[56]

79. At that time Fulgentius, bishop of the city of Ruspa, brought light to our doctrine.[57]

80. John Scytha and Paul were consuls. [498]. A certain Olympius, an Arian, was blaspheming the holy and consubstantial Trinity in the so-called Helian bathhouse in the Royal City, and while he was in the cold water bath, he was invisibly pierced by three arrows of fire, ministered by an angel, and finished his life impiously and at the same time in a marvelous manner.

81. Gibbus, a most famous man, was consul. [499] The Emperor Anastasius assembled a Synod in Constantinople,[58] with Flavian of Antioch and Philoxene of Hierapolis presiding, condemning Diodorus of Tarsis, Theodore of Mopsuestia with his writings, Theodoret of Cyrus, Ibas of Edessa, Andrew of Samosat, Eucherius, Bishops Quirus and John, and all the others who argue for two natures and two forms in Christ and those who do not believe in one crucifix for the Trinity, together with Leo, bishop of Rome, and his book, and persuaded them to apply anathema to the Synod of Chalcedon.

82. Patricius and Hypatius were consuls. [500] A certain Bishop Barbas supported the Arian heresy, and he presumed to say over a person needing baptism, contrary to the Law: 'Barbas baptizes you in the name of the Father through the Son in the Holy Spirit.' Straightaway the water from which he was going to baptize the man disappeared; in fact the vessel itself containing the water was shattered. When the man who was to be

---

[56] According to Victor of Vita, they exiled most Catholics to Corsica.

[57] The *claruit* plays on his name, *Fulgentius*, both words full of light.

[58] Hughes *Church in Crisis* 81-2; Hierapolis, 50 miles east of Cyrrhus, now Mabboug.

Arians and Vandals of the 4th-6th Centuries 147

baptized considered this, he at once ran to the Catholic one and received baptism in a lawful manner.

83. When Abienus and Pompey were consuls [501], the Emperor Anastasius removed from his Church Macedonius, bishop of Constantinople, with other clerics unwilling to condemn the decrees of Chalcedon, and he sent them into exile, and in his place he made the priest Timotheus a bishop. And Timotheus at once accepted for Mass those who condemned the Synod of Chalcedon.

84. While Abienus the Younger was consul [502], there was a great earthquake with mighty flashes of lightning and hail, and Heaven and Earth were shaken.

85. Cethegus, a most famous man, was consul. [503] Flavian, bishop of Antioch, with belated penitence, deserted the Emperor Anastasius, and leaving his throne, retired to his property called Platanus. The emperor then substituted Severus for Flavian, a man hostile to the Synod of Chalcedon, and he supplied the Eastern Church with great inducements to sin.[59]

85a During this consulship, a Circus was welcomed at Saragossa.[60]

86. Theodore, a most famous man, was consul. [504] Eugenius died, the bishop and confessor of Carthage. The Bishops Julian Bostrenus and John Paltensis retired from their Churches of their own accord, and others were placed in their Sees.[61]

87. Messalla was consul, a most famous man. [505] And in Constantinople, at the command of the Emperor Anastasius, the Holy

---

[59] The monk Severus (c. 465-538) gained the support of Anastasius for his monks being persecuted (Monophysites). Rewarded by the Emperor (in 512 rather than 503), he became Patriarch of Antioch, replacing Flavian, but he was deposed in 518 as Justin took over. A Monophysite and supporter of Chalcedon, he was finally excommunicated in 536. As the leader of the more moderate Monophysites, he left 125 homilies and 400 letters (through Syrian translations).

[60] This surprising item was added by the scholiast in Migne's edition. Under the Vandals the old circuses and amphitheatres were popular, over 60,00 watching races and games in Carthage (see Lachaux pp. 55-58, and Humphrey ch. 1).

[61] For the major rôle played by the inspirational Archbishop Eugenius under the Vandal occupation of Carthage, see Victor of Vita's work above.

148   B. Victor of Tonnena

Gospel was criticized as if written by ignorant evangelists, and was emended.

87a During his consulship, the Goths entered Dertosa, and Peter the tyrant was slain and his head was carried to Saragossa.[62]

88. Venantius and Celer were consuls. [508] Impure spirits took hold of the people of Alexandria and of all of Egypt, the poor and the great simultaneously, free men and slaves and clergy and monks, except for foreigners. And deprived of human speech, they began to bark all the days and nights like dogs, so much so that afterwards they were bound with iron chains and dragged to the Churches to recover their sanity. This was because they were all eating at the same time their own hands and their arms. With these things happening, an angel in the guise of a man appeared to some of the people, saying that this had come upon them as they had anathematized the Synod of Chalcedon, warning them not to presume anything of the sort thereafter.

88a During these days there was a battle between the Goths and Franks at Boglodor. King Alaric II was slain in battle by the Franks, and his kingdom of Toulouse was destroyed.[63]

89. Venantius the Younger, a most famous man, was consul. Cawades, king of the Persians, captured with the prayers of Christians the castle of Zumdaber, filled with many treasures from the beginning of its use, but where nobody could go inside, as it was subject to the lions of devils and was protected by a guard. He went inside and took out all the treasures from it.

89a After Alaric, King Gisalec became king, his son from his concubine, and he reigned for seven years.[64]

90. Importunus the Younger, a most famous man, was consul [509] Helias, the bishop of Jerusalem and a defender of the Chalcedonian Synod, was unwilling to receive Severus of Antioch for communion, as he was an enemy to the apostolic faith, and the Emperor Anastasius advised him not to, and he was exiled to the castle of Paraxenis. And in his place John, the

---

[62] See Vasaeus *ad a.* 506.
[63] See Isidore *Chron.* pp. 473, 384. The Arian king was defeated near Poitiers by the orthodox Clovis, king of the Franks, freeing the territory around Toulouse.
[64] See Isidore *Goth.* 37.

Arians and Vandals of the 4th-6th Centuries   149

guardian of the Cross, was ordained bishop, and he quickly received Severus of Antioch for communion and condemned the Synod of Chalcedon.

91. While Boethius, a really famous man, was consul[65][510] Vitalian, son of Patriciolus, when he recognized the subversion of the Catholic faith, the condemnation of the Synod of Chalcedon and the sackings of orthodox bishops replaced by heretical ones, collected a strong force of brave men and rebelled against the rule of Anastasius.

91a During his consulship, Gesalic killed Haericus in the palace of Barca, and in that year Helban, the general of Theoderic, king of Italy, forced the same Gesalic to flee from Spain and make for Africa. But the ally of Vedicus was killed at Barca.[66]

92. Felix, a most famous man, was consul. [511] Count Vitalian clashed with Patricius, grandson of the Emperor Anastasius and master of his Roman militia, and when sixty-seven of the militia had been killed, he captured Patricius alive and bound him with bronze chains and handed him over to be guarded in an iron cage, and afterwards tore him apart.

92a However, Count Veila was killed at Barca.

93. Paul and Muschianus were consuls. [512] Alamundar, the king of the Saracens, had been baptized by the defenders of the Synod of Chalcedon, and when Severus, the bishop of Antioch, sent him God-nurtured bishops with a letter, he concluded his proposition in a wonderful way in his foreign tongue, as he overcame them, and revealed the immortal God.

94. Anicius Probus[67] and Flavius Clementinus were consuls [513] At the command of Emperor Anastasius, Plato, the prefect of the State, and Maximus, ascended the pulpit of the Church of Saint Theodore, and there,

---

[65] The extremely famous Boethius was born in about 470, and became *magister officiorum* under Theoderic, but he was accused of treason and was imprisoned in Pavia. Before his execution in 524, he wrote his *De Consolatione Philosophiae*. His granddaughter, Rusticiana, and her family were very close friends of Pope Gregory the Great, and they were almost certainly liquidated by the military usurper to Maurice's throne, Phocas. For earlier links see my article 'A New Family Tree for Boethius' *Parergon*, 23 2006, 1-10.

[66] See Isidore also in his *Goth*. 37.

[67] See Minge's note on this Anicius Probus.

150 B. Victor of Tonnena

with the hymn which the Greeks call the τρισάγιον,[68] they made a new
addition saying 'he who was crucified for our sakes,'[69] and while they
were going through the forum of Constantine, singing the psalms, clouds
unexpectedly poured ashes over them instead of rain, and the ashes
covered the whole city and province. Due to that novelty, many evils fell
upon the city of Constantinople, and many suffered evil deaths. For
indeed the mobs of Green supporters and of the Blue ones were united
against the Emperor Anastasius, and among a thousand injuries and evils
they spread fires in the city, and it was burnt from the Bronze Statue,[70] all
the way to the forum of Constantine, along the whole length of that street
of the ninety-four columns.

94a During their consulships, Gisalec returned from Africa through fear of
Helban and made for Aquitania, where he remained in hiding for a year.[71]

94b After Alaric, Theoderic king of Italy, reigned over the Goths in Spain
for fifteen years, protecting the sweet young Amalaric.[72]

95. Senator, a most famous man, was consul. [516] Count Vitalian came
into Constantinople with a strong army of barbarians, and settled in
Sosthenes. He promised peace for the Emperor Anastasius without any
other demand except that he first restore to their proper Sees the defenders
of the Synod of Chalcedon, who had been sent into exile, and unify all of
the Churches of the East with the Church of Rome.

96. Florentius, a most famous man, was consul. [515] The Huns caused
atrocious damage to Armenia, Cappadocia, Galatia and Pontus.

97. At that time Euphemius, bishop of Constantinople, died in Ancyra, in
Galatia, and the Empress Ariadne died in the Royal City.

98. Peter, a most famous man, was consul. [516] All of the abbots and
desert monks across Palestine and the river Jordan wrote to the Emperor

---

[68] An ancient hymn especially used in the Eastern churches, beginning with the
three-fold invocation of the Lord God, with 'Holy, Holy, Holy.'

[69] In the Greek: ὁ σταυρωθεὶς δι᾽ ἡμᾶς.

[70] Suggested by the Greek phrase ἀπὸ τῆς χαλκῆς 'from the bronze statue,' as is
read in Antigonus Carystius *Mirabilia* 15 and Diogenes Laertius 9.39, 10.9.

[71] See Isidore *Goth.* 38.

[72] See Isidore *Goth.* 39.

Arians and Vandals of the 4th-6th Centuries 151

Anastasius defending the status of the Synod of Chalcedon, and attacking the impieties of Severus, the bishop of Antioch.

99. While Agapitus, a most famous man, was consul, [517] John, bishop of Alexandria, died, and Dioscorus was ordained in his place. Timotheus, the bishop of Constantinople and critic of the Synod of Chalcedon, died on April 5th, and Anastasius handed over the bishopric to John of Cappadocia, his cellmate. Before his ordination, Anastasius first of all made him condemn the Synod of Chalcedon.[73]

100. Agapitus, for the second time, and Magnus were consuls. [518] The Emperor Anastasius was inside his palace, but was put to flight by his fear of thunder and was struck by a bolt of lightning, and died in the bedroom where he had been hidden. And with ignominy and without the usual funeral rites, he was taken to a tomb in the eighty-eighth year of his life.
101. Justin I, the fifty-first emperor of the Romans, reigned for eight years and nine months. He was an Illyrian Catholic and a lover and at the same time a defender of the Chalcedonian Synod, whose wife was called Lupicina, but named Euphemia afterwards by the people of Constantinople, and whose nephew was called Justinian, a bodyguard of the candidate.

102. Justin and Heraclius were consuls. [519] The prefect Amantius stirred up sedition among the people and was touted as another emperor. At the command of the Emperor Justin he was killed, together with Andrew his chamber-servant, and thrown into the sea.

103. Rustitio, a most famous man, was consul. [520] John, who was chosen for supreme rule before Justin, was ordained bishop of Heraclia, and Justinian, the nephew of Emperor Justin, was appointed commander of the guard, as was usual for a candidate.

104. Valerius and Justinian were consuls. [521 At the death of Dioscorus, Timotheus succeeded him as bishop of Alexandria. But Severus of the Church of Antioch became the leading heretic, and John of the Church of Jerusalem. The Emperor Justin united the bishops of the East with those of the West, with due satisfaction, except for the depraved ones,[74] that is,

---

[73] Reading *Joanni Cappadoci Syncello proprio,* as was proposed by Wesselingius, rather than *Joannes Cappadox in Cella propria* in Migne that makes little sense.
[74] Reading *praeter pravos* as in U and P-E, that makes more sense than Mommsen's *propter pravos* ('because of the depraved ones'), read by Hartmann.

152 B. Victor of Tonnena

Acacius, a one-time bishop of Constantinople, Peter of Antioch and Peter of Alexandria, who were implicated in the original error, and he revived the decrees of the Chalcedonian Synod, that had been rejected in the time of the Emperors Zeno and Anastasius.

105. Symmachus and Boethius were consuls.[75] [522] Vitalian returned to Constantinople after taking an oath, and the Emperor Justin received him gratefully and made him a military commander, and allowed him to be made consul.

106. Maximus, a most famous man, was consul. Thrasamund, the king of the Vandals, died in Carthage. His wife Amalafrida fled to the barbarians, but after a military engagement she was captured near the desert area of Capsa and died in prison, deprived of food. The daughter of the Emperor Valentinian, who had been captured by Giseric and married to Ugneric, gave birth to Hilderic, who reigned for seven years and three months. And so he was bound by an oath of his predecessor Thrasamund, before he became king, neither to open the Churches in his kingdom to Catholics nor to restore their privileges. But to avoid neglecting the terms of the oath, he ordered the Catholic priests to return from exile, and consecrated Boniface as bishop of the Church of Carthage, who with his heavenly decrees was active enough for the supplication of the whole city.

107. It is said that Vitalian was murdered by a faction of the patrician Justinian inside the palace of Constantinople, in the place that they call Δέλφικον (Delphicon) in Greek.[76]

108. The Emperor Justin for the second time and Apio were consuls. [524] In the bishopric of the Church of Rome, Symmachus had died and was succeeded by Hormisda. Timotheus was still in charge of the Church of Alexandria. Severus, bishop of the Church of Antioch and critic of the Chalcedonian Synod, was sought by the Emperor Justin for punishment, but fled. In his place Paul was substituted. John was in charge of the Church of Jerusalem, but Epiphanius succeeded John as bishop of the Church of Constantinople.

---

[75] The consuls Flavius Boethius and Flavius Symmachus, were brothers, and sons of the very famous Anicius Severinus Manlius Boethius, and of Rusticiana, grandmother of the Rusticiana who was so dear to Pope Gregory.

[76] P-S and Mommsen's most unlikely δέλφακα ('a pig') was adopted by H, but P's Δέλφικον adopted by M, is more likely in the golden city ('tripod' or 'Delphian').

Arians and Vandals of the 4th-6th Centuries 153

108a While they were consuls, Amalaric was made king of the Goths. He reigned for five years.[77]

109. After the second consulship of Justin and Apio, the Emperor Justin unwillingly made his nephew Justinian joint emperor, at the senate's request.

109a Philoxenus and Probus were consuls. [525] [Twice].

110. Marbotius was consul. [527] The Emperor Justin died.

111. Justinian, fifty-second emperor of the Romans, ruled for thirtynine years and seven months. His wife was called Theodora.

112. The Emperor Justinian was consul. [528] The eastern Churches at the command of the same emperor, publicly adopted the four Synods of Constantinople, Ephesus I and Chalcedon, and the faith of one hundred and fifty Holy Fathers, with sacrifices present.

113. Decius, a most famous man, was consul. [529] Through the supporters of the Empress Theodora, he asserted that the passion of just one person of the Trinity should not be accepted at all, but in the Trinity absolutely, and he imposed this on all with a general law, and used force to obtain signatures from clerics and monks. For which reason a great many priests withdrew from the Church, and monks retired from their own monasteries, asserting they were happy with the faith of those who had met for the aforesaid four holy Synods.

113a During these days, Stephan was appointed prefect of the Spains. But in the third year of his prefecture, a Council held in the city of Gerona sacked him.[78]

114. Lampadas and Orestes were consuls. [530] Hypatius, the grandson of the Emperor Anastasius, claimed the throne of Constantinople, but when many thousands of men had been killed by the soldiers' swords in a Circus show, he was captured, and during the night he was killed with Pompey and thrown into the sea.

---

[77] See Isidore *Goth*. 40.

[78] Called Gerunda at that time. See Vasaeus *ad a*. 530. King Amalaric fled to Barcino, the modern Barcelona. Agathias, the sixth century historian, used the Greek word ἄγγων for a 'Frankish javelin.'

154   B. Victor of Tonnena

115. After the consulship of Lampadas and Orestes [531], Geilimer took over the throne in Africa with supreme power. And entering Carthage, he deprived Hilderic of his kingdom and consigned him with his children to prison, and executed Oamerdigus and many of the noblemen.

115a During their consulships, King Amalaric was defeated by Zidibert, king of the Franks, in Gaul, at the battle of Narbonne. He fled and came to Barcino, but there he was struck by a Frankish javelin by a man called Besso, and died.

116. After the third consulships of Lampadius and Orestes, Belisarius, commander of the Roman army, was defeated in two battles, but miraculously overcame the Persian Thrace.

117. The Emperor Justinian was consul for the third time. [533] The tyrant Geilimer cruelly killed many of the noblemen in the province of Africa, and stole the properties of many through Boniface.

118. Justinian was consul for the fourth time. [534] The Emperor Justinian was visited by the Bishop Laetus,[79] who later was martyred by Huneric the king of the Vandals, and he sent an army to Africa against the Vandals, led by his general Belisarius, and this same Belisarius defeated them in battle, and killed Gunthimer and Gebamund, the brothers of the King Gadinges, and put to flight King Geilimer himself, and captured Africa on the ninety-seventh anniversary of the Vandals' invasion. Also in that incursion by Belisarius, before he entered Africa, the tyrant Geilimer killed King Helderic along with the latter's family. Belisarius, the general and patrician, captured the tyrant Geilimer, and brought him to the Emperor Justinian with the riches he had acquired from their looting of Africa.[80]

---

[79] For the mission of Bishop Laetus, and his fiery death in Carthage, see ch. 50.

[80] Belisarius (c. 505-565) was far the most successful general under Justinian I, mostly in campaigns on the western frontiers and in North Africa, and against the Ostrogoths in Italy. He was so successful that he was recalled, to control the Eastern armies, replaced in the West by a one-time Court eunuch, Narses, who proved just as capable in battle, and an excellent governor of Italy. See ch. 151. For Belisarius' three consulships, see ch. 121 below. For Narses, see my 'The Eunuch Narses' in Chris Bishop (ed.) *Text and Transmission in Medieval Europe*, (Cambridge Scholars, Newcastle, 2007), 46-57.

Arians and Vandals of the 4th-6th Centuries   155

119. Belisarius, a most famous man, was consul. [535] After Boniface, Reparatus received the bishopric of Carthage. But Peter succeeded to the bishopric of the Church of Jerusalem after the death of John.

120. After the second consulship of Belisarius [536], the Emperor Justinian published tracts on the Incarnation of the Lord, and forced the bishops of Illyria to add their signatures.

121. After the third consulship of Belisarius [537], at the death of Epiphanius, successor to John as bishop of Constantinople, Anthemius, bishop of Eutychianista[81] in Trapezum, with the support of the Empress Theodora, took control of the Church of Constantinople.

122. John, a most famous man, was consul. [538] For the Church of Rome, after Hormisda, John was ordained as bishop, after him, Felix, after Felix, Boniface, after him, another John, and after that John, Agapitus.

123. In the Church of Alexandria, at the death of Timotheus, who had succeeded Dioscorus the Younger, two heretical bishops were ordained by popular choice on the same day, namely Theodosius and Gaianus. When they were ordained, Alexandria was divided between enemies of Christ on both sides: from Theodosius, they wanted to be called Theodosians, and from Gaianus, Gaianians. Both in equal measure rejected the Synod of Chalcedon and endorsed the errors of Eutyches and Dioscorus.

124. Apio, a most famous man, was consul. [539] Severus, bishop of Antioch, the leader of a heretical group called the 'Severians,' and Julian, the bishop of Halicarnassus, attacked the Apostolic Faith and the Chalcedonian Synod, claiming that Christ was one nature from two persons. And while Severus added that this nature was corruptible and Julian that it was incorruptible, Alexandria, Egypt and Libya were divided on both sides between enemies of Christ, as the Theodosians followed Severus and the Gaianians followed Julian. But two other heresies came from the Theodosians, one of the Agnoetae and the other of the Tritheitae. For indeed they added to the perversity of the Agnoetae, from which they came, the claim that the divinity of Christ was ignorant of what had been written for the future concerning the final day and hour. But the Tritheitae added that there are three Gods in the Trinity, just as there are three

---

[81] *Eutychianista* in U and M, is rightly supported by Mommsen, and is preferable to the *Eutychia Justa* in P-E.

156   B. Victor of Tonnena

persons in it, contrary to what has been written: 'Listen, Israel: your Lord is one God.' And again: 'There is no God, unless one,' and 'I am God, and there is no God beside me.'

125. Justin, a most famous man was consul. [540] Agapitus, the archbishop of Rome, came to Constantinople, and deposed Anthemius, the bishop of Constantinople and corrupter of the Church and enemy of the Chalcedonian Synod. He deprived the Empress Theodora, his patron, of communion. In addition he at once made Menas bishop of the Church of Constantinople.

126. Theodosius and Gaianus, the bishops of Alexandria, were condemned and transported into exile together with their heresy. But Theodosius, relegated to the Sykai district in Constantinople,[82] corrupted almost the whole palace and the greatest part of the Royal City with his perfidy. This circumstance allowed almost every heresy, to such an extent that not only the Theodosians but also the Gaianians constructed monasteries and oratories in the Royal City. For the aforesaid heretic, Theodosius, lived until the first consulship of the Emperor Justinian the Younger.

127. In that year, while Paul the bishop of Antioch was still alive, Euphrasius was put in his place.

128. Basil, a most famous man, was consul. [541] Agapitus, the archbishop of Rome, died in Constantinople, and Silverius was ordained in his place. But as for the Church of Alexandria, with Theodosius and Gaianus in exile, Paul, the prior in charge of the monks of Zabennensiotae, celebrating the demotion of his predecessor, the heretical Dioscorus, was demoted by the Council of Palestine, and Zoilus was ordained bishop in his place.[83]

129. In the aforesaid consulship, Stuzas assumed the throne in Africa in the districts of the desert and ruled tyrannically. [542]

---

[82] This was an unsavory suburb on the outskirts of the city, where its Jews lived, forced to endure the nauseating smells emitted by the city's tanneries. See ch. 162 below, for the Bulgarian attack being held up in the narrow streets of this old district.

[83] The text is uncertain in this passage, but H's text is acceptable with two changes. *Paulus prior* seems far more apposite than *Peter Prestor* (in U) or *pretor* (P-S), and the monks probably inhabited the *Zabennensiotae* monastery, as in P-S.

Arians and Vandals of the 4th-6th Centuries   157

130. In the second year after the consulship of Basilius, a most famous man [543], through the support of the Empress Theodora, who had never ceased to be secretly hostile to the Chalcedonian Synod since her reign had begun, deceitful confiscations were prepared. The bishop of Rome, Silverius, was sent into exile, and Vigilius was ordained in his place. And before he became Pope, the Empress Theodora mentioned above arranged with a hidden surety that the Pope would condemn the Three Chapters, the outcome of the records of the Chalcedonian Synod. That is the letter of Ibas of Edessa to the Persian Maris, that was approved of by the judgment of the Chalcedonian Synod and judged to be orthodox, and in accord with the Synods held before. Then Theodore, bishop of Mopsuesta, was praised in the acts similarly of the Synod in Antioch under John of that Church, and in Chalcedon. And the words of Theodoret, bishop of Cyrus, were praised by the acts of the Synod of Chalcedon with the same Theoderet. And so this Pope Vigilius, encouraged by Antonina, the patrician wife of Belisarius,[84] was compelled to write to Theodosius at Alexandria, Anthemius at Constantinople and Severus at Antioch, long since condemned by the Apostolic See, as if he was writing to true Catholics, and feel about their faith just as they did. The gist of that letter is proved to be as follows:[85]

'Bishop Vigilius greets my lords and brothers, united in the love of Christ our God and Saviour, Bishops Theodosius, Anthemius and Severus. I know indeed that a belief in my faith reached Your Holinesses before, with God's help.[86] But my glorious mistress[87] and my most Christian, patrician daughter, has made me be filled with a desire now, that I might send over this letter to Your Fraternities, so paying my respects to you, with the grace whereby we are joined together in Christ our Lord and Saviour, I signify that I have held and am holding that faith which you hold, with God's help, as you know that we preach and read this between us, because we have one soul and one heart in God. I have hurried to

---

[84] For a most unflattering portrait of Antonina (and of Belisarius) see G. A. Williamson (tr.) *Procopius: The Secret History* (Penguin Classics, 1981^2), pp 41-65.

[85] The ed. in Migne emended this letter from a copy of it in the *Liberati Breviar*, ch. 22.

[86] The *quia* ('that') in U with *pervenit* ('reached') is more likely than the *quae* (in P-E and M), and *antea* and *adjuvante* are preferable to *ante* and *juvante*, but add nothing extra to the sense.

[87] The *domina* ('mistress') is not in the *Breviar* but it well suits an imperial agent behind the Pope. Mommsen added *Antonina*, rightly bracketed in H.

158 B. Victor of Tonnena

announce to you the joy of my promotion,[88] which is yours, with the help of God,[89] as I know well in my mind that Your Fraternities are willing to embrace what you longed for.[90] And so nobody ought to know what I am writing to you, but rather, let Your Wisdom judge that it respects me more highly than all others, so that it may complete more easily what God has begun to do.'[91]

The subscript was: 'Pray for me, my lords and brothers, bound together by the love of Christ, our Lord and Saviour.'[92]

130a During this year, five kings of the Franks entered the Spains through Pamplona and reached Saragosa. They besieged it for three days, and totally destroyed it, along with the province of Tarracco, with their pillaging.[93]

130b During these days a plague affecting the groin harmed almost the whole of Spain. A general mortality of the World followed the beginning of these evils, and most of the people were killed by an attack on the groin.[94]

131. In the third year after the consulship of Basil, a most famous man [544], the tyrant Stuza drew together a multitude of people, led by the general Solomon, the patrician chief of the Roman militia in Africa, and they attacked Cilius. When a clash took place, through the sins of Africa, the militia of the Roman State and Solomon, leader of both, were defeated.

---

[88] The 'promotion' in *provectus* in the *Breviar,* is preferable to *profectus* ('profit'), read by the other editions, and the imperfect is preferable to the present *optat*.

[89] With *adiuvante* as above (*iuvante* U) rather than the *iubente*. The plural *scientes* that follows with a *quia* as in the *Breviar*, improve on the syntax of *sciens* and *quae*.

[90] The *Breviar* improves the syntax and sense with *sciens.libenter amplecti*, rather than *licenter amplectitur*. H keeps *sciens* in brackets, yet Mommsen supported it.

[91] The *Breviar* has *existimet*, perhaps preferable to *aestimet* in the text, but to have the Pope finishing what God has begun is more likely than doing it on his own, as the *Breviar* comments with *possim haec quae coepi operare et perficere*.

[92] The Breviar ends with some different readings, with *nobis* for *me, mihi* for *mei, Christi .. Servatoris* for *in Christo Domino* and *coniuncti* for *connexi* (preferable).

[93] See Isidore *Goth.* 41, and Vasaeus *ad a.* 542.

[94] Reading *necatur* ('killed') as in Scaliger and M, rather than the weak *vocatur* ('called') in the MSS, or Burkard's *vexatur* ('disturbed')that was adopted by H. Neither explains the 'mortality.'

Arians and Vandals of the 4th-6th Centuries 159

132. In the fourth year after the consulship of Basil, a most famous man [545], the Emperor Justinian was aroused by the thefts of the Acephali,[95] and he carefully forced Vigilius, bishop of Rome, to hurry to the Royal City and condemn the Three Chapters under the guise of a congregation of those divided from union with the Church.

133. Macarios took over the bishopric of the Church of Jerusalem after Peter.

133a At the death of Thiudis, Thiudisolus ruled the Goths for one year and seven months.[96]

134. In the fifth year after the consulship of Basil, a most famous man [546], the tyrant Stuza in Africa had a battle at the gate of Tacea, and was struck by the javelin of John, a Roman general, and at the same time John was struck by Stuza's. And at once they both fell from each other's sword, and they died on the Lord's Day, on which the battle took place.

134a At the death of Thiudisolus, Agila ruled over the Goths for five years and seven months.[97]

135. In the sixth year after the consulship of Basil, a most famous man [547], Ferrandus, a deacon of the Church of Carthage, was deemed famous.

136. In Carthage, inside the palace, during the night a general Guntarith murdered Ariobindas, a patrician and leader of the Roman militia in Africa, sent there at that time by the emperor, and he took over the kingdom with a tyranny. But a duke of Carthage, Artabanus, killed him when he was dining on the thirty-sixth day of his reign.

137. In the eighth year after the consulship of Basil, a most famous man [548], the Emperor Justinian wrote most earnestly to the various provinces established within the boundaries of his kingdom, and he compelled all the bishops to condemn the Three Chapters.

138. Doninus succeeded Antiochus as bishop of Antioch.

---

[95] The *Acephali*, 'lacking a leader,' were Monophysites who rejected all authority.
[96] From Isidore *Goth.* 44, and see Vasaeus *ad a.* 548.
[97] Again from Isidore *Goth.* 45, and see Vasaeus *ad a.* 549.

160 B. Victor of Tonnena

139. In the ninth year after the consulship of Basil, a most famous man [549], a Synod in Illyria, in defense of the Three Chapters, wrote to the Emperor Justinian, condemning Benenatus, the bishop of the city of Prima Justiniana, for objecting to the same Three Chapters.

140. The Empress Theodora, an enemy of the Chalcedonian Synod, with her body totally riddled with cancer, ended her life in an unnatural manner.

141. In the tenth year after the consulship of Basil, a most famous man [550], the bishops of Africa banned Vigilius, the bishop of Rome, from Catholic Communion, for condemning the Three Chapters in a Synod, reserving a place for him to repent, and in defense of the Three Chapters just mentioned, they sent a sufficiently suitable letter to the Emperor Justinian, through Olympius, a teacher.

142. During that time the twelve books[98] of Facundus, bishop of the Church of Hermiane, were enlightening.[99] In them he declared with great clarity that the oft-mentioned Three Chapters had been condemned by the command of the Catholic faith and Apostolic Council of Chalcedon.

143. In the eleventh year after the consulship of Basil, a most famous man [551], Reparatus, archbishop of the Church of Carthage, Firmus, primate of the bishops of Numidia and Primasius and Verecundus, bishops in charge of the Council of Byzacenum, for the reason of their faith were called to the Royal City by the command of that Emperor.

144. Apollinarius was became bishop of Alexandria, replacing Zoilus, who was unwilling to condemn the Three Chapters mentioned above.

145. In the twelfth year after the consulship of Basil, a most famous man [552], Reparatus, the archbishop, was attacked by a great many calumnies for the fact that he had not given his assent to the condemnation of Three Chapters as mentioned above, and he was stripped of his office, and sent into exile in Euchaita.[100] Primasius, his deacon and emissary, after condemning whatever had been defended in Synods and in general, even though the bishop was still alive and it was contrary both to the wishes of the clergy and of the people, was ordained as bishop of the Church of

---

[98] The *libri* may well be read from the *VII* in P-E.
[99] Hermiane was on the Southeastern coast of the Peloponnese.
[100] The text has *Eucayda*, for *Euchaita*, it appears, as Euphemius of Constantinople was to be exiled there in 496 by the Emperor Anastasius.

Arians and Vandals of the 4th-6th Centuries 161

Carthage. Firmus, the Primate of the Council of Numidia, corrupted by the gifts of the emperor, gave his assent to the condemnation of those Chapters, but while returning to his own place by ship, perished with a most shameful death. Primasius of Aquimetia was also relegated to a monastery, but when Boethius became Primate of Byzacenum,[101] he was prevented by death from being his successor, and Primasius at once assented to the condemnation mentioned above. Reverting to his own place, he attacked with the strongest of persecutions what he had been defending before, while concocting calumnies against the faithful and robbing them of their possessions. But the way in which he had sinned could not remain hidden. For indeed he was condemned by the Catholic bishops of his own Council for his legal transgressions, and was punished with an unfortunate death. And what he had fraudulently amassed was removed honestly by his judges. But Verecundus, the bishop of the Church of Nicaea, persisting in his defense of the Three Chapters mentioned above, in the city of Chalcedon where he had sought refuge, departed from this life in a hostelry of the glorious martyr Euphemia, where he joined the Lord.[102]

146. Macarios, bishop of Jerusalem, was ejected, and while he was still alive, Eustochius was ordained.

147. In the thirteenth year after the consulship of Basil, a most famous man [553], a Synod was assembled at Constantinople, on the order of the Emperor Justinian.[103] Among the holders of Sees there were: Vigilius, the bishop of Rome, although ordained while Silverius was still alive;

---

[101] This reference to another Boethius who was temporarily primate of Byzacenum, in North Africa, in 552, is most intriguing. The son of the great Anicius Boethius, a Flavius Boethius was consul in 522 together with his brother Symmachus, and he probably became praetorian prefect of Africa in 560-561, as shown in T. S. Brown *Gentlemen and Officers*, Rome, 1984, pp 29-30. He briefly mentions this Primate, and I suggest that he may have been a younger brother, serving in the Church of North Africa. Flavius' daughter was the patrician lady Rusticiana, as we have seen, a close friend of Pope Gregory the Great. He later chided her for her solo tour of Mount Sinai, in North Africa, at risk to her health, in letter 4.44 (August, 594).

[102] The scholiast rightly supports *martyris,* for the *matris* in the text, and almost all hostelries then were managed by or for the Church. Euphemia, a 4th century martyred virgin, was highly revered in Chalcedonia, as patroness of the great church in Chalcedon where the Synods held their sessions, and where plenty of accommodation was needed.

[103] See P. Hughes *The Church in Crisis* ch 5.

162   B. Victor of Tonnena

Apollinaris of Alexandria, promoted while Zoilus was alive; Dominus of Antioch; Eustochius, made bishop after the removal of Macarios as bishop of Jerusalem; and Eutychius of Constantinople, who had replaced Menas. There they subjected the often mentioned Three Chapters and those defending them to condemnation, and for themselves they banned any reversal with penitential penalties, binding themselves perpetually with such an anathema, if they should try to absolve themselves at some time. And they placed this below a sentence of condemnation. Rusticus, Deacon of the Church of Rome and Felix, Abbot of the monastery of Guillum in the province of Africa, argued against their decrees in writing, and were sent into exile to Thebez with their supporters.[104]

And so, after these doings, an earthquake shook the Royal City from its foundations, and then it toppled a great many buildings and porticos, and flattened almost all the altars, while the basilicas remained standing.[105]

148. In the fourteenth year after the consulship of Basil, a most famous man [554], Bishop Frontinus was summoned to the Royal City, and because of his defense of the same Three Chapters, was sent off in exile to the first city of Thebes, Antinoê[106] In his place, Peter was ordained by the heretics as bishop of the Church of Salona.

149. Priests of the proconsular Council of the province of Africa, were deluded by the artfulness of the Chapters' critics, the Bishops Rufinus and Vinus, and Archbishop Reparatus, and greeted them as defenders of the faith, and through the communion of Primasius, a false bishop of the Church of Carthage, they polluted all except for very few.

150. Dacius, the bishop of Milan, came to Constantinople, and because he consented to the condemnation of the same Three Chapters, he was struck down and died that day.

151. The eunuch Narses, a patrician and an ex-prefect, in battle, quite miraculously overcame the king of the Goths, Totila, in Italy, and killed him and took all of his riches.[107]

---

[104] Thebez, in the desert of Palestine, seems very likely with *Thebaida*.

[105] The opening *itaque* suggests that the earthquake was a divine punishment.

[106] The *Antinoensi* in U and H seems much more likely than *Antiochensi* in P and Migne, which has no real connection at all with Egyptian Thebes.

[107] Narses (c. 473-573), coming from Armenia, became keeper of the privy-purse in Justinian's palace, and was sent over to Italy to help Belisarius, and finally

Arians and Vandals of the 4th-6th Centuries 163

152. In the fifteenth year after the consulship of Basil, a most famous man [554], the bishops of the Council of Numidia gathered together in the same way as the proconsular priests and came to Carthage. They were polluted by the communion of Primasius, the same false bishop of the Church, and made sinners, before they returned to their places.

153. Victor, the bishop of the Church of Tonnena and author of this work, suffered imprisonments and simultaneous beatings on the Balearic Islands, and in the monastery of Mandracium as well.[108] His first and second exiles on the island of Aegimuritanae,[109] and his third exile in Alexandria, were shared with Theodore, bishop of the Church of Cebarsusitum. He was also sent into exile and thrown into the prison of the castle of Diocletian, after the praetorian prison, and all of this was due to his defense of the aforesaid Three Chapters.

154. Anastasius succeeded Domninus as bishop of Antioch.

155. In the sixteenth year after the consulship of Basil, a most famous man [556], Primasius, who had usurped the Church of Carthage, afflicted those who were unwilling to agree with him now with clubs and now with imprisonments and now also with exiles.

---

replaced him. While the Ostrogoths held the sea, he met their army at Taginae in 552 and destroyed it and its King Totila. Narses freed Rome, and at the battle of Mons Lactarius defeated and killed Totila's brave son, Teias, and ended the Gothic power in Italy. As the prefect of Italy he was a very capable administrator, and defeated the Alimanni, invading from the North, at the battle of Capua, but his taxes were too severe and unpopular, and the new Emperor Justin recalled him. If Victor is right, he was originally a Court eunuch (like Farinelli at the Spanish Court, entrusted with matters of State), and he lived to the very old age of 96, it seems. Some historians seem unaware of his early life as a eunuch in the palace, a contrast to his later life as a patrician, praetor and extremely successful general. For the great general Belisarius, see chapters 118-121 above. For a rare but brief biography of the capable and generous Narses, see Randers-Pehrson pp 215-218. For my recent study of the brilliant eunuch's career, see the note above.

[108] As suggested by Mommsen and adopted by H (*in insulis Balearis* from *in Sala est Valericis*). Sala is very possible (modern Sale), on the coast of Mauretania, near to Casablanca, but *Valericis* cannot be located. The text of Procopius supports Mandracium as a port of Carthage, from the meaningless *de mandra* in the text. This is the errant writer's first *cris-de-coeur*.

[109] This island is quite close to Carthage, now called Zembra.

164   B. Victor of Tonnena

156. Victor and Theodore, aforesaid bishops from Africa, were freed from their prison, and after continuous discussions in the bishop's palace for fifteen days, they were sent to another place of custody, the monastery of Tabenensiotae, situated in Canopus, twelve miles from the city of Alexandria.[110]

157. In the seventeenth year after the consulship of Basil, a most famous man [557], Vigilius of Rome died in the island of Sicily.

158. At that time Felix, Abbot of the monastery of Gallitanum, being exiled in Sinope, departed from this life to join the Lord.[111]

159. In the eighteenth year after the consulship of Basil, a most famous man [558], Pelagius, Archdeacon of Rome and a defender of the aforesaid Three Chapters, returned from exile, persuaded by the Emperor Justinian, and condemning what he had recently defended with great consistency, was ordained by sinners as the bishop of the Church of Rome, and was Pope for five years.

160. In the nineteenth year after the consulship of Basil, a most famous man [559], the bishops of Illyria, except for some small monasteries and a few of the faithful, were in agreement in allowing persecutions, reneging on their earlier faith.

161. At that time the Huns did very serious damage to Armenia.

162. In the twentieth year after the consulship of Basil, a most famous man [560], the Bulgarians invaded Thrace and they penetrated as far as the Sykai district of Constantinople,[112] and they captured the patrician Sergius, who had recently been commander of the African militia, and at once dismembered him. But the armies of the patrician Belisarius resisted them

---

[110] Theodosius in Migne is most unlikely here, with Theodore as a previous fellow victim of the emperor, especially with a third appearance together in chapter 169. The *praetorio* could well refer to the Emperor's palace, as these African bishops got no further than Alexandria, it appears. Its bishop then was Apollinaris, who joined in the condemnation of the Three Chapters. In first century Roman times, Canopus was synonymous with luxury and debauchery.

[111] Sinope was on the SE coast of the Euxine in Paphlagonia (mod Sinop, Turkey).

[112] See ch 126 above for this unsavory Jewish district of Constantinople, where the Bulgarians were 'bogged down.'

Arians and Vandals of the 4th-6th Centuries 165

bravely in battle, and put them to flight, and the Bulgarians retreated over the Danube.

163. In the twenty-first year after the consulship of Basil, a most famous man [561], the body of Saint Andrew the Hermit was found and taken to Alexandria with very great honour, and located with full honour in the Basilica of Saint John the Baptist.

164. In the twenty-second year after the consulship of Basil, a most famous man [562], Frontinianus, the bishop of Salona, was moved from exile in Antinoê to Ancyra in Galatia. Peter, the usurper of his Church, died, and Prodinus was substituted in his place.

165. In the twenty-third year after the consulship of Basil, a most famous man [563], Reparatus, archbishop of the Church of Carthage, in exile at Euchaita, with a glorious confession passed over to the Lord on the fifth day of January.

166. In that year the Emperor Justinian was the first to receive the legates of the people of Arabia and had them return to where they had come from with very great presents.[113]

167. In the thirty-seventh year of the rule of the aforesaid Emperor Justinian, Pelagius was ordained bishop of Rome, and was Pope for eleven years.[114]

168. Eustochius, bishop of Jerusalem, who had been ordained in the place of Macarios who was still alive, was ejected, and the bishopric of Macarios was renewed again.

169. In the thirty-eighth year of the same emperor [564], Bishops Musicus, Brumasius, Donatus and Chrysonius from Africa, and Bishops Victor and Theodorus from Egypt likewise, were summoned to the Royal City at the emperor's command. And while they were present in the presence of the same Emperor Justinian, and afterwards, while the bishop of the Royal City, Eutychius, argued with them, they resisted the new heresy, and they

---

[113] P & Migne left out the text from 'first' to 'return,' copied in P by another hand.
[114] Until he was killed by the plague that welcomed his reluctant successor, Gregory the Great, who very nearly followed Pope Pelagius to the grave, during his memorable seven-fold procession.

166   B. Victor of Tonnena

were segregated in turn and incarcerated in one of the monasteries of that city.[115]

170. In the thirty-ninth year of his reign [565], Justinian sent into exile the bishop of Constantinople, Eutychius, who condemned the Three Chapters, supported by the deacons of the hermit Evagrius and the monks of Didymus and of the confessor of Alexandria, whose praises I sang above, with the authority of famous men, and in his place he appointed John, a similar bishop with the same error.

171. In that year the Greens in the Royal City started a civil war, and with their sword blows they put to death many of the State's citizens. But afterwards the prefect Julian executed most of the perpetrators of these atrocities.

172. In the fortieth year of his reign [566], Justinian came to the end of his life in the fifteenth indiction.

173. Theodore, the bishop of Cebarsusitum and defender of the Three Chapters, exiled to the Royal City, died on the same month and day as Justinian. And he was buried next to the confessors whose tongues had been cut out by the king of the Vandals, Ugneric.

174. Justin junior, the son of Vigilantia, the sister of the Emperor Justinian, and born from a most charming father, took over the great scepter of the Empire with popular support. His wife Sophia was said to be the granddaughter of the Empress Theodora.

175. All the years from the first human Adam were collected up to the incarnation of Jesus Christ our Lord, which is 1,199 years. But from the nativity of Jesus Christ our Lord, which was in the 43rd year of the rule of Augustus Octavian Caesar, up to the first year of Justin, the emperor of Rome, who was the successor to the rule of Justinian, is 567 years. From Adam at the same time down to the first year of the emperor of Rome just mentioned is 1,766 years.

---

[115] This is the last reference to his fate by Victor, but as the preface shows, it seems most unlikely that he continued to refuse to toe the official Catholic line for much longer.

C. VICTOR OF CARTENNA

ON PENITENCE

Preface

The third Bishop Victor was the bishop of Cartenna, and he lived from 428-477 in North Africa, where he wrote a book of thirty-three chapters (pp 1060-1094 in Migne) on Penitence (*De Poenitentia: Liber Unus*). Although a few early scholars were unsure as to the authorship of this work (wrongly included as an appendix to the works of St Ambrose), the last chapter ends with a personal appeal from a Victor (*memento mei; ... et quaeso ut in orationibus tuis nulla capiaris oblivione Victoris*: 'Remember me; ... and I ask that in your prayers you are not affected by any forgetfulness'), and Migne (pp 1057-1058) supports the authorship of Victor of Cartenna, as first proposed by Gennadius, although he had seen a manuscript with an improbable *Victoris ... Tonensis* as author. In his useful book on Penitence in the Western Church of the late antiquity, Poschmann had a chapter on Victor's *De Poenitentia* and agreed the work was his and came from the fifth century, despite uncertainty on the part of French scholar Batiffol. By contrast, in Lewis and Short, a few unique words appear assigned to the *De Poenitentia*, but by some 'Victor of Tonnena.'[1] This important and interesting work on Penitence was lucky to survive, and has never been translated into any modern language, despite its inclusion in the Appendix to the works of the celebrated Saint Ambrose. For mediaeval historians and theologians this should prove a useful text now that it can be read in English.[2]

---

[1] Bernard Poschmann *Abendländische Kirchenbüsse* (München, 1928).
[2] See W. H. C. Frend, *The Donatist Church: A Movement of Protest in Roman North Africa* (Oxford, Clar. Pr., 2nd ed.,1985). His comment (pp 305-6) is of interest: 'The legacy of Donatism may be preserved in the puritanical work of Victor of Cartenna on the subject of penance. The *De Paenitentia* cannot be claimed for certain as Donatist, but written from Cartenna, the centre of Rogastic exclusiveness, it betrays the harsh and uncompromising attitude towards the sinner

168 C. Victor of Cartenna

The bishop's literary style and imagery suggest that he was well trained in rhetoric and in law. His frequent and mostly effective use of anaphora, antithesis and parataxis is very evident, and he keeps his late Latin usages to the minimum, although there are four on the first page, *intenebrat*, *veniabile, reatus* (as 'guilt') and *nundinat* (passive in Classical Latin). He is also very partial to polysyllabic words, in many cases very long abstracts. But he uses subjunctives and gerundives correctly by Classical standards and has many complex periods. The text is mostly reliable, but a few changes were needed to make sense, commented on in my notes.

His choice of quotations is nearly always apt, and it reflects a very usual habit of that time. He clearly quotes from memory, at a time where mnemonic drills were inevitable for any bright student, and he finds it harder to find the accurate originals in his memory bank for the books of the Hebrew Testament (except for the very basic work of the clerical mnemonic drills, the *Psalms*) than he does for those of the Greek Scriptures, especially the four gospels. Some of his quotations are carefully adapted to his argument, with some necessary alterations, others are little more than approximations, even for some quite well known passages. He is fond of dramatic renderings of stories in the Hebrew Scriptures, sometimes for their own sake, it seems, although a link with penitence is made at some point usually at the end. He does not overdo biblical quotations, however, unlike in the defense of the Catholic faith in what was almost certainly the bishop of Vita's account of the contest between the Vandal King Huneric and Eugenius, archbishop of Carthage.[3]

Chapter 1

My dearest brother, as I am about to describe the duties and merits of penitence, I think that there is no need for words but for action. For a matter that is beneficial and necessary should not be stated so much as taught. Penitence might have an element of total bitterness in its nature, but it bears the fruit of sweetness in its outcome, and it sticks in the throat while it bestows a salutary remedy for the heart. Penitence, I say, is the condemnation of a former life and a correction promised for the future.[4] And one's way of living is brought as it were to a new life, while a pious

---

which one associates with the Donatists.' For the most part, Victor's work is neither harsh nor uncompromising.

[3] Book 3 in the *Historia Persecutionis Africanae Provinciae* by the Bishop of Vita.

[4] Poschmann picked out this neat antithesis for his summary of the tract.

Arians and Vandals of the 4th-6th Centuries   169

mind does not look back to what lies behind in its rear. I do not teach this in this way with words I have said, just as I practice it with things I have done. And although a person of justice may not agree, yet I accuse myself at the start of my speech.

For a cautious confession of a sin has an element of justice, because it is lawful, as you teach, that God should punish sins committed, yet penitence practiced with humility comes before the sentence of the Judge. For it has been written: 'To the penitent he has given a way to justice, and he has confirmed those failing to endure and has promised them a path to justice.'[5] Come, therefore, penitent sinner, confess your own sins, open unto God the secrets of your wickedness, open wide the secrets of your heart, and remove anything that covers your internal transgressions. God knows everything that you have done secretly, and if your tongue will not proclaim it, your conscience cannot conceal it. In vain do you delude yourself with a secret consolation, and think that what you have committed without a witness can be hidden. Everything that is hidden is revealed to God, and whatever shines in the open, a night of hidden thought makes dark.

Make yourself your own defendant in an act of confession, and prepare your case in your view, with yourself accusing. Pass a severe sentence on yourself, before you feel the anger of the Judge, and to enjoy compassion,[6] exercise beforehand censure of yourself. Believe me, all that you are suspected of becomes pardonable at once, when penitence with this sort of justice has been found in you, as the Scripture says: 'To the penitent he has given a way to justice, and he has confirmed those failing to endure and has promised them a path to justice.' Behold, the Lord awaits the gift of confession, provided guilt does not apply to the person confessing. As man's conscience may be known to God's senses, a tongue prefers to admit what hidden parts of a heart cannot conceal.

Penitence, therefore, is what combines different offices in one act; for from one point-of-view it reveals the man confessing, from the other it recalls an innocent confession. From one point-of-view it sells guilt, from the other it excuses crime. From one it brings sins nearer to one praying, from the other it demands forgiveness for the penitent. Nor does the Lord allow a confession to be punished, as he knows how to recall the

---

[5] Close to *Sirach* 17.19. However the Vulgate gives us *viam* for its *partem justitiae, confirmavit* for *corrogavit* and *illis sortem* for *illos in sortem.*
[6] Victor uses *mulgeas* (lit. 'milk') metaphorically.

170 C. Victor of Cartenna

condemned man who is penitent. O magnificent treasure-house of heavenly goodness! O singular ordinance of a most forgiving Judge! He wants to extort a spoken confession from defendants for this reason, so that he may find nothing that he should have to punish. And although a man confessing before temporal judges is soon directed to punishment, one confessing before the Lord at once obtains a pardon. And He does not extract it from those confessing under any tortures, when the person suffering seems to carry out an office of terror in his own mind. For the groans of a person confessing, are a gain for the holy Judge, and a confession without complaint is a joy for the Advocate. What is not punished in a servant, is taken on by his master,[7] and much is conferred on the Creator if anyone is condemned to a penalty, but is granted a pardon. For he wants to have a loss in the punishment, but does not want a loss in his clemency. A person does not hope to be punished who is prepared to be pitied, as He himself says about himself through a prophet: 'I do not want the death of him who is dying, as that he should come back and live.'[8]

The Wisdom of Solomon agrees with this, saying: 'God did not make death, nor does he rejoice in the destruction of the living.[9] 'Therefore, our Judge's merciful nature hopes that the guilty do not perish in their life, but perish in their thoughts, and he does not desire the end of a person dying, but hastens rather to preserve the one who has confessed. 'I do not want the death,' he says, 'of him who is dying, but that he should come back and live.' Behold the true source of life, who does not want the death of him who is dying, but his laments, when converted,[10] and he wants himself, being compassionate always, to be a benefit, so that justice does not hold him after judgment.

Chapter 2

And so a loss is experienced in a man's death, as He does not rejoice in any demise.[11] For in the giving of life, reason for grief must come from death, not as if he descended by the law of bodily sensation, as he would be saddened by the person who is lost and dying. But when he cannot

---

[7] Reading the neat *servo* in a MS from Rome rather than the editors' *inferno*.

[8] *Ezech* 18.32. In the Vulgate two plural imperatives are used (*revertimini et vivite*), here *ut* with the third person subjunctives *revertatur et vivat*.

[9] *Wisdom* 1.13.

[10] I suggest *converti* for *conversi* in the sense of 'be converted.'

[11] Following the editor, who prefers *in uno* to *in vivo* in cod. Rem.

Arians and Vandals of the 4th-6th Centuries   171

obtain any joy from the death of someone perishing, the act of sadness is easy, as if the affection of someone feeling sorry, not the anxiety of someone mourning, and the source of the sadness is piety,[12] not any external pain from suffering. Therefore it follows that he who rejoices over one found, would grieve over one lost, and he who gives thanks over a living person would not be made happy over a dead one. The Lord makes this clear through a parable in the gospel: 'But you must celebrate and rejoice, since your brother was dead and is alive again; he was lost and has been found.'[13] And again he says: 'Thus there will be joy in Heaven before your Father and his angels over one sinner who repents.'[14] From this the Lord demands penitence with the Prophet Isaiah's words: 'It is I who wipe out your iniquities, and I shall not remember them. But you must not forget, and we shall be judged. Declare your iniquities first, so that you may be justified.'[15] And what could be more pleasing, I ask you, than this promise? What could be found sweeter than this invitation? To summon the Judge and speak before him on your behalf as defendant, not so that he punishes you, but absolves you, not to censure your confession, but to justify the guilt found in you by him himself? But I shall not remember, and you must not forget; that is to say: The memory of your deed will not remain in my mind, if you do not forget your own sin, and the infamy of your crime will be destroyed, if you do not cease to confess it to my ears, compelled by its recall.

And so you see God intent on the crimes of a sinner, if there is no sign of an act of penitence, and you see the anger of a just judge threatening the neck of a defendant, if the groans of his confession should not please him. Consign to oblivion whatever you cannot publicize, and abolish the stigma of a crime, provided you do not wound your conscience with silence. 'It is I who wipe out your iniquities, and I shall not remember them. But you

---

[12] Following *ex pietate* in the editors' texts, rather than *expiata,* in Rem. He is very partial to succinct antitheses, and here *pietate* neatly balances the *passione.*

[13] *Luke* 15.32. The Vulgate reads: *epulari .. oportebat, quia .. hic .. erat* for the text's *gratulari ... te oportet, quoniam .. fuerat.*

[14] *Luke* 15.7. Again the text adapts the Vulgate quite freely in places. Victor would have known Holy Writ very well, and he appears to quote from memory, with mainly minor changes. He is usually more accurate than the Bishop of Vita. Both are far more accurate with Greek Scriptures than with Hebrew ones.

[15] *Isaiah* 43.25-26. Again, it is a very free adaptation of the Latin in the Vulgate, mainly due to omissions. In the Letters of Saint Gregory the Great, he has just the same accuracy with quotes from the Greek Scriptures, but like the Victors and Ambrose, his adaptations of Hebraic ones are far freer.

172   C. Victor of Cartenna

must not forget.' He wanted there to be no point of time, no moment of a moment, in which forgetfulness of your sins might steal into your heart, but so that you might curse the sins you committed before, not so that you might be captured by the pleasure of former misdeeds. And let a sigh come from you not from a longing for things past but from a remembrance of grief. You should always put your case before your eyes and mourn, and bewail your death at every moment, and sense continually that you are already dead, and know without doubt that you are going to die. Our Lord will not lead you to a punishment but will turn you away to glory. And you will be remembered, even as you forget those deeds that you did sinfully before, about to provide for yourself eternal and unending consolations for your temporal grief.

Although your sins may escape unpunished, in His own words: 'Blessed are they that now mourn, for they shall be comforted.'[16] 'But you must not forget, and we shall be judged.' He means 'meanwhile, we shall be judged.' Will the Lord be judged, who says that he should be judged with a sinner? Heaven forbid! 'Let us be judged' He says, 'you confessing and I forgiving, you offering what you should, I by granting your sins, you admitting your iniquities and I justifying you for your show of piety. Finally see what follows: 'Declare your iniquities first,' he says, 'so that you may be justified,' not so that you may be condemned; so that a reward for conversion remains for you, not a punishment for what you confessed, so that the judgment of justice accompanies you, not the ignominy of condemnation. And you will be free of all your iniquities then, when you stand before yourself as your witness and accuser. 'Declare your iniquities first,' he says, 'so that you may be justified.' But should He challenge you, my brother, to confess your iniquities, as if he were ignorant, when he knows them before they take place? And should he hope to hear them from you, as if not knowing them, when he is accustomed to judging those not yet born with his foreknowledge? Or do you not know that in the womb of holy Rebecca, a twin birth was conceived,[17] and it was born at the same time, but by the notion of foreknowledge he gave a judgment of very different merits?

---

[16] *Matthew* 5.4. The text adds the *nunc* ('now').
[17] Rebecca's discordant twins were of course Esau and Jacob.

Chapter 3

And so He wants you be more aware of what is going on inside you, just as, when you describe your ailment to a doctor, he would prescribe an antidote necessary for you; for then you will be able to obtain a perfect medical cure, if you avoid concealing the wounds in your conscience. But what sort of cure will you have if you do not reveal what is hidden inside you? For in my view, unless the doctor is fully informed, a sick person cannot be cured. Let him wait a long time for the reasons for your pain to be shown to him, so that you understand the medical remedy when already cured. For you will consider what may be owed to the doctor with a just valuation,[18] if you know the disease inside you beforehand. And to avoid delaying you any more, your penitent confession is the medicine, and that cures you, that gives you new life. It does not allow your wound to contain putridity, but as soon as you have groaned over it, it then spreads a knotty scar tissue over the wound.[19]

Today if some bodily disease should affect you, and you should feel your limbs suffering from an inner sickness, or if you find out that your wound is cancerous with the putridity of foul puss, you at once run to the doctor and seek a remedy from his art, you are up early before the sleeping doctor's front-door, and you stand before his home as a morning caller, keen to beg him with prayers, promise gifts, offer favors and hand over your whole fortune for the sake of your health. And very often when the doctor's inexperience or weariness overcomes him, or certainly it is put off for a long time, nevertheless you persist with an assiduous watch, and hope for a late remedy, man from man, and are full of hope that help is at hand, although so far you may feel no effect of renewed strength.[20]

Yet you do not run to God, your free doctor, to a voluntary dealer in drugs, who while curing the illnesses of your soul knows how to endure contempt, and expects no reward for your health, but desires rather to enrich the one he has cured with a reward. And in any case a temporal

---

[18] The MSS Rem and Sorb. read *juxta aestimationem* ('according to estimation'), but the editors' *justa aestimatione* seems to suit the theme better.

[19] The Cod. Rem as adopted by Migne has *nodabilem*, the other MSS & editions *notabilem*. This is the only use of *nodabilis* in surviving works, but it suits the medical imagery perfectly. Lewis & Short ascribe it to Victor of Tonnena. The use of *putredo* is late Latin, used met. by Ambrosius with *peccatorum* (*in Luc.* 5.27).

[20] The word *corroboratio* is only found here, but its sense is obvious.

174 C. Victor of Cartenna

doctor only cures the rest that concerns the body. God cures the soul, which is wounded by sins, and the human doctor offers remedies that will help for the present, while God applies a perpetual medical cure. And yet the human doctor cannot even help himself unless God gives him assistance. For the cleverness of medicine very often labors in vain, if God is unwilling to prolong a sick man's life. And we shall see these doctors sometimes unable to save themselves, when through their corporeal vices they are robbed of the benefit of salvation. And so there will be no benefit in medicine when the medicine does not help the doctor himself. Believe me, no one restores you to better health than He who made you, nor does anyone do justice to you other than he who cures you with a lashing. He alone knows how to sew up fractures in his creation and how to re-form the broken appearance of our clay into the substance of our pristine state, as He himself says through the prophet: 'As the clay is in the potter's hand, so are you in my hand.'[21]

This itself is not done after an interval of time, for as soon as you have told him your vice he at once bestows assistance also, and almost no time intervenes for begging for help and providing cures. He only waits for you to confess. There will be no delay in your cure. 'Declare your iniquities first,' he says, 'to be justified.' With these words the same Spirit, speaking through the Prophet Ezekiel, renews his promise to the unjust: 'On whatever day the impious man is converted from injustice and acts justly, on that very day all of his injustices will vanish; he will not die in the injustice of his own action.' And elsewhere: 'When you have been converted, then will you be saved.'[22]

Chapter 4

But you may perhaps say: 'I have no confidant, and any crimes I have committed are not open to anyone at all. Why then, if you have no confidant, are you unaware anyhow that God is the inevitable confidant for your conscience? And if no human being knows your deeds, of course God knows ahead what you have done and are still going to do. For what is there that he does not see, as he sees everywhere and everything, as he himself says to Job: 'Who would think that anything escapes my notice? Give me a place where God is absent, who is totally hidden, and you too

---

[21] *Jeremiah* 18.6. The Vulgate has *in manu* with *figuli*, with *estis* understood.

[22] These two quotations are from *Ezekiel* 18.26-8 and from *Isaiah* 30.15. The first is freely adapted from the original, and the second likewise.

Arians and Vandals of the 4th-6th Centuries

will be hidden in your deeds, as you think.[23] But God is everywhere and all in all, as He himself says: 'The sky is my seat, but the earth is the footstool for my feet,' and 'I fill the sky and the earth.' On this the Prophet David also said: 'Where shall I go from your Spirit and where shall I flee from your face? If I shall ascend into Heaven, you are there, if I shall descend into Hell, you will come there. If I shall receive my wings directly, to inhabit the furthest of the seas, there indeed will your hand, Lord, lead me and your right hand shall contain me.'[24]

And so you say in vain that you have no witness, although you hear that all of God is everywhere, and spread through everything by the display of his majesty, and He would know well whatever is thought to be hidden. 'But I do not have a witness,' you will say. You would have said this rightly if you did not have the example of Cain, the first of the parricides. With his parricidal impiety he had persuaded his pious brother to go with him into a field, and his rough and ready brother, not bothering to be on his guard over his brother, obeyed his orders with the goodness of sincerity. The two brothers walked side by side with a single escort, and the unfortunate parricide as it were chose a place without a witness to carry out the wicked crime he had thought of. As if indeed, if he did not have a human witness, he could have escaped at all the eyes of God! Or could conceal it with his concern over solitude, when nothing could be concealed from our Creator's vision! But when the primitive creator of an unutterable crime judged the place suitable for perpetrating a crime, he leapt on him madly and, inspired by the devil, slew his most patient brother as he failed to fight back. The affair was in fact evident in its outcome, but as far as Cain had thought, his crime lay hidden without a witness. And the cruelest of men believed that without a witness he could not be said to have committed the crime, although he acknowledged the crime by the very fact that he wanted to conceal it. But behold the Lord of all things, for whom whatever is thought hidden is clear to see, and for

---

[23] The Rom editor reads a marginal gloss of *oculus* ('eye'), thus missing the very pointed repetition of *occultus*.

[24] These three quotes come from *Isaiah* 66.1, *Jeremiah* 23.24, and *Psalms* 138.7-10. Except for a *vero* for the *autem* in the Vulgate, the first two are accurate, but in *Psalms* 138, the Latin is very different: *tu illic es; si descendero in infernum, ades; si sumpsero pennas meas diluculo* ('at dawn') *et habitavero in extremis maris ... tua deducet me et tenebit me.* The text has *tu ibi es ... in inferos, tu ibi venies? Si recepero ... directas, ut inhabitem in novissimo maris; ... tua, Domine, ...continebit me.* This again shows that the Bishop's memory was not always accurate, but the *diluculo* and *recepero* are quite surprising with such a well-known passage.

176   C. Victor of Cartenna

whom whatever is done within the secrecy of thoughts cannot escape his notice, as the Scripture says: 'The thought of man will trust in you,' and again, 'your eyes saw my imperfection and in your book shall all be written,' and again, 'God looking close at our hearts and kidneys.' On this the same Prophet David said: 'You saw my thoughts from afar.'[25]

God called for the parricide with an indignant voice, and knowing that he would deny the atrocious spirit shown by him in his fierce deed, to increase the guilt of the impious parricide, pretended that he was ignorant, as it were, of the crime that had been committed. 'And the Lord said to Cain,' he said, "Where is your brother Abel?" and Cain said: "I know not. Am I my brother's keeper?"'[26] O most hateful madness! O singular audacity! He denies the crime that he has committed without a witness, with confidence. He believed that the crime could not be made public without a witness, yet the very denial betrayed his guilty conscience all the more.[27] What are you doing, unlucky Cain? You have no human witness; but behold, you have the shedding of blood as a betrayer, which publicizes and accuses you by itself. Its voice summons you before the Creator, and the flow of blood creates odium, in case the parricide should escape punishment by hiding. 'What have you done? Behold, the voice of your brother's blood cries unto me from the ground.'

But when the parricide sensed that what he thought was hidden was revealed, and was convicted by the witness of the blood of having made up arrogant deceits, in vain, he confessed his crime. He hoped that a more severe judgment would be passed on him, since his conscience could not excuse the parricide he had committed. But meanwhile the more severe penalty was put off, so that a long-lasting thought should torture the author of so great a crime, and the quickness of the punishment demanded by him should not be seen more as a sparing. And it would reach a great age with long lasting punishment, which would extend the crime of parricide for the

---

[25] These four quotes from the *Psalms* (75.11, 138.16, 7.10 and 138.3) are used to prove that God reads man's thoughts. The first three are accurate, the last just replacing *intellexisti* with *vidisti*. Every monk (and priest) was expected to know the *Psalms* off by heart, at least, as Pope Gregory the Great regularly demanded.

[26] *Genesis* 4.9. There are four changes from the Vulgate (*ait/dixit; qui respondit/et dixit; num/numquid*).

[27] Reading *ipsa negatio* in the Rom edition, rather than *ipso negotio* ('by the business itself') in the other MSS and Migne.

Arians and Vandals of the 4th-6th Centuries   177

dying villain.[28] How then do you deceive yourself over this, arguing that you do not have a witness, although Cain was convicted and punished likewise due to the testimony of innocent blood?[29]

Chapter 5

'But I have no witness,' you will say, 'to divulge my deeds.' I ask you, please tell me, if you do not have a witness, do you lack the witness of your conscience? Or can you escape from yourself and avoid your conscience? I mean by conscience, the place where all that we do does not die, which accuses and judges us in our deeds. And although it may not have the use of speech, yet it knows not how to keep silent. A witness can be moved away, a witness can help you for a time by his absence. Conscience is always with you, and without you it does not exist. It clings to your heart and it never deserts you, and like some handmaid, it departs from you for no period of time. It holds you as its prisoner and its captive, forever under its jurisdiction. If at some stage a more pleasant and successful action diverts you, and happiness over the deed begins to delight your senses,[30] then that conscience suddenly arouses you, it strikes you deep inside and obstructs your senses, and it interrupts the joy, and disturbs the whole region of your heart with tearful sighs. And as if it were held wounded by disgrace, no remedy is found for a person as a cure, since it is always offended when another person is castigated and is itself first struck when another is wounded.

Then do you want to know how great the severity of conscience is? Your witness can be corrupted by gold, can be bought by money, but conscience allows no amount of corruption, its testimony remains intact, protected by the total strength of faith. What is more, a defense is hired against a witness, and subtle arguments are sought for a clever defense, and the truth of the testimony is perverted by the cunning of immoral eloquence; the

---

[28] With *extenuaret* ('shorten') in MSS and editions, the argument is nonsensical. I suggest the rare verb *extentaret* ('would extend'), explained by the *marginalia* in Gill: *poena diuturnitate longaevior, quod lentitudine moriendi aestimaret facinus parricidii* ('a punishment of greater age in its length, as the crime of parricide would be estimated by the slowness of his death').

[29] Victor's treatment of the Cain and Abel conflict from *Genesis* 4.2-15 is given far greater dramatic force and is neatly used to prevent the reader from thinking a crime can be committed in safety if there is no human witness. God can read your thoughts, he argues, even those in the future.

[30] An infin. is needed with *coeperit*. I suggest *delectare* rather than *delectatione*.

178 C. Victor of Cartenna

judge too is bought off, to avoid the true nature of the deed. But when conscience is important, all of these are irrelevant. And when a man is dying, his conscience certainly does not die, as it is judged with his soul after the death of his body. And do you think that it is to your advantage not to have a witness, when you sense the daily and perpetual judgment of your conscience? But quite clearly divine punishment will not accompany him whom his own conscience has judged. For he will be free there of the judge's power, necessarily so, where a defendant shall be his own witness and accuser against himself. For without doubt the case of a sin will be doubled if an insolent conscience shall be unwilling to confess its misdeeds. For then a person becomes impious from his sinning, if he proves to be obdurate in confessing his sins. And so that he punishes his sins with a worthy sentence, let a stubborn conscience pay a penalty for obstinacy. For the agitation of a judge is broken, when the earnest strictness of a severe repentance is softened by the attack of a confession, and a judgment drawn up with indignation is overturned through satisfaction, and the intention of a threatening oration is tempered by the modesty of a very humble one.

Learn this from the people of Nineveh, by whose confession a sentence already delivered was cancelled, and the threat of God's anger was turned aside, so that their penitent confession should not be fruitless. A fearful sentence from Heaven was already hanging over the wretched city, and the axe of divine punishment was threatening the necks of the unlucky people. The Heavenly sword had already been drawn from its scabbard, and vehement anger was raging for the punishment of crimes that they had committed. The herald's voice threatened death for the people and the prophet's cry announced death close by for all who were about to perish. 'After three days,' he said, 'the city of Nineveh will be overthrown too.'[31]

'Alas, why do you exact crimes from God and what sins do you obtain from him? You have passed over that most merciful holiness of our God, from whom you have exacted such a close and untimely punishment. So I think I can see what great distress was oppressing our wretched people, and what sort of necessity had seized them with trembling.' Fear had excluded good advice and despair had no remedy. For the quickness of the time had been so precipitate that the charge would not relax the dreadful suspicion of crime even for a short time. 'After three days,' he

---

[31] *Jonah* 3.4. In fact they had forty days to repent. Jonah's journey took three days.

Arians and Vandals of the 4th-6th Centuries 179

said, 'the city of Nineveh will be overthrown.' And what sort of destruction was it going to be, that is indicated to those about to die? It did not signify a hostile incursion at any rate, nor the din of weapons, nor the terrible blare of trumpets, which they could perhaps meet with the defense of those resisting, or could join battle after declaring contests of the parties, or could extend the fate of captives with the help of flight. But a death is proclaimed from divine indignation and heavenly punishment, for which he had to be punished and not be removed by flight, nor was care to be given to the warlike arts of defense. For who could refuse the death imposed on them, which a heavenly thunderclap began to pour forth?

Chapter 6

But behold, a plan did not desert the citizens in their fear, and a remedy from their danger was found in their desperation. As they returned home, they interrogated their consciences in the manner of a trial, and ran to the ramparts of penitence, and holding their shields of confession before them, they diverted the arrows. They all went to take care of confessing their crimes and the crowd exposed to death worked together on an office of satisfaction. About to perish, they indicate that fasting was necessary for them, and castigated their souls with the whip of humility on their own bodies. They wore goats' hair instead of vests, and besprinkled their bodies with ashes instead of perfumes, and lying prostrate they licked the dust. They celebrated their deaths with tears and they carried on their lives with lamentations;[32] they publicized their guilt with groans and broadcasted the hidden sins of their actions. Every age and sex adapted itself to offices of mourning, all alike. All elegance was laid aside, and smart apparel was rejected. But that mean attire on their bodies were clearly ornaments of penitence, and their virtuous appearances were the highest glory of confession. And nourishment was even denied to the suckling children themselves, and infants not yet infected by their own sins put up with the burdens of others. The dumb herd hungered for their food and the brute animals did not receive their natural fodder. A single wail by different natures was heard all along the walls of the city, and the weeping lamentations of mourners resounded throughout all the city's buildings. And to say it once, the earth sustained the groans of those confessing, but the stars themselves also rang with the very voice of

---

[32] The noun *plangimonium* is only found here, but is wrongly ascribed to Victor of Tonnena by Lewis and Short.

180   C. Victor of Cartenna

penitence. What was written was fulfilled: 'The prayer of those humbling themselves will penetrate the clouds.'[33]

Finally, they so placated an embittered God, so softened his rigidity, so calmed his anger, that he buried his sword of punishment in its scabbard, as their conscience judged their own case. Their confession snatched the sinners from being penalized, and penitence claimed for itself those already given up for punishment. The tears of those confessing at once deleted the record of their condemnation, and those guilty of sin were acquitted by their assent and confession over their crimes. Holy God saw that the penitents had taken his judgment on to themselves, and as they condemned the errors of their conscience with that assent, he at once granted those pardon whom he had planned to punish, and thereupon he spared the afflicted, so that exempt from punishment, they might become rewards for piety. The testimony of the prophet was proved, which we quoted a little before in the previous chapter: 'It is I who wipe out your iniquities, and I shall not remember them. But you must not forget, and we shall be judged. Declare your iniquities first,' he said, 'so that you may be justified,' and again: 'When you have returned and have lamented, then will you be saved,' and again: 'Turn to your Lord God, for he is merciful and pious, long-suffering and with much compassion, and he turns his sentences against the infliction of ill-will.'[34]

On this the most blessed David also said: 'I know my sin and I have not covered over my iniquity. I said, I shall confess before me my injustice to the Lord, and you have remitted the iniquity of my sin,' and again: 'Because I know my iniquity, and my sin is always before me.'[35] And so, you see that the sinner needs a daily judgment against himself, whereby when his conscience is laid bare, it is wide open.[36] And although all that we do may be known to God and it cannot be hidden to his sense even before it happens, yet he prefers to lay bare the secret of your heart and to reveal the sins on your conscience, so that he may open the bare nature of wickedness to his indulgence as a gift. How does he want to send away

---

[33] *Eccles* 35.21. I have accepted the Vulgate's *penetrabit* rather than the text's prf. This account is again a more dramatic and expanded retelling of the original, the King of Nineveh's proclamation in *Jonah* 3.6-9, based on penitence.

[34] The first quote from *Isaiah* 43.25-6, appeared in chapter 2 above. The second is a very free adaptation of *Isaiah* 30.15, and the last one is close to *Joel* 2.13.

[35] Both are close to the Vulgate, for *Psalms* 32(31).5 and 51(50).5.

[36] The text is difficult, as an open conscience is hardly closed (*operitur* in the text). Gill suggests *aperitur*, rightly adopted, it seems, by the Rom. edition.

Arians and Vandals of the 4th-6th Centuries 181

one who confesses when stripped of mercy? The most blessed prophet sang about such men, saying: 'Blessed are they whose transgressions are forgiven and whose sins are covered up,'[37] although both the iniquities and sins are hidden and covered, for no faithless confession holds a true place of pardon, and a penitent conscience is safe if it doubts not the remission of indulgence.

Chapter 7

But by contrast, if what is done is denied, a mass of sins is built up, as we mentioned above in the action of Cain. For when he has decided to deny his crime to his Creator, he is not slow to remove himself from a penalty, so that his conscience, in the atrocity of his deed, would frustrate the fruit of penitence due to his denial. For by denying he was convicted, and by not confessing voluntarily, his insolence was punished over his crime, because a penitent confession did not follow his interrogation. And so he is pleased to open a sevenfold argument, step by step, over that punishment, and to show what case would force such a harsh sentence to be built up, with the approval of an obvious defendant, in case, due to the enormity of the punishment, a path of calumny might lead to a suspicion of injustice. Although a severe punishment ought to accompany the discovery of a new crime, as it would be an example among posterity far longer. For a person who thinks that parricide is contained in just one charge is mistaken, since within the testimony of the same crime all wrongdoings have been compressed. For I hear that the Lord has said: 'You shall love the Lord your God with all your heart and with all your soul; and you shall love your neighbour as yourself. On these two commandments hang all the law and the prophets.'[38]

Since, therefore, on these two commandments everything to do with the law may hang, and I may see that Cain neither loved his God, whose creation he first violated, and strongly hated his brother, whom he killed with an impulse of impiety, it appears that he has not yet paid a service of punishment, in whose deed all crimes are found to come together. And the sevenfold punishment was rightly revealed in his case, as the universal crimes had their beginning in him. And yet I detect seven sins in him specifically, for each of which specific torments have been allotted. For his first crime was that he did not divide rightly, that is he first ate of the

---

[37] *Psalms* 31.1.
[38] *Matthew* 22. 37, 39 and 40.

182   C. Victor of Cartenna

primitive fruits of the earth, before offering them. Secondly because, when he seemed to have received a rejection of his gift which he deserved, he conceived an insolent spirit, and although there was no fault of a gift being rejected by his pious brother, the unfortunate man believed that he should be defended as it were by the Creator, if he was seen to kill his brother approved by God for this reason. His third crime is that, when he was imbued with the gall of envy and poisoned by the bitterness of malice, he was jealous of his most innocent brother with a fierce hatred. The fourth is that he deceived him, tricking him into following him so as to walk side by side into the field, where the just brother would enter into his martyrdom with the simplicity of a sheep, and the unjust one would defile the soil with parricide. The fifth is that the wicked inspirer of trust murdered his brother. The sixth is that, when he had committed his crime, he both denied it as well, and thought that God was ignorant of some deeds, although he felt that he had punished the secret of his conscience, when he had offered a suitable reply in the rejection of his offering. The seventh crime is that after the death, when betrayed, he did not think he should be punished for parricide, since due to the infamy of the reported crime, for the present moment he asked to be killed.

And so a sevenfold punishment was rightly inflicted on Cain, on whom as many injuries were applied as the number of causes, so that justice would not exceed the due punishment, and a suitable retribution should not surpass the number of crimes.

Chapter 8

I have suspected for some time that I have deviated from the proposed path of the work that I began, and have turned the quick course of my diction into another topic. But a return to what has been omitted is easy, and the path through material left aside is quickly regained, since the argument does not turn away from the conclusion of the proof introduced. 'And so I acknowledged my sin unto you,' he said, 'and mine iniquity have I not hid. I said, I shall confess my transgressions unto the Lord and you have forgiven the iniquity of my sin;' and again: 'For I acknowledge my transgressions, and my sin is ever before me.'[39] He taught this not only with words but carried it out with deeds, since it is not sufficient to put virtue before the words of spiritual wisdom for consummation, unless

---

[39] From *Psalms* 32(31).5 and *Psalms* 51(50).3.

Arians and Vandals of the 4th-6th Centuries 183

learning is adorned with actions, for suitable authority is only then attributed to the teaching if it is based on a proper example.

Finally the Lord says through the evangelist: 'Whoever shall do so, and shall teach them, shall be called very great in the kingdom of Heaven,'[40] so that both learning may be strengthened through deed, and the faith in deeds may receive a testimony from the learning. Otherwise the learning will not be based on the strength of effort, if it abuses the glory of virtue with verbal trappings. For the tongue will be rich in eloquence, but the conscience will not be filled with the riches of deeds.

Let us see, therefore, what the man achieved who sang such words. And thus, at the same time, the king[41] had succumbed to two sins, and his uncontrolled rule had enticed the prince into perpetrating a crime. For when he wanted to conceal his adultery, he committed the crime of homicide. But he carried out both neither due to the violence of a royal descent, nor due to the ambition of greater power. For, although the adultery debased him with the license of incest, yet the homicide had not been perpetrated due to hatred. And thus a prophet[42] was sent by the Lord to preach before him about the case of adultery and the death of the slain husband, and to extract a judgment from an unsuspecting king, under the cover of a parable that he had composed.[43] However, when the prophet explained the fable that he had told, David was most upset and passed an unintentional[44] but justifiable sentence on himself, and as a judge unknowingly proposed a punishment on his own head. Furthermore, when the accused advocate saw that he was being condemned by his own judgment, and the singularly just examiner accepted himself as his defendant, and felt that he could not avoid the penalty of a judgment in which the judge himself was detained in the role of one condemned, he

---

[40] *Matthew* 5.19.

[41] This is David, the second king of Israel, who had killed Goliath. He seduced the beautiful Bathsheba, and when she told him she was bearing his child, he arranged for her husband, Uriah the Hittite, to be killed in the front line of battle (the 'homicide'). See *2 Samuel* 11-12.24, where her second child is Solomon.

[42] This was the uncompromising prophet, Nathan.

[43] The parable followed the marriage of David and Bathsheba. In it, a wealthy man with many flocks picks a poor man's sole lamb and family pet to feed a visitor. David exclaims with dramatic irony: 'as the Lord liveth, the man who has done this thing shall surely die.' 'Thou art the man' is Nathan's chilling reply (12.1-7).

[44] The *indesignatam* is unique here, as recorded in Lewis & Short ('undesigned').

184 C. Victor of Cartenna

adopted a most salutary decision under such great duress, and fled to the refuge of penitence. He knew that his sin was betrayed and did not hide his wickedness with any complex denial. At once he stated the evidence against himself, and emitting the words of confession, he at once obtained a pardon for his sins: 'For I have sinned, he said, against the Lord.'[45] But that prophet imposed no delay in absolving him nor did he put off the execution of remission. As soon as the obvious defendant had made his confession, Nathan obtained indulgence for the crimes by the will of God, saying: 'The Lord has absolved your sin.' This was fulfilled as he sang in the psalm, saying: 'I acknowledged my sin and my iniquity have I not hid. I said, I will confess my injustice unto the Lord against me, and you forgave the iniquity of my sin.'[46]

Chapter 9

Let us look at another example of penitence in the case of holy David. For outstanding in the practice of a life that was worthy of imitation,[47] this king had so subjected himself to a faithful service to heavenly worship, that he would leave us examples not of his morality, but of his monuments. For he had ordered the people to be numbered, contrary to a prohibition, as he had wanted to know the size of the whole army. The king's will was obeyed and the collected number of the whole army was reported to him, and he began to know splendidly what was harmful to him. He proclaimed his good fortune with his people's increases, and numbered the gain of the multiplied strength of his army among his principal joys. Soon another prophet came to him and the case for wrongdoing was subtly put forward, but not for him, as it was first presented, but a choice of a penalty was now proposed for a deed. 'And the word of God came unto the Prophet Gad, saying: "Go and say unto David, thus said the Lord, I offer you three things; choose one of them so that I may do it unto you." So Gad came to David and told him, and said unto him: "Shall seven years of famine come unto you in your land, or will you flee from the face of your enemies for three months while they pursue you, or shall there be three days of deaths in your land? Now decide, and see what answer I shall return to him who sent me." '[48] Then what sort of

---

[45] *2 Samuel* 12.13.

[46] *Psalms* 32(31).5.

[47] The edd and Sorb read *vitae .... institutor* ('teacher'), but Minge rightly reads the text's *instituto*.

[48] *2 Samuel* 24.11-13. The events leading up to this point appear in verses 1-10.

Arians and Vandals of the 4th-6th Centuries 185

battle now arose in his mind over his decision? On one side the fear of his enemies terrified him, on the other the devastation of famine and on the third the blow of divine anger. He did not want any of these to happen, but his offences could not remain unpunished.

Among such great difficulties of choice, since he was being restricted by the nature of each of the dangers, being taught by the example of the preceding pardon, he chose a more bitter punishment in his very uncertainty, and consigned himself to a more severe penalty, so that he could request clemency. For the strictness of justice is softened when applied to pity, and the first case of piety was dealt with before the most merciful of judges. For he who forgives those confessing their sins does not condemn the stubborn over their will. And for that reason that devoted king, when fluctuating over a critical decision, did not dismiss the anchor of penitence. And confident over the piety of the terrifying prophet, he did not consider the greatness of his punishment. 'And David said unto God, I am in great straits over those three choices, but it is better for me to fall into the hands of the Lord, as his mercy is very great; let me not fall into the hands of men.'[49]

At once a punishment followed his agreement, and an appeasing penalty accompanied his appeasing choice. There was a countless loss of life, and a great many people were killed by an angel's blows. Seventy thousand died in the army, and miserable destruction oppressed the sweet spirit of the camp with ruin. David admitted that he was the cause of the deed with its weapon of punishment, and he put on the breastplate of confession against the savage sword of justice, exclaiming that he deserved more instant punishment than those punished, and prayed that their sentence be turned against him, so that he might save the people from their destruction. 'Behold, I the shepherd have sinned and I have acted wickedly. But these sheep, what have they done? Turn your hand against me and against my father's house.'[50] Behold, the penalty was overturned by the duty of apology, and the indignation was restrained by the arms of confession, so that punishment no longer proceeded against him, and the affliction that poured against the people from Heaven, abated. With the one act of penitence he obtained piety for himself also, and he at once ended the punishment for his people, so that presented with the gift of pardon, he sang this, saying: 'I said, I will confess my transgressions unto the Lord,

---

[49] *2 Samuel* 24.14.

[50] *II Kings* 24.17.

186 C. Victor of Cartenna

and you forgave the iniquity of my sin,'[51] for while he bowed beneath the despair of conviction, he deserved expiation, being worthy of reconsideration. But the enormity of your sins oppresses you, and captivated by their power, you do not dare to raise your eyes to Heaven. Indeed I approve of a conscientious fear, I do not applaud mere advice, but I prefer you to be suspect over the pursuit of indulgence, not totally in despair over the renewal of salvation.

Chapter 10

Now confusion over supplication affects an aspect of confession, which being conscious of its sins has no doubt over the Creator's remission of sins, but it blushes over the magnitude of its transgression, for to have recognized one's guilt is the beginning of confession, and comes next to pardon, that repentance encourages. But you will say that the abundance of my sins drives me backwards. Rather, you should apply yourself all the more to the least office of confession, the more you have been burdened with loads of sins, so that what you are not worthy to exact through friendship, you may be able to obtain through lack of shame. For you hear in the evangelist that the Lord said that 'to whom little is forgiven, loves less.'[52] Then you make God unholy if you should think that He repudiates a conversion, and denies compassion for one returning to the fold, so that from this you may know that the lost are searched for with loving pity. The apostle supports this, saying: 'And if we are unfaithful, yet He will abide faithful, he cannot deny himself.'[53]

Or are you unaware that when tempted nine times in the desert, the Lord put off Moses' freedom, and he could not have condemned his hard treatment over that tenth temptation in turn, if the people had not showed repentance over the nine previous faults, as he himself says: 'Behold, in this wilderness they have tempted me now ten times.'[54] Read the book of Judges and you will find that Israel's sons on countless occasions did unseemly things in the Lord's presence, and were handed over to invading nations. But when the people are again converted through chosen men, you will lead them out of various captivities, and their wrongdoings may not be punished, if a suitable penitence follows what was done so often.

---

[51] *Psalms* 32(31).5, as above.
[52] *Luke* 7.47.
[53] *2 Timothy* 2.13.
[54] *Psalms* 32(31).5, as above.

Arians and Vandals of the 4th-6th Centuries

For although a correcting punishment was not lacking, yet there was no removal through perdition, but a prayer of conversion. For when a son is beaten but is received with affection, he has certainly been admonished to provide satisfaction, but has not been punished. It seems to be a correction due not to hatred, but to love. For often, when he comes back after a beating, he is not denied the rights of piety. Finally, hear the Lord condemning through his prophet the harlot Israel, with a scourging of this sort, as he wanted to bring her to him with the right of conversion, besotted and polluted by contagion as she was: 'And I said, after she had played the harlot like this, turn back to me; and the disordered Judah did not return.'[55]

The Lord manifests the same in the gospel, when he rails at hard hearts, saying: 'O Jerusalem, Jerusalem, you that killed the prophets, and stoned those sent unto you, how often would I have gathered together your children, even as a hen gathers her chicks under her wings, and you were not willing.'[56] Believe me, the Lord awaits the very last act of our life, and as our final departure finds us, just so will he judge us. Certainly, if you are surrounded by all sorts of wrongdoings and a fog of crimes darkens[57] your eyes, and your neck bends beneath a yoke of sin, and within the sanctuary of your conscience a disgraceful wound from foul acts would forthwith corrupt you, and if you do not yield your soul to the vileness of despair, when you pour out just one prayer confessing the secret close to your heart, He will not deny you a remedy of pardon, he who came to save souls, not to destroy them. And because He does not want the dying man's death, without doubt he persuades the convert to a new life, as the Lord says: 'The Son of man is not come to destroy men's lives, but to save them,'[58] and again: 'For the Son of man is come to seek and to save that which was lost.'[59] Unless you make the devil all-powerful, if you should think that the Lord cannot snatch you when captured from his jaws; and just as he is always vigilant so as to destroy, so the Lord is not too busy to acquire souls.

---

[55] Freely adapted from *Jeremiah* 3.6-7.

[56] *Matthew* 23.37.

[57] The word *pernubilo* is only found here, and is credited rightly to this *Paenitentia* in Lewis & Short, but wrongly to Victor Turonensis.

[58] *Luke* 9.56.

[59] *Numbers* 14.22.

Chapter 11

And so in this faith of the present world let the final confession as it were of the robber persuade you, and let the very last confession on the cross of one not despairing for the desperate men provide you with the greatest of hope. Therefore that man had made all of his past life bloody with robberies, had always acted as the shield-bearer in a life of devilish savagery, had never remembered God and had listened to no legal commands, or certainly if he had listened, had taken no notice, being more inclined to crimes; that man placed all his hope in a desperate life and he practiced cruelty in the manner of criminal accomplices; for he was condemned to the cross because of this, and he hung fixed to the wood together with those crimes. Finally the desperate man came to his senses, and situated in that punishment, he obtained a great profit for himself from his death. He trembled before the future Judge at his side, made public the crimes on his conscience and straightaway acquired baptism with a flow of blood, and as he confessed, he entered into paradise with the Lord, dressed in purple. This is a true case of penitence, this is a special, legal definition of confession, if you should believe that the Son of God, whom you know to be our Creator, is our judge also, as he himself says: 'For the Father judges no man, but has given all judgment unto the Son,' and to obtain hope of perpetual salvation, he does not consider his present life but thinks about a future judgment.[60]

For at the first sight of the judge the condemned man exposed himself, and confessed his crimes, fulfilling the office of penitence. Then when he saw the punishment of the cross, he realized that the judgment was the same for the man fixed beside him, but not its cause. But then he believed that he was God, when the Jews had persistently rejected him. And not forgetting the future on the cross of justice, he commended his memory to the judgment of the man about to reign. The gospel makes this clear: 'But the other malefactor answering rebuked him, saying, "Do you not fear God, seeing that you are in the same condemnation? And we indeed justly, as we receive the due reward of our deeds; but this man has done nothing evil." And he said to Jesus: "Lord, remember me when you come into your kingdom." '[61] Be quick to see what he deserved, what he heard from the mouth of Truth, and what he accepted, thanks to the judgment: 'Verily I say unto you, today you will be with me in Paradise.'

---

[60] *John* 5.22.
[61] *Luke* 23.42.

Chapter 12

But you say to me: 'I have added sins to sins, and have been upright but am now falling, and again I have fallen, and a wound on my conscience now almost cured, has broken out again with the exulceration of sinfulness.' Why are you nervous? Of what are you afraid? He is always the same who cured you before, you will not change your doctor. He will not labor to explore the cause of your sickness, nor will he try to examine the strength of some new medicine, but he will cure you with a well-known antidote. He does not wait for an experiment of an assistant, as he knows the source of your weakness. From what you have been cured in the past, from that you will be cured once more. And you will not be suspect over a remedy that cures you, and the doctor will be without concern over your renewal. He will find fault with your intemperance, quite clearly, and he will attack your impatience with a harsh reproof, but he will not deny you help, as he does not despise the sick man. Hear the prophet saying: 'Will he not help him who sleeps to arise?'[62] And if a man has been shipwrecked, does he not sail a ship in like manner? Or one who has lost his harvest, is he without hope once and for all, does he not either plough or sow once more?

This voyage of ours is tossed about on some worldly ocean, and we have to navigate, and sails must be placed on the masts' stretchers. A storm rages, the wind rises up, the tempest is savage. But if you hold on to the rudder in such a way that you do not release your ship's hawsers, you will reach port, with profits unimpaired. But if however, with the waves in your face, you are driven on to rocks that envelop you, and are obstructed by blasts of wind, and you are shipwrecked among the clashing straits of a swollen flood, then must you go back to the Subura[63] and the first task is repairing the ship and purchasing the goods, and again one must undergo dangers, and past disasters must be refunded through law suits. And so that you may recover what you have lost, you will not hesitate to entrust yourself to the former danger with uncertain hope. For without doubt you will become a beggar, if after shipwreck you are unwilling to return to the practice of business. Nor will you be able afterwards to complain about your need and hardships, if caught by the misfortune of shipwreck, due to

---

[62] *Psalms* 41[40].8.

[63] It was the main shopping district (of Rome). The text has *saburram* ('sand'), which does not agree with *redeundum* and 'ballast' is certainly not the first requirement, anyway.

190 C. Victor of Cartenna

the stupidity of sloth you are made a beggar by the calamity.[64]And if this is the concern of a worldly businessman that usually, after the loss of a shipwreck, he would not despair of restoring his past losses through industrious exertion. And if stripped of funds by attacks on him, he does not let his shortage be detected, but is keen to increase his funds more from a small start, and with doubtful hopes he strives to acquire greater profits, as his sinfulness increases. How much more should you think about the losses to your soul, and you should recover from perdition instantly, wherein the losses of future hopes are counted, and the search for eternal life is unhappily thrown away.

Chapter 13

You must go to the money-chest of a suitable banker, and offering the interest of penitence and usury for satisfaction, write a promissory note and provide a signature, and from him buy for yourself glowing gold, as a gift for God, and fill your ship with goods of whatever sort, if not precious, and spend your fortune in buying that precious pearl, with which you might decorate the baseness of your soul, so that when you come to a great city, where your goods are offered for sale, you are more equipped with quite valuable riches and very costly goods. For if stupid sloth overcomes you, and bodily laziness begins to overcome your senses, and you seek no arguments for the restoration of your soul, you will be subjected to the creditor's tortures and will be detained as answerable to the money-lender. That noble sentence will be given, and you will be unable to escape it, conscious of yourself, nor could you suspend it by interjecting with an appeal: 'Unto everyone that has shall be given, and he shall have abundance, but from him that hath not shall be taken away even that which he has;' and, 'cast you the unprofitable servant into the outer darkness; there shall there be weeping and gnashing of teeth.'[65]

You are not to be allowed to wear your tunic, made by the weaving of the cheapest worker, and your clothing, ugly with stains, looks horrible to you. And yet does your soul not seem horrible to you, as it has been polluted by sordid sins and defiling crimes? Except that, at that very moment, you quickly wash your tunic, so that you may put it on nice and clean and without any foul spots. But do you not want to recover the candor of your soul, when infected with the foulness of crimes, do you not hope for your

---

[64] Reading *mendicus* with *efficiaris*, rather than the text's *mendici*.
[65] *Matthew* 25.29-30.

Arians and Vandals of the 4th-6th Centuries

conscience to be washed clean, when you know that it is muddy with the filth of sins and contamination of crimes? Who, I ask, collapses and does not try to get up? Who is sick and does not want to regain his health? Who is in danger and does not hope to escape? Who is brought to poverty and does not desire to recover his patrimony? If the nature of things allows this, that for disasters of that sort that emerge, some cannot return to the condition of their former state, vie with previous acts to perceive the worse ones, drop your hands and close your eyes, foolishly half-awake, fall asleep, never to be wakeful, lie down, never to get up and destroy your mind, sluggish with the stupor of sleep. Afterwards you will repent over your stupidity, when you can think of nothing that may benefit your soul. You will always be lying down as an invalid, naked, worn out by poverty and, so to speak, intoxicated with the drunkenness of sleep, and you will hear that phrase which you should never forget: 'They have slept their sleep, and they have found nothing.'[66]

Rise up, my brother, rise up and drive out the torpor of an insane counsel. Be vigilant, always be vigilant, and be concerned over your salvation, not so as to sleep without hope. Beware the thief at night, in case he digs through the wall of your home, and avoid the man shooting a flying arrow at midday, for careless security is wide open to incursions, and a man sleeping is easily robbed and struck a deadly blow. Confidence is in wakefulness, there is no safety in sleep. It suits a sober mind to have sleep as its servant, not its master. An enemy flees from a man he does not find asleep. 'And blessed is that servant whom his lord shall find watchful when he comes,' as he said: 'Awake from that sleep, and arise from the dead,' and come to Christ.[67]

Chapter 14

But I do not dare to pray, you will say, because my conscience holds me back. For not once, but more often and frequently have I erred. But I shall say: 'If embarrassment over praying holds you back, end the constancy of your sinning and there will be a benefit from your fear, not a hopeless case of which you are afraid. For to fear the power of the Judge, will not be a sign of embarrassment, but a sign of shame. For although freedom to sin may be frequent, yet a conscience becomes excusable that timidity endures in a sinner's memory. Let Ahab show you the example of

---

[66] *Psalms* 76(75).5.
[67] *Matthew* 24.46 and *Ephesians* 5.14.

192 C. Victor of Cartenna

a most impious king. For this king coveted the vineyard of Naboth the Jezreelite, as it bordered on his own property.[68] He offered a price, or certainly a substitute amount of vineyard, but Naboth ignored the offer, asserting that he could not for any reason transfer his inheritance to another person. Irritated by this repulse, the king returned home sadly, as his keen desire had proved fruitless.

Then his wife, the sacrilegious Jezebel, asked the reason for her husband's sadness, and when she found out, she provided the tinder of consolation, as it were, for his wounded heart. Through the cunning counsel of the impure woman, several calumnies were produced, and the innocent Naboth was stoned to death. After completing the crime of her deadly vow, the woman went to her husband as if victorious, to describe to him her joy over the death of the slain man. And so that she would not be involved alone in the crime, the cunning of the first born woman brought it about that she forced her husband to be privy to the crime, and a single chain of crime bound two guilty partners in marriage.[69] She said: 'Arise, take possession of the vineyard of Naboth the Jezreelite, which he refused to give you for money; for behold he is dead.'[70] But he was upset over providing the occasion for the murdered man's death and was horrified at the reports of the crime, and acquired the reason for the man's death with tearful grief. For tearing apart his royal garments, he clothed himself in funereal clothing, which attested not so much to his conscience of guilt as to his penitence over his first thoughts. 'And it came to pass, when Ahab heard that Naboth the Jezreelite was dead, he rent his clothes and put sackcloth on his body.' And so Ahab could be free of the blame for the shedding of blood, because he had been penitent over the purpose, not over the murder, but for the profane woman, the impious act of homicide had remained, as she thought she was right to buy the vineyard with a payment of bloodshed. But behold, just as the dog returns to its vomit, he became hateful.

Ahab forgot his penitence, and giving up his grief at once, went on to possess the vineyard of the dead man. And he lost his merit of innocence, for he was enticed by his desire for the vineyard and joined his consent to the killing of the slain man. Soon the venerable Prophet Elijah gave God's

---

[68] See *1 Kings* 21.1-29 for the story of Naboth, Ahab and Jezebel – or in the text Achab and Jezabel. The prophet below, Elijah the Tishbite, appears as Elias.

[69] The usual attack on Eve, here a prototype for the murderous Jezebel.

[70] From *1 Kings* 21.15. The following quotation from this story is misleading, combining vv 16 and 27 (when Elijah had passed on the Lord's chilling message).

Arians and Vandals of the 4th-6th Centuries 193

command to him, and a sentence was indignantly brought against him, demanding that his former repentance be annulled and that the double presumption of his crime provide a reason for his punishment. And Elijah said to Ahab: 'So says the Lord. Behold, I bring evil upon you, and I shall take away your posterity, and I shall cut off from Ahab him who pisses against the wall, and he who is despised and left in Israel. And I shall make the house of Ahab like the house of Jeroboam the son of Nabat, and like the house of Baasha the son of Ahijah, for all those things with which you provoked me and made Israel sin.'[71] But once the king was unable to escape the impact of the sentence, he suddenly changed his mind to his former penitence, confessing his guilt with tears, and he reduced his royal rule with a goat's hair shirt, put on a sackcloth of penitence, and fearing the face of the man threatening him, with a silent groan made his offence public and did not excuse his conscience. He said: 'It came to pass, when Ahab heard these words, he humbled himself before the face of the Lord, and went weeping and rent his clothes and put sackcloth on his flesh. Then the Lord said to Elijah: Did you see how Ahab humbled himself before my face? I shall bring no evil in his days, but in his son's days I shall bring it.'[72]

See how reverence made him fearful, and how great his severity was that was broken by his fear! Not through a pompous speech, nor polished words, nor copious eloquence did he please God, but with many tearful prayers. His mouth was silent but his heart groaned, he wept with his eyes and mourned in his conscience, and the Creator's piety applauded the shame of his repentance. It was insufficient for the defendant to have escaped his due penalty, if his laudable reverence had not accepted a witness. And he who was condemned for a crime was praised for his fear. And his mourning before the death of the slain man was significant. But he purged a sin often repeated with a repeated lamentation.

---

[71] Again from the same story, vv 21-22, adapted, with different spellings for Baasha (Baasa) and Ahija (Abiae), and with *Deum* for *me*.
[72] Adapted from *1 Kings* 21.15, vv 27-29.

Chapter 15

King Manasseh, the son of Hezechiah,[73] deserves to be mentioned, as he surpassed the audacity of all the profane. Turning his impious hands against God, and degenerating from his father's morality, he madly erected a cult of idols for all to worship, without exception. This man, possessed by sacrilegious madness, erected altars of execrable superstition, polluted them with statues of devils, filled the church's holy high altars with stone figures, worshipped a grove, dedicated his sons to a profane fire, sought out auguries, defiled his life with evil deeds, led his people to the worship of idols, polluted them with his rites, delivered them up to the devil, and practiced everything banned by divine laws, going beyond all the insolence of a desperate mind.

Because of the great number and seriousness of these sins, he was taken in war and bound with chains and weighed down with fetters, as he endured the punishment of captivity. He was transported to Babylon and paid the penalty for his impiety, brought to a realization of divine punishment, which he did not remember having endured before. Finally, when struck by an appropriate whip, he was converted, and recognized God when in a state of punishment, whom he had not sought before, while placed on the throne. Affliction assisted his desperation and his wickedness was corrected as he realized it from the painful correction. That punishment cured his lost mind and the beating contributed greatly to his salvation, as it struck the impious man to such an extent that it made him acceptable to God, although the devil had made him another's property through his impotence. And what was inflicted on his vanity helped his soul to recover.

Faith in the Lord's Scripture admits this: 'And the Lord spoke, he said, against Manasseh, and bound him with chains and fetters and led him into Babylon. And soon, when afflicted, he besought the Lord his God, and was greatly humiliated before the face of the God of his fathers, and he prayed to God, and the Lord heard him and called him back to Jerusalem, to his throne. And Manasseh knew that the Lord he was God. Behold,

---

[73] The son of the pious Hezekiah, Manasseh succeeded him as king of Judah (697 to 642), but he was guilty of idolatry and wickedness, until a captive in Babylon, where he repented. The 'Prayer of Hezekiah' is apocryphal. The text has Manasses and '*filius Ezechiae.*' For Hezekiah's good reign, see *2 Kings* 18-20. For his son's idolatry, see *2 Kings* 21.1-18, and *2 Chronicles* 33.1-20 also (for his conversion).

with how much sudden lamentation did he weep for his sin with a converted heart, and atoned for it, and wiped clean with his tears the wickedness that he had done. But he prayed conscious of his guilt, and deserved to purchase his pardon with satisfaction, to such an extent that he restored to their former veneration those sacred objects that he had polluted before with the contamination of a profane act. Through the consummation of his conversion, that prophetic oracle of the divine mouth was implemented: 'When you have been converted and have mourned, then will you be saved.'[74]

Chapter 16

But why should I mention those kings, whose laudable origin from a chosen race did not allow them to depart from a city of holy religion, despite most wicked persuasion? Although that deadly and alien prince, Nebuchadnezzar, was penalized by divine punishment, so that through corrective punishment he would be forced to acknowledge Him whom he had dared to reject with his violation of sacred things, and would believe in Him with his virtues whom he had not known before, due to the ferocity of his spirit. This went so far that he who had not feared before to proclaim himself as a god, puffed up as he was by his most vigorous spirit, did not dare afterwards to lie about His incomparable majesty. For corrected with great admiration for what was done to him, he did not cease to confess the true God alone with all his heart and with decrees publicly proclaimed.

But if you fear to pray, due to your bad conscience, you have the teaching of the publican. Although of a suspect race,[75] when you pray over your sins, do you not deserve to be heard? When he had entered the temple, with his neck bent down under a mass of sins, and with the eyelids of both eyes held tight shut with a heavy illness of wickedness, he did not dare to look up to Heaven. He fearfully stepped back and placed himself at the very rear, not so much in a location, as in a court trying his conscience. And he did not irreverently push himself forwards for a supplication, prompted by audacity, but held back any movement of his footsteps. The publican with frequent blows on his chest reminded them shamefully that

---

[74] Adapted from *Isaiah* 30.15.
[75] The text's *suspectum generi*s agreeing with *merearis* is wrong. I suggest instead *suspecti generis* ('of a suspect race').

196 C. Victor of Cartenna

he was on trial,[76] as he chastised his guilty heart with his fist. Words were not heard from his mouth, but groans were, and his whole confession was made with only five words. The Lord manifests this in the gospel, saying: 'Two men went up into the temple to pray, and one was a pharisee, and the other a publican. And the pharisee stood, and prayed thus with himself, saying: "God, I thank you that I am not as other men are, unjust, extortionists, adulterers, or even as this publican. I fast twice on the Sabbath, and I give a tenth of all that I possess." The publican was standing far off, and would not lift up so much as his eyes unto Heaven, but smote his breast saying: "God, be merciful to me a sinner." '[77]

But notice what his reverent supplication asked from the inspector of his heart. His modesty perceived God, with a munificent reward, as he wanted to win his favor. And his modesty deserved to be justified at once, proved when he confessed so humbly, as the Lord said: 'I tell you, this man went down to his house justified, rather than that pharisee, for everyone who exalts himself shall be humbled, and he that humbles himself shall be exalted.'[78]

Chapter 17

Where then do you place the example of that sinful woman, who seemed to have exposed her crimes, not with her words but with her tears, and while her tongue was silently praying, she confessed what was on her conscience with her act of penitence? For the Lord was lying down in the home of a certain pharisee, who had prepared a temporary meal, as it were, for the person he had invited. Finding this, the woman who was a prostitute audaciously entered the home of the pharisee, and fell at the feet of the Lord lying there, and washed his holy feet with her tears and dried them with her hair, and kissed their soles incessantly, and soaked his feet with precious ointment, and she washed clean the stains of her sins with almost all the parts of her body with which she had sinned before. Then the Lord, before whom our bones have been separated, spoke through his prophet: 'All my bones shall say, Lord, who is like unto you?[79] The pharisee's murmur chides the woman's hidden plan, but the Lord praises

---

[76] The text in Migne cannot be construed properly (*publicans verecundiam reum pectus percussum crebro*). I suggest an improvement on the earlier editors with *publicanus se verecundia reum pectoris percussione crebra.*

[77] Taken with minor changes from the parable in *Luke* 18.10-13.

[78] *Luke* 18.14.

[79] *Psalms* 35[34].10.

Arians and Vandals of the 4th-6th Centuries 197

her obvious faith with remarkable approval, and prefers her humble confession to his host's apparatus, delighted more by the woman's action than by the meal, as he preferred to be pleased by her conversion rather than be fed, for he is not influenced at all by a desire for food, but would feed on the feast of a confession, saying: 'Do you see this woman? I entered into your house and you gave me no kiss, no water for my feet, but from the time she came in, she has not ceased kissing my feet. You did not anoint my head with oil, but this woman has anointed my feet with ointment. Wherefore I say unto you, her sins, which are many, are forgiven, because she loved greatly.' And turning to the woman he said: 'Your sins are forgiven.' Is this a small thing? But see what she heard afterwards: 'Daughter, your faith has saved you, go in peace.'[80]

The young woman, a long time sinner, was soon forgiven, and when forgiven she was quickly transferred to the peace of the Lord. after she had been devastated by the battle with her own crimes. This is that prophetic oracle: 'When you have converted and have lamented, then will you be saved,'[81] and again: 'First describe your iniquities that you may be justified.'[82] And so, when you realize from all of these different documents that He is delighted by a sacrifice of penitence, you should not fear that the reward for a contrite heart and humbled spirit might vanish before a pious judge, just as the Scripture tells us: 'The sacrifice to God is a broken spirit, God does not despise a contrite and humble heart.'[83] Why do you not hasten to emerge from the depths of luxuries and from the whirlpool of earthly pleasure, and to cease from drunken acts so as to enjoy the duties of penitence? Nor should you think because you have removed yourself far from God, for that reason his ear is closed to you. Soon he will open the doorway when you have knocked on it, and showing pity he will include you in his enclosed court, to be pitied. The further you have removed yourself the more quickly will He come close, as the prophet says: 'God is close unto them that are of a broken heart, and will save those of a contrite spirit.'[84] About this, the Lord God says in the gospel: 'Blessed are they that mourn, for they shall be comforted.'[85]

---

[80] Adapted from *Luke* 7.44-50.

[81] Adapted to suit his argument, from *Isaiah* 30.15 (Vulgate: *si revertamini et quiescatis, salvi eritis*. There is no sign of any lamentation).

[82] Again adapted from *Isaiah* 43.26 (Vulgate *narra si quid habes ut justificeris*).

[83] *Psalms* 51.17[50.19].

[84] *Psalms* 34.18[33.19].

[85] *Matthew* 5.4.

Chapter 18

But penitence seems bitter to you after secular pleasures. It is true, I sense the damage to your health, I see the illness of your mind, but if you desire to be cured, you should not wait for an attack on your healing nor be afraid of a remedy. When He applies a knife to your wound, the cutting causes a quicker cure. For a careful cure is very badly handled, unless the suppurating decay is cut out at once. The taste of an antidote is bitter, but what is rough on the throat provides a healthy life. The Lord cures us, but not as foreigners, though he will preserve for himself whatever foreign sinners he cures. At every hour, on every day, he is intent on curing people, nor is he impeded by any delays that get in his way. His virtue is then clearly impeded, when he cannot find anyone to cure. For the Lord's kindness must be absent when no one exists needing pity.

The punishment in penitence is rough, but it becomes smoother if the manner of the fault should be dealt with. Ambition over earthly pomp has long since delighted you, and secular tyranny has claimed you as its slave, now languid in luxury, now sunk in wine-bibbing. Some have seen you intent in the harassed manner of a gamester, others have seen your gluttony, others your addiction to whores, those have seen that you have sold yourself to brothels, are soaked with perfumes and smeared with spices, and they saw you infected with foreign eye-shadow. You were resplendent in your robes, glowing with gold and decorated with jewels and most precious pearls. Therefore, restore state for state, and at least belatedly pay compensation of time for time; separate your life alternately in each action with equal moderation. You then belonged to the devil, now belong to God, or rather be yourself now as you were a stranger formerly. And if perhaps you were to consider it, you have wasted a great deal of time, so that a short time reduces the little left.

Take time off now for yourself, not for a time; take time off, I said, not to be idle but to pursue the business of confession. Revert to the path from the byways of which you had strayed, and seek the losses that you had made. First find yourself as you were, so that you find what you seek. And if you find yourself, seek nothing from yourself. Put on sackcloth and sprinkle it with ashes, pray always while fasting, fast while preaching. These are more precious, with which the body is affected, so that the beauty of the mind may be regained. A humble vest looks rough, but this is extremely proper, as it is not displeasing to God. The body's clothing is cheap, but it is the special attire of holiness. And would you perhaps now

Arians and Vandals of the 4th-6th Centuries   199

ask about the indignity of the clothing, if you had lost your wedding garment? And when you appear ugly with your foul nakedness, do you not think how you should be clothed continually? Do not fear, I beg you, that when the man invited to the royal dinner has entered with the garment, you may be driven from the group of diners, reproached with a similar condemnation, and hear it being said to you: 'Friend, how came you in here not having a wedding garment?' And when you do not find an argument to excuse yourself, he would say: 'Bind him hand and foot and take him away, and cast him into outer darkness, and there shall be weeping and gnashing of teeth.'[86]

Chapter 19

But I believe that you doubt whether clothing that has been lost cannot be found again, or that when you seek it, it can be refused by the person who had recently given it. See in the gospel, that the younger son who has wasted his patrimony and is begging, has been brought to such a pass that he was willing to be a swineherd, due to his pressing need.[87] Worn out by an extreme lack of food and poverty, since he was not even allowed to feed on the husks of the swine, he reverted to his early health of mind as he began to burn with desire for his former way of life, and thinking of the abundance of his father's home, he started to condemn his guilt with a consideration of conversion. And so, having penitential thoughts at last and speaking to himself with a private feeling of satisfaction, he returned to his father's household gods, a naked exile, as if by right of return. Then that father, who had seen the decision made in his son's heart, before his lost son could pour forth words of confession, anticipated the affection of the grieving boy, and raised him compassionately as he returned. He fell on his neck and reconciled him with kisses, and the father assured him wonderfully as he was fearful and silent. But that most contented and penitent son, and splendid confessor, secure in his father's promise, and still suspect for his own satisfaction, opened a well thought out order of confession, explaining with words what he had pondered over in his heart: 'Father, I have sinned against Heaven and in your sight and am now unworthy to be called your son. Make me as one of your hired servants.'[88] So the father was placated by the prayers of his confession, and ordered the best robe to be brought, and told them to dress his bare body at once,

---

[86] *Matthew* 22.13. It ends: 'For many are called, but few are chosen.'
[87] All this section is a paraphrase of the parable of the two sons in *Luke* 15.11-32.
[88] Combined from *Luke* 15.19 and 21.

200 C. Victor of Cartenna

as the boy's garment had recently been lost. He ordered them to give him a ring also, renewing his seal with its sign, and enclosed his feet with the protection of slippers,[89] and for his son's restoration he ordered a fatted calf to be slaughtered, that is, he ordered a most welcome sacrifice to be offered for their reconciliation, which would have been acceptable in Heaven and the angelic host.

His more severe perseverance had aroused his elder brother to hatred of his blood brother, and as elder son he spoke against him, criticizing his crimes as he was received. But his commission was not revoked, the father's piety did not alter, his brother was defended, the son was made an heir; and he aroused full affection in his father for himself, as he showed perfect judgment in his penitence. 'I am delighted, he said, and I rejoice, because this your brother had been dead, and is alive again, and he was lost, and is found.'[90] And so you see that, when the son was converted, a pristine robe was restored by the merchandise of penitence, and that the father celebrated with all his prayers the return of the son who confessed. For his lost patrimony would affect his oath of baptism, on which all the buildings of the heavenly kingdoms are based. That son, a faithful Christian obtaining freedom from his father, had lost this through the contagion of lust and luxury, and placed far from his God, had polluted himself quite foully with his shameful acts, and as servant of the devil, to whom he had given himself through his most abandoned way of life, began to pasture swine, that is unclean spirits, and when he was not allowed to feed on their food, because through the tightness of his flesh, he could not be fed on devilish husks, and deserted on both sides, and destitute in every way, he was worn out and fatigued by lack of good fruit. But returning home, he received at once everything of which he had been deprived, and the substance of his former possession remained, ascribed to his father's concord. Therefore you return too, brother, return, and from being dead be alive again, and renew yourself from what you have lost.[91]

---

[89] The *praeceptorum* ('of teachers') is very strange, and it suggests a scribal error, an anagram of the far more likely *crepidarum* ('slippers'), for the *calceamenta* in the Vulgate text.

[90] *Luke* 15.24 and 32.

[91] After the imperative *revivisce* I suggest that the final words should read *repara te* ('renew yourself'), rather than the infinitive *repara-re*.

Arians and Vandals of the 4th-6th Centuries 201

Chapter 20

The good shepherd searches for his lost sheep, and is more delighted over its discovery than over those that are not lost.[92] He bears it back on his shoulders and replaces it in the company of its flock, and shuts it in the lodging-place of its former security. He does not attend to the main body of those left, as he seeks to complete the entire hundred with the return of the one lost sheep. A woman searched for a lost drachma energetically, and lit a lamp, and cleaned her house with a broom, and she invited those who were dear to her and her neighbours equally for the joy over finding the silver coin. And does anyone think that God is not delighted over the restoration of a convert, when he considers a parable especially suited to the person showing penitence? As he himself says: 'I say to you, so there will be joy in the presence of the angels of God over one sinner that repents.'[93] But notice that singular comment of the Lord, as he said: 'They that be whole, need not a physician, but they that are sick. For I have not come to call the righteous, but sinners to repentance.'[94] So the Lord summons sinners to repentance, and our physician hopes to help those sickly rather than the healthy. But he does not therefore ignore the just, because he welcomes sinners. For the life of the just is a heavenly vocation, just as the man who looked for one lost sheep left ninety-nine sheep behind on the mountains, to confer a benefit of mercy on them. The apostle proves this, saying: 'But to him who does not work, but believes in him who justifies the ungodly, his faith is counted for justice, following his proposal of grace.'[95]

Finally, when you hear with what javelins the Lord strikes the hearts of the sinners in the gospel, you will understand how highly he valued the sacrament of penitence, as he says: 'There were present some who told him of the Galilaeans, whose blood had mingled with their sacrifices. Then Jesus said unto them: Do you suppose that these Galilaeans were sinners above all Galilaeans, because they suffered such things? I tell you, unless you repent, you shall all perish likewise. Or those eighteen, upon whom the tower of Siloam fell and killed them, do you suppose that they were sinners above all men who dwelt in Jerusalem? I say unto you, unless you repent, you shall all perish like them.'[96] And so as to prove his

---

[92] For the 'lost sheep' parable, see *Luke* 15.4-7, and for the lost silver coin, 8-9.
[93] *Luke* 16.10.
[94] *Matthew* 9.12-13.
[95] *Romans* 4.5.
[96] *Romans* 4.5.

202   C. Victor of Cartenna

case, he added an example beneath this for a comparison, mentioning the fig tree, which when sterile of fruit and unfruitful is ordered to be cut down, but the farmer intervened, and was allowed to put off its demise, while by digging around it with suitable cultivation and applying a basket of dung, a delay would be made to produce the fruit of penitence.[97] Furthermore, if that tree which had not produced any fruit of its kind was ordered to be cut down before that time, with what sort of implement should it now be chopped down, or cut with an axe, if it was covered by thorn-bushes and choked by various types of bramble, and had no cultivation in its restoration? For the example of the tree is similar to the man of faith, who deprived of the fruit of his faith, thought of nothing that would benefit him with a hopefully profitable future. For it had been planted in a vineyard, and the vineyard specially denotes the Church, in which that tree had been planted. But the cultivator of this vineyard seems to express the person of that priest, who would make use of a trench for an unfruitful nursery, using the cultivation of the Lord's precepts. And the practice of penitence is signified by the basket of manure. But if after a long wait, fruit could not be found in the vineyard at all, in future vines should be torn out by the roots and left to dry, that is, cut off for a future judgment, as if a worthless block of useless wood, and would burn, turned into the fodder of eternal fire. And yet this could be understood about Christ also and about the Jewish people.

Chapter 21

I believe that it has been sufficiently and abundantly clear to your senses, through these proofs which we put forward with a great devotion to the infirm to arouse and encourage your mind, that God, the fountain of mercy, does not want to have the destruction of sinners, but rather the correction of sin, in such a way that the greater the amount of offences, the more penitence is in action. The man who has returned should not despair of a quick renewal of himself, as he hears the Lord himself encouraging the sinner to repent. The Revelation of John the Divine explains this more clearly, in which he accuses the Churches' angels of yielding to laments of penitence when deceived by early errors. For the Lord is thus proved to desire the ruin of no man, as he presses penitence on the person falling. Finally, he says to the angel of the Church of Ephesus: 'Remember from where you have fallen, and repent, and do the first works; or else I shall come unto you, and I shall move your candlestick out of its place, unless

---

[97] The barren fig-tree parable appears in *Luke* 13.6-9.

you repent.'[98] And yet, behold, the angel is mentioned to whom the care of penitence and conversion is entrusted, and is persuaded to complete her prior works, so that it is made known that she has lost nothing from all of her merits.

But there is a graver threat in warning someone who does not repent, if one puts up with the obstinacy of a hardened person. For the severity of the punishment will be inexcusable, if the first correction does not bend an ungovernable neck; and the man reminded beforehand by the authority of one threatening him, will perish through his wickedness, by not subjecting his most vigorous neck to the yoke of satisfaction. He certainly claims that the man will return to his past state, who is corrected by the proper humility of a confession, to run the course of a true life. This is declared more fully a little further on, when the angel of the church of Thyatira is chastised by a stinging rebuke, saying: 'I have many things against you, because you suffered that woman Jezebel, who calls herself a prophetess, and teaches and seduces my servants to commit fornication and to eat from things sacrificed. And I gave her time to show repentance, and she was unwilling to repent of her fornications; and I shall put her into a bed, and those who commit adultery with her will be in great tribulation, unless they repent of all their deeds. And I shall kill her children with a sword, and all the churches will know that I am the searcher of heart and loins, and I return to each of you according to your works.'[99]
But what could be said more humanely, what more mercifully? As he said: 'And I gave her time to show repentance, and she was unwilling to repent.' You do not have any excuse, sinner, you do not have any; there is none if you are doubtful with a reason, there is none if you despair without a good reason. With these examples, gird yourself to make your confession, with these proofs arm yourself for penitence.

Chapter 22

For the Lord puts off punishing so as to find penitence, and while using periods of time, he delays suffering, so that his clemency does not lose what ought to become censure. He does not look at past bad deeds nor corrects mistakes, but applauds what is corrected. You have a promise, as he persuades you to repent, if you are not punished, he will credit it to you. 'And he gave her time to show repentance,' he said, 'and she was

---

[98] *Revelation (or Apocalypse) of John the Divine* 2.5.
[99] Adapted from *Jeremiah* 3.7.

204   C. Victor of Cartenna

unwilling to repent.' Similar to this is that prophesy: 'And I said after she had committed all these fornications: "Turn to me," and she was unwilling to turn to me.' But if you hurl yourself into an abyss of despair, whirled around by the enormity of your sins, or hesitate to root out your pile of wealth with a restrained step on your journey, or declining more downward with the collapse of a perverse mind, you produce decadent steps with a slippery motion, then instantly your hope of renewal is snatched away and lost, a sucking whirlpool of crimes will pull you into its gulf,[100] and your eyes will be closed with the night of sin, so that they cannot see the gleaming beam of the true light. The blindness of death will present itself, and through some trickery the deceiving angels will lead you around from here and from there. All the sins will become welcome to you, and the freedom to sin will be wholly pleasing to you; the devil will hold you addicted to his sort of freedom, so that you are free to sin, but not to live.[101]

The devil will not let you look back to what you were before, when he has called you away most deceitfully with the charm of sinning and the sweetness of crime. And to say it just once, he will so deceive you with the pleasantness of dying, that it seems more pleasant for you to die, than return to God. For no sin is committed without its delightfulness, and it cannot otherwise ensnare the mind unless it entices with the sweetness of desire the person it would deceive. For it is necessary for the deadly preparation of a lethal cup to be a sweet and smooth mixture to the throat, so that a first taste of bitterness does not warn off the drinker.

Thus finally that tree's poison seemed good to the very first woman to look at, and sweet to taste, and after she had lied about this sweetness on her lips as she ate it, its subtle violence infected her swallowing, as she lost her spiritual life, and destroyed what was still vigorous and full of life. As her prayers relapsed in the opposite way through lack of control, He ejected her from her blessed paradise and her secure estate, to an exile in the world as a spectacle for all time.[102]

---

[100] The imagery closely echoes the terrifying Charybdis in Virgil *Aeneid* 3.422.

[101] Following the editors' *diabolus suae libertati addictum*. Minge's text is weak.

[102] As usual, Eve is condemned rather than the lying snake, and 'woman' becomes a spectacle, guilty for evermore.

Chapter 23

I beg you, brother, fear this, flee from it and be terrified by it. Do not allow an enemy to rejoice over your perdition, or to raise a victorious eyebrow in the sight of God. Beware of the return of the seven unclean spirits, to which the eighth joined himself, as prince of all evils. And since nobody puts up with even one demon, who could bear to be dominated by eight? As the Lord says: 'When the unclean spirit has gone out of a man, he walks through dry places seeking rest, and finds none. Then he says: "I will return to my house, from which I came out." And when he is come, he finds it empty, swept and in good order. Then he goes and takes with him seven other spirits wickeder than himself, and they enter in and dwell there. And the last state of that man will be worse than the first.'[103]

If a hostile force had trapped you, when surrounded by a military blockade, and under a barbaric attack a robber's troop had held you captive,[104] what groans would you utter, what cries would you give what laments would you emit? You would utter sighs all day and night, would not seek food, would not miss drinking, and exhausted by thirst and worn out by hunger, on you just dryness of rough skin would appear, and a wrinkled thinness, your hair would be stiff, thick with filth, and the rough hair on your stiffened head and limbs marked with a long beard would look terrible. Under the sword of the man who is releasing you, you would give him your inheritance, and hesitating, you would walk about naked, poor and stripped of every sense. You would have tried to escape, or if an opening were offered for flight, uncertain and at great risk you would ponder how to overcome the danger.

The source of crimes holds you captive, not with iron chains, but he has you bound with the fetters of criminality. He has placed shackles of lust on you, and on all sides has surrounded you with a tighter guard. He has given you a law that you think everything legal that is not allowed. A pit of eternal death has submerged you while still alive. And do you not groan over the damage to your salvation, the loss of eternal hope and loss of eternal life? You walk along decked with a fine array of clothes, you frequent dinner-parties with opulent food, you are drunk with wine, you make your soul fat with daily feasts, and you do not stop cultivating the

---

[103] *Matthew* 12.43-45.

[104] I propose reading *turma* rather than the *urna* in all the MSS and the text, its sense of 'urn' or metaphorical 'fate' far from appropriate here. With the very appropriate but technical term *turma* 'troop,' the *t* could have easily dropped out.

206 C. Victor of Cartenna

gluttony of a fleshy body; as for your other crimes, I'll keep quiet about them for the moment. Do you think also, do you imagine that this is not a sign of heavenly punishment, in that you know not how you should repent over your sins? The apostle approves, as he says: 'As they did not retain God in their knowledge, He gave them over to a reprobate mind, to do what is not convenient,' and again, 'because they received not the love of the truth, that they might be saved, for this cause God sent them strong delusion, that they might be damned, as they did not believe the truth.'[105] From comments like these the apostle was finally afraid that on reaching Corinth, he would join many from these who showed no penitence over the unclean acts they did, and fornication and lasciviousness.[106]

Chapter 24

Think of the sumptuous dinners of that wealthy man, and the abundant affluence of his rich banquets, as clothed in purple, a richer purple, and bright woven silk, he deals totally with the hope of present time, but not at all with the future. Hear what is reserved for him after all those luxuries. After purple, a flame, after banquets, indigence, so that he seeks a miserable drop of water, who before had drained a draught of precious nectar, and sought from it, but did not receive, the solace of the tip of a damp finger, to which he had denied the crumbs of his own feasts in his lifetime. Confess, I beg you, everything of which you remember you are guilty, confess, and come before the face of God with satisfactory service, humble your heart before him and bend your neck in his sight; bend your knees and fall to the ground striking your face. That heavenly Advocate will at once accept your groan, and will not put off addressing his Father for your sake, as He has grown accustomed to providing a sure patronage for the penitent. He will not plead his case with proofs, with a prescribed style of eloquence, but he will at once obtain the benefit of a pardon, as God would not expect any fee from a defeated client. The apostle proves this, saying: 'Who will accuse against God's elect? It is God who justifies. Who is he that condemns? It is Christ that died, but also that is risen again, who is at the right hand of God, who also makes intercession for us.' The most blessed Apostle John placed this in his letter, agreeing with him, and said: 'If we say that we have no sin, we deceive ourselves and the truth is not in us, but if we confess our sins, God is faithful and

---

[105] The first quote is from *Romans* 1.28, the second, *II Thessalonians* 2. 10-12, a rather free adaptation.
[106] See *II Corinthians* 12.21.

Arians and Vandals of the 4th-6th Centuries 207

just to forgive us our sins, and to cleanse us from all unrighteousness. If we say that we have not sinned, we make Him a liar, and his Word is not in us. My little children, these things I write unto you, that you sin not. And if any man sin, we have an advocate with the Father, Jesus, and he is the propitiation for our sins.'[107]

Everything said by the Son of God, the Lord Jesus Christ, who is the way, the truth and the light, is the law, and by his example he taught us that what he entrusted to us in the Scripture took place, for He would not want anything to be done by us which he either did not do himself, or about which he would not be pleased if we were doing it. But what he himself had commanded could not be displeasing, because he would have done first what he had commanded. For the command's learning would become futile, if in the deed the authority of the teacher did not come first. But whatever the Lord has ordered and has done, will not be futile, as he ordered that it should be done through imitating him. And so the same Lord put forward these words for his disciples to guard: 'Take heed to yourselves; if your brother sins against you, forgive him; and if he sins against you seven times in a day, and seven times turns again to you saying: "I repent," forgive him, and he will be forgiven by you.'[108] And when He had been consulted over a case, by the Holy Apostle Peter, and said: 'Lord, if my brother sinned against me, how many times shall I forgive him? Up to seven times?' Jesus said unto him: 'I do not say to you up to seven times, but up to seventy times seven.'[109] Then does not God, who orders us to give a due dismissal to a brother who sins against us seven times, preserve a form of this order of his for us? Or who said: 'I want mercy more than a sacrifice.' Can He deny us a treasure house of mercifulness? As I said before, when praying for pardon, this is to believe that Lord Jesus made everything up that he taught us, if he were unwilling to look after a form of his precepts that concerned us.[110]

---

[107] The first quote is from *Romans* 8.33, the second is adapted from *I John* 1.8-10, II.1-2.

[108] From *Luke* 17.3, 4. The Vulgate reads *increpa illum* ('rebuke him.'), for the first *dimitte illi,* and does not include the last sentence (otiose).

[109] *Matthew* 18.21,22.

[110] The quotation is from the prophet *Osee* 6.6, included in the Vulgate (but not the NAB), with Victor's *sacrificium* for the Vulgate's more powerful *holocausta*.

Chapter 25

And it does well to apply to this argument a quick comparison with the parable, of course, of the two young servants, one of whom was bankrupt, due to a large debt, and was ordered to be sold together with his wife and children, and he prostrated himself before his master's feet and begged for his patience, that if allowed some time, he would have paid back all the debt, and through his master's mercifulness he would have deserved to have the debt granted to him. Under such a condition, he was kept ready for torture. But he was unwilling to pity a fellow slave who owed him money, because he forgot the benefit conferred on him very recently. He was at once handed over to the torturers, and from his torments, he repaid what he had been given to him earlier. It is from that that the Lord placed an order on prayers of this sort, as He said: 'Forgive us our debts as we forgive our debtors,'[111] so that you may know that you can be forgiven as much as you have forgiven your own debtor. Or rather, so that you seem to spare yourself, when you have pardoned another when requested. For you will be judged by your own judgment without doubt, if you yourself desire to be forgiven but are unwilling to forgive another, as the Lord says: 'With what judgment you judge, you will be judged; and with what measure your make, it shall be measured to you again.'[112]

I want you to read more attentively the beginning of the Prophet Zechariah, and there you will find what will animate you more robustly: 'The Lord,' he said, 'has been angry with our fathers with a great anger.'[113] Who would not tremble on hearing this? Who would not turn white, terrified by the thunder of this voice? Or what sense would this intimate indignation not disturb? For what state of sanity could be kept when such vehement anger of the Creator was being denounced? And it was not enough to have said 'anger,' unless 'and great' was announced, as if, supposing it was not 'great,' a somewhat milder anger could have been tolerated. But let us see what ending such a great commotion may proclaim. 'I believe,' he said, 'I shall disturb you with the tumults of war, and punish you with the savage condition of captivity, I shall affect you with famine and shake you with disease and consume you with death, the unexpected devastation by wild animals and beasts will ravage you and exile will agitate those fugitives dispersed everywhere.' For this remains

---

[111] The parable appears rather differently in *Matthew* 18.23-34, as there the first of the slaves has his debt forgiven, until he has cast his fellow-slave into prison. The other quote is from *Matthew* 6.12.

[112] *Matthew* 7.2.

[113] *Zehariah* 1.2 with 3 below.

Arians and Vandals of the 4th-6th Centuries   209

to be understood, that great anger should be followed by a more vehement punishment. 'The Lord,' he said, 'has been angry with our fathers with a great anger, saying to them:' let us hear what he said: 'Turn unto me and I will turn unto you.' O, what indignation, flowing from piety! O, what great anger, that brings in mercy! I ask him, how does he feel pity when so angry? Or if he shows pity in this way, how is he indignantly angry? Another prophet predicts this: 'Revert, Israel, to your Lord, because you are weakened by your iniquities. Say to him: You can remit our sins, not that you accept iniquity, but that you accept goodness; and return to him the fruits of your labors,' and your heart will dine among the good. And elsewhere: 'Return,' he said, 'transgressing men,' said the Lord, and again: 'Return you backsliding children, and I will heal your backslidings.' The blessed David sang of consolations for sins in harmony with these: 'Confess to the Lord, since he is good, for his mercy endures for ever.'[114]

Chapter 26

Nor did I say this so that I should seem to have given very much looser reins to license, and under the pretext of awarding pardon divinely, to have provided more of the Creator's penitence as tinder for sinning. For with these words of mine, I lift up the one falling, and do not throw down the one standing. Nor do I make a prejudgment over innocence as I exhort a sinner to penitence. If indeed, as I have just said above, innocence exacts from God the reward owed to one's life, but penitence expects the blessing of mercy. For not sinning is being afraid, but to be penitent is more than to be afraid. For usually secure good-fortune lies under complaints, but it is made more cautious in avoiding the past, as fear improves it, because it will always be more concerned, as it takes care not to fall constantly where it has already fallen before. Even so by experiencing dangers, a helmsman is made concerned, and sometimes he fears to enter offensive ports, after he has just once sailed in one, to be secure from shipwreck. Finally the Holy Writ tells us: 'One never tried out, knows little,'[115] to show that in a case of trying something out, what is tried is always done with more caution, and a person is corrected more through fear, who before was not cautious through knowledge from trying something out. But the Lord hopes to pardon sinners as far as possible, as he does not want the death of

---

[114] The last four quotes are from *Osee* 14.2-3, *Isaiah* 46.8, *Jeremiah* 3.22 and from *Psalms* 106(105).1. The prophet Osee's adapted text in the Vulgate has *vitulos labiorum* ('the calves of your lips'), where Victor's *fructus* is preferable ('fruits').
[115] *Sirach* 34.10.

210 C. Victor of Cartenna

one dying as much as his return to faith and life. As He at once hastens to pardon those whom he has several times condemned to punishment for their sins, when interrupted by penitence. And to bury his sword in its sheath, He commutes a sentence of punishment with satisfaction.

Chapter 27

And although this was proved above from the deed of the people of Nineveh, yet accept the witness of the Prophet Jeremiah over it, so that from his testimonies a clearer example may be proved for you. He said: 'The word came to Jeremiah from the Lord, saying: "Arise and go down to the potter's house, and there you will hear my words." And I went down to the potter's house, and, behold, he was making a work on his wheels, and the vessel that he was making fell from his hands; and again he made another vessel, as it seemed good for him to do so forthwith. And the word of the Lord came to me, saying: "O house of Israel, will I not be able to fashion you like that potter? Behold, as the clay in the potter's hands, so are you in my hands, just as if I should speak about a nation or about a kingdom, to raise them up, and to destroy them, even if that nation has turned from its evil thoughts, I shall repent of the evils that I planned to do to them, and I shall not do them. Now speak to the men of Judah and to the inhabitants of Jerusalem, saying: Behold I frame evils against you, and I hatch a plan against you. Let each one of you return from his evil way, and make your thoughts better." '[116]

And so our potter persuades us to turn away from really bad ways and thoughts, so that a conversion through penitence might mould our fractures and vices into another vessel. And he does not want the substance of his work to perish in penitence, in case a sentence holds a defendant, whom a confession would excuse. With this the Wisdom of Solomon agrees, saying: 'But have mercy on all, Lord, because you can do all things, and you overlook the sins of men, for their repentance, for you can do so when you wish to, and since you are the Lord of all, you make yourself pardon all men.'[117] So let us convert, and confess to the Lord, as we live in this passage of time, and let us prepare our payment of penitence for our Judge. Do not let the careers of our time be unprofitable, nor let us live together as born for sinning, but for doing good. Or if we

---

[116] Another lengthy episode from the Hebrew Scriptures. fairly close to *Jeremiah* 18.1-11.
[117] A very free adaptation of *Wisdom* 11.23 and 27.

Arians and Vandals of the 4th-6th Centuries

are subject to sin, since it in this theatre of the world we cannot avoid sinning, let us remember ourselves, so that we long to escape from the steep descent to Hell. Let us repent, therefore, from our faith, and pray from our heart, and weep from our bowels, and as the prophet says: 'Let us worship, bow down and weep before the Lord our maker,' since 'they that sow in tears shall reap in joy.'[118] Lucky, oh all too lucky, the duty of tears, with which rewards are gathered in future time! And blessed the progeny of seed, which is poured out in weeping so as to be cut down in joy! For it has been written: 'Lucky the man who acknowledges his wailing.' Let us raise our eyes to the mountains, from where help will come for us, because 'as the eyes of servants look to the hands of their masters, and as the eyes of a slave-girl look to the hands of her mistress; so our eyes also wait upon the Lord our God, until he has mercy upon us.'[119]

Chapter 28

Let us not prolong our planned conversion with temporal delights, in such a way that with a skill in sinning and a delight in self-destruction, we sink into an abyss of crimes right up to extreme old age, since the terminus that would end the length of life allotted to us by divine consideration, would be thought uncertain. And perhaps this that is either thought the beginning or the middle of life, the limit of an imminent sunset would now settle, and the due finish for the Lord, indignant over the slowness of conversion, would be a calling. Since indeed, from its suggestion that delays in conversion should be broken, an oracle would seem to have been proposed: 'Delay not your conversion to the Lord, put it not off from day to day, for suddenly his anger will come; at the time of punishment you will be destroyed,' and again: 'My Son, if you have sinned, do so no more, but for your past sins pray to be forgiven, and do not pile sin upon sin, nor say: "The compassion of God is great; for mercy and anger are alike with him." '[120] Nor should we allow ourselves to become slaves right up to death and give up our bodies to the control of crimes, but we should obey the apostle as he says: 'Do not let sin reign in your mortal body, so that you should obey it.'[121]

---

[118] The two quotes are from *Psalms* 95(94).6 and 126(125).5.

[119] The two quotes are from *Sirach* 14.2 (partly) and *Psalms* 123(122).2.

[120] Three quotes from *Sirach*, 5.8-9, 21.1 and adapted from 5.5-7.

[121] *Romans* 6.12.

212   C. Victor of Cartenna

Although sins cannot be absent, they certainly should not reign, that is, a hasty license to sin should not be had, without considering an escape from it. Or certainly, if someone thinks that there is still time left for him to sin, and when he has had his fill of lust and his bodily strength has ordered his mind to return then to a decision of being penitent, let him establish for me the ultimate time of his life, and as he calculates it, he will have learnt, as he recommends it, he will have understood it, so that he rightly flatters himself, I must say, over a period of time. But although we may have an unexpected and terminal exit, and there may be a doubtful course for our life, thanks to ignorance about our death, how does each person think that there is plenty of time for confession when ignorant of the length of his time, although he might hear anyway the Scripture saying: 'You will confess while alive and well, and you will praise God, and with the living and those confessing you will take part in a time of holiness.'[122] For let a delay in time create a confession, and not give birth to despair. For damnation is increased by its delay, as he thinks of divine patience with stubborn animosity.

This was done, as has been shown, in the times of holy Noah, when God's patience, extended over a hundred years, poured an implacable cataclysm over the rotating world, as His censure inundated it. From this the holy apostle says: 'Or do you despise the richness of his goodness, and his longsuffering, not knowing that the goodness of God leads you to repentance? But following your hardness and impenitent heart, you treasure up wrath against yourself, for the day of anger and revelation of the righteous judgment of God, who will render to every man according to his deeds.

Chapter 29

I want you to tell me what the glory is of present things, what the fruit is of this time, what the use is of transitory things. The power of a throne is ended by death, as I have said, canvassing for control is frustrated by succession, an abundance of riches is very often squandered by us while alive, an effect of pleasure is destroyed by the intervention of sadness, the delight of joys is violated by the threat of fear, and everything which is captured by desire, longed for by body or soul, is cut away by time's final scythe. Nor can one obtain the perfect privilege of beatitude, unless surrounded by infinite eternity; for what is measured by unavoidable

---

[122] A very free adaptation of *Sirach* 17.23-24.

Arians and Vandals of the 4th-6th Centuries 213

necessity must be transitory. Without doubt one will remain punishable and fickle and weak, whose life is sometimes interrupted by a fortuitous event. So for all of these that end in death, what is proper for us in death itself?

If we shall have nothing that may be healed[123] by one's conscience, with the help of a good deed, and if we could have nothing good from ourselves, what should we take with us when returning to our final home? How naked and ugly our soul will remain if we do not at least protect it with a covering of penitence, and with cloaks of confession! Unless, because we are in a hurry to hide our wickedness, and do not strive to conceal the nakedness of our soul, although its beauty may be invisible by nature, its ugliness will become visible with the filth of sins.

Chapter 30

Those wares must be taken up, those riches must be embraced, that power must be seized which time does not snatch away, place does not withdraw, person does not remove, but which remain in a perpetual state, are preserved with eternal privilege, are not subject to an end and are neither pressed down by the yoke of death nor burdened by it. For there the goodness of conscience is safe, where one will no longer be allowed to sin, after the evil doings of the present time, where there is no access for the devil, where there is no place for darkness, but neither he who deceives nor he who could be deceived, are found. Therein all things are good, therein everything is fortunate, therein there is universal prosperity. The day will not be changeable in its increase of light, the sun will not be slower in rising, but will appear brighter in shining and darker in setting; the night will be totally absent, there will be no moon, nor will the glittering stars shine more brightly. Nobody will feel hungry, tears will be wiped away, with no fear, no sign of terror, as happiness possesses all things, peace everything, and joy whatever was guilty of sadness. The Prophet Isaiah clearly explains it all.[124]

Then what glory is there for the fortunate, what punishments for the wretched, what groans, what sighs for the sinners, what blessedness for the saints? These have fellowship with God, those are presented with the

---

[123] The verb *subsarcinare* (from *sarcire*, 'to repair') is only found here, a late Latin compound (see Lewis & Short). Its metaphorical use here is effective.

[124] This series of antitheses (with a neat chiasmus directly after the quotation) is loosely based on *Isaiah* 60. The 'refreshed' above is from *indefessos* ('not worn out'); the *a* was not needed with the instrument *rivulis*.

214 C. Victor of Cartenna

torment of the flames of Hell, these enjoy an incomparable consolation, those are destroyed by an indomitable furnace, these are delighted by the fountains of Paradise and the groves' tall trees, refreshed by the rivulets, those are hemmed in by pools of fire and a burning flood, and darkness of black night, and are oppressed by inescapable punishments. At the end, these enjoy heavenly goodness, those are consumed by the voracious jaw of the whole of Hell and eternal death.

Chapter 31

If anyone now, as far as today is concerned, while weak with ruinous poverty, should not have the recourses from which he might support his gnawing hunger, and should see others loading tables with rich banquets, and drinking from jeweled goblets when filled with feasting, and greatly extend their brightly coloured conviviality with its foreign elegance, competing in rich display, what sighs do you think he raises from the depths of his innards, what complaints does he utter from his painful guts? Sometimes he also pours out tears, when he begins to be seized a little more fully by his desire for what he has seen, and senses that his ineffective desire burns more and more from that desire.

Therefore, what groans will come from the unfortunate then, what torments with inconsolable grief over that comparison, when they have seen a crowd of blessed souls enjoying heavenly supplies and perennial riches, and themselves defrauded of a drop of water falling from a finger, and enduring an inextinguishable flame as well, kept with no hope of pardon?

We cannot bear the burning heat of the sun, we cannot endure the heat of a bath at all, as we are sensitive to the blaze of furnaces and keep far away from them. Who could bear raging Hell, and who will be able to endure the roar of the smoking abyss, burning on the furnaces of Hell, and put up with the fire-balls of infernal darkness, where the howling of those burning is the only sound heard, as the wailing resounds of those cruelly punished? I pray you, how must these be escaped, how must they be guarded against and rejected with total strength and all of one's spirit and mind!

Chapter 32

When, therefore, the gates of pardon are opened wide, when the port of penitence is offered to those fluctuating, tossed about by a storm of crimes,

Arians and Vandals of the 4th-6th Centuries — 215

when care is promised for languishing minds, and of his own accord the Creator promises vital medicine for the wounded, when mercy is ready at hand, before justice pulls out a dagger, as far as its hilt, let us take up the arms of penitence, and soften the Judge's rigor with satisfying service. For anyone allowed to be penitent has the certain gift of pardon, as without doubt one is not allowed to confess if one has retained no piety. This is proved by the condemnation of the old serpent at the very beginning of the world, when driven out by the thunderbolt of an unheard sentence, and absolute severity pulled it down from the status it possessed, much against its wishes. For this they say the regions of Sodom and Gomorrah were burnt to the ground by a heavenly fire, for which no penitence was reserved because of their excessive sins, so that they were perhaps unable to avoid the justice of their punishment, despite being warned. The death of the Pharaoh cries this out in Exodus, the unexpected deaths of Korah, Dathan and Abiram bear witness to this, the punishments of Antioch and of Herod proclaim this, the shipwreck of Ananias and Sapphira indicate this, with their sudden punishment. No modern defense has let them off, and a pardon has been denied. The accompanying severity has cut them off.[125]

May the day of our departure not find us unready, and may the time of that winter or Sabbath not enclose us inside the devil's camp. Let us be vigilant against the deceitful traps of the 'old enemy' and his open threats. For towards those converted he is aroused more keenly, and he pursues those fleeing him more severely, as if ridiculed by them. Then he had inveigled them with flattery, so as to deceive them, now he disturbs them with temptations and cruelties. Then he had been like a friend, now like an enemy, he is angry with them; and he has made the one broken down by chance more cautious, but sometimes the one broken down is accustomed to breaking down the one who breaks him down. Let us flee from the pompous snares of the world, and totally reject its ambitions. The Apostle John says this persuasively: 'Love not the world, nor the things that are in the world. If any man loves the world, the love of the Father is not in him; for all that is in the world, is the lust of the flesh and the lust of the eyes, and the pride of life, which is not of the Father, but is of the lust of the world. And the world passes away, and the lust thereof.

---

[125] Those punished were the citizens of Sodom and Gomorrah in *Genesis* 19.1-25, the Pharaoh in *Exodus* 14.26-28, Korah, Dathan and Abiram, in *Numbers* 16.1-32 and Ananias and Sapphira, in *Acts* 5.1-10. Ananias gets a full treatment in Victor of Vita's work on the Vandals, book 3 section 14, but Sapphira is left out there.

216 C. Victor of Cartenna

But he that does the will of God, abides for eternity; as God also abides for eternity.'[126]

Let us be washed with the baptism of penitence, so that we can see our Lord with a pure heart. Let us remove our evil thoughts from our minds and from the sight of the eyes of God, and let us learn how to act justly; let us inquire into a judgment, saving the person treated unjustly, let us judge for an orphan, justify a widow, and we shall discuss it with the Lord. And if our sins are like purple, He will purify them like snow. But if like scarlet, He will make them like white wool. And because he will sprinkle us with hyssop, we shall also be clean, he will wash us and we shall be whiter than snow.[127]

Chapter 33

There are three things that the Lord preserves for us, established by his decision. I mean goodness, mercifulness and justice. Goodness is whereby we have now begun to exist; mercifulness, whereby we are called to penitence; justice, whereby we shall be judged at a future date. These meanwhile guard a sequence of times in themselves: past, in which with the Lord as Creator, we are created and are born; present, in which we are converted and would provide mercy; future, in which we shall be rewarded according to our works, decided by justice. And so when we have the rule of mercy in our hands, the gifts of piety are also placed under our control. Here let us purge our consciences of all wickedness, and fit our selves hereafter with spiritual qualities, through a good way of life. Let us avoid desires that fight against our souls, and let us in no way endure a profane conscience. Let us follow all that we believe from our faith, if we may prepare ourselves through just acts with a life without blame. We shall deserve the remission of all our sins, we shall rise to eternal life in the resurrection of believers, and with the audacity to presume to speak more, we shall enter into the kingdoms of Heaven with the just, with which we have deserved to have a part through penitence, as the Scripture says: 'But to the penitent he gave a part in justice, and brought together those losing hope to sustain them, and destined to them the fortune of truth.[128]

---

[126] *I John* 2.15-17. The last sentence has been added to the Latin in the Vulgate.

[127] Based on *Psalms* 51(50).7.

[128] *Ecclesiasticus* 17.20, but with *partem* for *viam* ('path of justice'), *corrogavit* for *confirmavit* ('confirmed those...') and *illos in* for *illis* ('destined for them').

I have written down as much as the mediocrity of my intellect could gather from the readings of the Lord, most beloved brother, by which I might be encouraged to practice penitence equally with you. And if you now attend to them, in my opinion, with keenness of mind and your own purpose, and sitting on the chariot of confession, you reach His forgiveness, then accept me as a companion with you in this project, so that, with the addition of a shared fellowship, we may hasten to the goal of remission, or if, shackled by the inertia of sloth, I cannot keep up with your swiftness, remember me. And when you earn a reward from the generosity of God, I beg that in your prayers, you do not fail to remember your Victor.[129]

---

[129] The final word at least gives the modest author's correct name.

D. Athanasius

Expositio Fidei (Εκθεσισ Πίστεωσ)

Preface

The composer of this brief defense of the Catholic faith certainly uses much the same language as Athanasius, but sees the Word and the man Jesus as relatively distinguished from each other, in many places, and the Word is given a comparably higher standing. For his helpful comments on this defense and on my English version of it, I am indebted to Dr Andrew Hamilton, a specialist in early Greek doctrine and a lecturer at the Jesuit Theological College in Parkville, in Melbourne.

Chapter 1

1. We believe in one unbegotten God, Father Almighty, maker of all things visible and invisible, who has his existence from himself.

2. And we believe in one unique Word, Wisdom, the Son, begotten from the Father without a beginning and for evermore, and a Word not uttered, not in the mind, not an effluence from what is perfect, not a section of the unchangeable nature nor its extrusion, but a Son complete in himself, both living and active, the true image of the Father, equal in honour and glory.

3. 'For this,' He says, 'is the will of the Father. That just as they honour the Father, so should they honour the Son also,'[1] the true God from a true God, as John says in his epistle: 'and we are in him that is true, and in his Son Jesus Christ. This is the true God and eternal life.'[2]

He is an almighty God from an almighty God, for he governs and rules all that his Father governs and rules. He is whole from whole.

---

[1] *John* 5.23.
[2] *I John* 5.20.

Arians and Vandals of the 4th-6th Centuries 219

5. And like the Father, as the Lord says: 'He that has seen me has seen the Father,'[3] and he was begotten unutterably and inconceivably; 'for who shall declare his generation?'[4]

6. For coming down from the bosom of his Father and from   the immaculate Virgin Mary, at the completion of the ages, He took upon himself our human form, as Jesus Christ, whom He gave to suffer for our sakes by his own choice, as the Lord says: 'No man takes my soul from me. I have the power to lay it down, and I have the power to take it back again.'

7. Being crucified in this His human form and dying for our sakes He rose from the dead and ascended into Heaven; as the beginning for our ways, while still on earth he revealed to us light out of darkness, safety out of error, life from the dead, and a way into Paradise, from where Adam was thrown out, and into which he again entered through the robber, as the Lord said: 'Today you will be   with me in Paradise,'[5] which Paul also entered, and an ascent into Heaven, 'where the forerunner entered for our sakes,'[6] the Lord-Man, in whom He will judge the living and the dead.

Chapter 2

1. We likewise believe in the Holy Spirit, 'that searches all things, even the deep things of God,'[7] and we anathematize the beliefs that are opposed to this.

2. Neither do we believe that the Spirit is a Father-Son, as the Sabellians do,[8] saying that the Son is the same being as the Father, and not the same in being,[9] thus stripping away the being of the Son.

3. Nor do we attribute to the Father the suffering body that the Son bore for the salvation of the whole world.

---

[3] *John* 14.9.

[4] *Acts* 8.33 (as in *Isaiah* 53.8).

[5] *Luke* 23.43.

[6] *Hebrews* 6.20.

[7] *I Corinthians* 2.10.

[8] For the Sabellian heresy, see note 194 above.

[9] Yet again the definitive word (ὁμοιούσιον) is used for the orthodox Catholics, as in Victor of Vita's narrative and in the defenses of their faith by Archbishop Eugenius and by Saint Ambrose.

220   D. Athanasius

4. Nor is it possible to consider the three substances as divided from each other, in the bodily way proper to human beings, so we do not believe in many gods as do the pagans.

5. But as a river, that takes its birth from a spring, is not divided, although it may carry two names and two forms of names.

6. For neither is the Father the Son, nor is the Son the Father. For the Father is father of the son and the Son is the son of the Father.

7. For just as the spring is not a river and a river is not a spring, but each is one and the same water, which runs down a channel from the spring into the river, even so the divine nature comes from the Father into the Son without change and indivisibly.

8. For the Lord says: 'I came forth from the Father and I have come.'[10]And He is always with his Father, being in his bosom.

9. And the Father's bosom was never emptied of the Son's divinity. For he says: 'I was by him as one bound to him.'

10. But we do not think that the Son who is before all Creator of all, and God from God, is something made, created or from non-Being. He is Being from Being, one God from one God, since, like glory and power, all things were created eternally from the Father. For 'he that has seen me has seen the Father.'[11]

11. Clearly all things were created through the Son, but he is not a creation, as Paul says concerning the Lord: 'For by Him were all things created, and He is before all things.'[12]
12. But he does not say that 'he was created' before all things, but that he exists before all things. Being created, at any rate, is the lot of all things. To exist before all things befits the Son alone.

---

[10] *John* 16.28.
[11] *John* 14.9.
[12] *Colossians* 1.16-17.

Chapter 3

1. Well then, the one who was begotten by nature perfect from the perfect one, was born 'before all mountains,'[13] that is before all rational and intellectual existence. For in another place also Paul calls Him: 'The firstborn of all creation.'[14]

2. Yet he shows that the firstborn is not just a creature, but the one begotten of the Father. For to be called a creature is alien to his divinity.

3. For all things were created by the Father through the Son, but the Son alone was born from the Father from eternity.

4. Wherefore the divine Word 'is the firstborn of all creation,' unchangeable from an unchangeable Father. The creature is the body that he bore for our sakes.

5. On this, Jeremiah speaks in the version made by the seventy interpreters: 'The Lord created for us a new salvation as an impregnation, and men will be driven into this salvation.'[15]

6. Aquila's version of the same passage reads:[16]'The Lord created something new in the female.'[17] And the salvation created for us as an impregnation, that is new and not ancient, and that is for us and not before us, and it is Jesus, who became man to save us.

7. And He interprets it partly as salvation and partly as saviour. And salvation comes from the Saviour in the way that radiance comes from light.

8. Thus the new salvation created from the Saviour, as Jeremiah says: 'created for us a new salvation,' and as Aquila says: 'The Lord created something new in the female,' that is in Mary.

---

[13] *Proverbs* 8.25.
[14] *Colossians* 1.15
[15] *Jeremiah* 38.22 (Aquila).
[16] Ponticus Aquila translated the Hebrew Scriptures into Greek. A native of Sinope, he flourished in about 130. Converted to Christianity, he ended as a Jew.
[17] *Jeremiah* 38.22 (Aquila).

222 D. Athanasius

9. For nothing new was created in the female other than the Lord's body born from the Virgin Mary, without intercourse.

10. And as he says in the Proverbs, in the person of Jesus: 'The Lord created me at the beginning of his way to his works,'[18] he does not say 'he created me for his works,' so that no one should select the quotation for the divine nature of the Word.

Chapter 4

1. Well then, each of the quotations about the creation has been written corporeally for Jesus. For at the beginning of His ways was created the Lord-Man, whom he revealed to us for our salvation. The Lord and man was created as the beginning of the way, and He revealed it to us for our salvation.

2. Through Him we have access to the Father. For He is the way, as he says: 'I am the way,'[19] which leads us to his Father.

3. But the way is an object of bodily sight, the Lord-Man. At any rate, the Word of God created everything, not being a creation but a birth.

For nothing that was created, created something equal or similar to itself. It is natural for a father to beget, for a craftsman to make something.

5. The body that the Lord bore for us is something made and a creature, that was created for us, 'who was begotten for us,' as Paul says, 'as wisdom, sanctification, righteousness and redemption.'[20]Yet for us and for all creation the wisdom of the Father was and remains the Word.

6. And the Holy Ghost, being the one who proceeds from the Father, is always in the hands of the Father who sends it and of the Son who bears it, and through whom he accomplished all things.

7. The Father, having existence from himself, did not create but begat the Son, as we said, and he did not create him like a river from a spring or a shoot from a root or a radiance from a light, which nature knows to be

---

[18] *Proverbs* 8.22
[19] *John* 14.6.
[20] *I Corinthians* 1.30.

indivisible, through the Son there was glory for the Father and power, and greatness to all ages and unto all the ages of ages. Amen.

SELECT BIBLIOGRAPHY

Alexiou, Margaret *The Ritual Element in Greek Tradition* (C.U.P., 1974)

Arbesmann, Rudolf with E. L. Daly and E. A. Quain (tr.) *Tertullian: Disciplinary, Moral and Ascetical Works* (Fathers of the Church no. 40, New York, 1985[2])

Barker, John W. *Justinian and the Later Roman Empire* (Univ. Wisconsin Press, 1966)

Barnes, M.R. and D.H. Williams (eds), *Arianism after Arius* (Edinburgh: T&T Clark, 1993)

Barnes, Timothy D. *Tertullian: A Historical and Literary Study* (O.U.P., 1971)

Barret, Helen M. *Boethius. Some Aspects of his Times and Work* (C.U.P., 1940)

Barry, Colman *Readings in Church History* (New York, 1965[2]), vol 1

Battifol, Pierre *La Paix Constantinienne et le Catholicisme*; 312-359 (1914[3])

——. *Le Siège Apostolique; 359-451*

Baxter, Kenneth W. *Christian Martyrs in Muslim Spain* (C.U,P., 1988)

Beck, Henry G. J. *The Pastoral Care of Souls in South-East France during the Sixth Century* (*Analecta Gregoriana* 51, Rome, 1950)

Bloch, Herbert 'The Pagan Revival in the West at the End of the Fourth Century,' in A. Momigliano (ed.) *The Conflict between Paganism and Christianity in the Fourth Century* (O. U. P., reprint 1970), pp. 193-218

Bremmer, Rolf H. *et al* (edd) *Rome and the North: The Early Reception of Gregory the Great in Germanic Europe* (Peeters, Paris, Leuven, 2001)

Brisson, Jean-Paul *Autonomisme et christianisme dans l'Afrique romaine de Septime Sévère à l'invasion vandale* (Paris, 1958)

Brown, Peter R. L. *Augustine of Hippo* (Univ. California Press, 2000[2])

——. *The World of Late Antiquity: From Marcus Aurelius to Muhammed* (London, 1971)

——. *Religion and Society in the Age of Saint Augustine* (London/New York, 1972)

——. *The Making of Late Antiquity* (Harvard University Press, 1978)

——. *Poverty and Leadership in the Later Roman Empire* (2001)

—. *The Rise of Western Christendom: Triumph and Diversity A.D. 200-1000* (Blackwell, 2003[2])

Brown, T. S. *Gentlemen and Officers: Imperial Administration and Aristocratic Power in Byzantine Italy, 544-800* (London, 1984)

Browning, R. *Justin and Theodora* (London, 1971)

Bury, J. B. *History of the Later Roman Empire from the Death of Theodosius I to the Death of Justinian,* 2 vols. (N.Y., reprint, 1958)

Cameron, Alan *Circus Factions: Blues and Greens at Rome and Byzantium* (O.U.P., 1970)

Cameron, Averil (tr., introd.) *Procopius: History of the wars, Secret history, Buildings* in 7 vols (N.Y., Washington Square, 1967)

—. 'The early religious policies of Justin II' *Studies in Church History,* 13, 1976, 51-67

—. 'Images of Authority: Elites and Icons in Late Sixth-Century' *Past and Present* 84, 1979, 3-35

—. *Continuity and change in sixth century Byzantium* (London, Variorum Reprints, 1981)

—. *Procopius and the sixth century* (London, Duckworth, 1985)

—. *The Later Roman Empire: AD 284-430* (London, Fontana, 1993)

—. *The Mediterranean World in late antiquity. AD 395-600* (London & N.Y., Routledge, 1993)

—. *Late Antiquity: empire and successors AD 425-600*, with Ward-Perkins, Bryan and Whitby, Michael (C.U.P., 2000)

—. *Fifty years of prosopography: the later Roman Empire, Byzantium and beyond* (O.U.P., 2003)

Carr, Karen E. *Vandals to Visigoths: Rural settlement patterns in Early Medieval Spain* (Michigan, Ann Arbor, 2002)

Cherry, David *Frontier and Society in Roman North Africa* (O.U.P., 1998)

Collins, Roger *Visigothic Spain: New Approaches* (Oxford, 1980)

—. *Early Medieval Spain: Unity in Diversity 400-1000* (N.Y., 1983)

—. *Visigothic Spain 409-711* (N.Y., 2004)

Courcelle, P. *Late Latin Writers and their Greek Sources* (Cambridge, Mass., 1969)

Courtois, Christian *Les Vandales et l'Afrique* (Darmstadt, 1964[2])

—. *Victor de Vita et son oeuvre* (Algiers, 1954)

Cuming, C. J. (ed.) *Studies in Church History* I-III (Leiden, 1964-1966)

Cuoq, Joseph *L'église d'Afrique du Nord; du deuxième au douzième siècle* (Paris, 1984)

—. *Histoire de l'islamisation de l'Afrique de l'Ouest des origènes à la fin du XVIe siècle* (Paris, 1984)

226 Select Bibliography

Dalton, O. M., trans. *The History of the Franks by Gregory of Tours,* 2 vols (O.U.P., 1927)

Deanesly, Margaret *A History of the Medieval Church, 590-1500* (London, 1960^5)

Dewing, H. B. (tr.) *Procopius History of the Wars, Secret history, Buildings* in 7 vols (Loeb Class. Library, Cambridge Mass, Harvard Univ. Press, 1953-1962)

Diehl, Charles, *L'Afrique byzantine: histoire de la domination byzantine en Afrique (533-709)* (Paris, 1896)

—. *Théodora, impératrice de Byzance* (Paris, 1904)

—. *History of the Byzantine Empire* tr. G. R. Ives, (N.Y. 1984^2)

Dudden, F. Homes *Gregory the Great: His Place in History and Thought* 2 vols (N.Y., Russell & Russell, 1967^2)

Duval, Noël ed *L'Afrique Vandale et Byzantine, Antiquité Tardive* 10 (C.N.R.S., Paris, Brepols, 2002)

Evans, G.R., *The first Christian theologians* (Maldon; Oxford; Carlton: Blackwell Publishing, 2004)

Every, G. *The Byzantine Patriarchate, 451-1204* (London, 1962^2)

Louis Duchesne *L'Église au VIè siècle* (1925)

Fage, J. D. (ed.) *Cambridge History of Africa* Vol. 2 (C.U.P., 1978)

Finley, M. I. *The Ancient Economy* (Univ. California Press, 1973)

Fontaine, Jacques *Isidore de Séville et la culture classique dans l'Espagne wisigothique* 2 vols (Paris, 1959)

—. (ed.) *Grégoire le Grand* (Paris, 1986)

Foulke, William Dudley (tr.) *History of the Lombards: Paul the Deacon* (Univ. Pennsylvania Press, 1974)

Frank, R. I. *Scholae Palatinae: The Palace Guards of the Later Roman Empire* (Rome, 1969)

Frank, Tenney *Economic Survey of Ancient Rome* (John Hopkins Univ. Press, 1940)

Frend, W. H. C. *Martyrdom and Persecution in the Early Church* (Oxford, Blackwell, 1965)

—.'The early Christian church in Carthage' in *Excavations at Carthage* 3, 1977, 21-40

—. *The Donatist Church: A Movement of protest in Roman North Africa* (Oxford, Clarendon Press, 1985^2)

—. *Orthodoxy, Paganism and Dissent in the Early Christian Centuries,* article VIII (Aldershot, Ashgate, 2002)

—. *The Rise of Christianity* (London, 1984)

—. *Saints and Sinners in the early church: differing and conflicting traditions in the first six centuries* (London, 1985)

Gibbon, Edward *The Decline and Fall of the Roman Empire* 3 vols ed. Smeaton, Oliver (N.Y.)

Goffart, Walter *Barbarians and Romans A.D. 418-548: The techniques of accommodation* (Princeton, 1980)

—. 'Byzantine Policy in the West under Tiberius II and Maurice: The Pretenders Hermenegild and Gundovald (597-585),' *Traditio,* 13, 1957, 73-118

Gray, Patrick T. R. *The Defense of Chalcedon in the East (451-553)* (Leiden, Brill, 1979)

Grossi, Vittorino (ed.) *Gregorio Magno e il suo tempo* 2 volumes, Institutum Patristicum Augustinianum (Roma, 1991)

Gsell, Stéphanie *Histoire ancienne de l'Afrique du Nord* 8 vols (Paris, Hachette, 1913-1928)

Haldon, John F. *Byzantium and the Seventh Century: The Transformation of a Culture* (C.U.P., rev. 1997)

Hanson, R. P. C., *The search for the Christian doctrine of God* (Edinburgh: T&T Clark, 1988)

Hefele, Carl J. and Leclerq, Henri *History of the Councils* (1907-1921)

Hillgarth, J. N. (ed.) *Christianity and Paganism, 350-750; the Conversion of Western Europe* (Univ. of Pennsylvania Press, 1986)

Hughes, Philip *The Church in Crisis: The Twenty Great Councils* (London, 1960)

Humphrey, J. (ed.) *The Circus and Byzantine Cemetery at Carthage* Vol 1 (Univ. of Michigan Press, 1988)

Hussey, J. M. *The Byzantine World* (Harper pbk, N.Y., 1962)

James, Edward (ed.) *Visigothic Spain* (O.U.P., 1980)

Jones, A. H. M. 'Church Finance in the Fifth and Sixth Centuries' *Journal of Theological Studies*, 11, 1960, 84-94

—. 'The Constitutional Position of Odoacer and Theoderic' *J.R.S.*, 52, 1962, 126-130

—. *The Later Roman Empire, 284-602: A Social, Economic and Administrative Survey*, 3 vols (O.U.P., 1964)

—. *The Decline of the Ancient World* (London/N.Y., 1966)

—. *The Cities of the Eastern Roman Provinces* (Oxford, Clarendon Press, 1971²)

—. with Martindale, J. R. & Morris, J. *The Prosopography of the Later Roman Empire*, 3 vols (C.U.P., 1971-1992)

Julien, Charles André *Histoire de l'Afrique du Nord: Tunisie, Algérie, Maroc*, 2nd edit., 2 vols (Paris, Payot, 1951-1952)

Rouet de Journel, M. J. *Enchiridion Patristicum*

Kaegi, W. 'Arianism and the Byzantine Army in Africa, 533-546' *Traditio*, 21, 1965, 23-53

Kaniecka, Mary Simplicia (tr.) *Vita Sancti Ambrisii Mediolanensis Episcopi a Paulino eius notario ad beatum Augustinum conscripta* (Catholic Univ. of America, Washington, 1928)

Kirch, C. *Enchiridion fontium Historiae Ecclesiasticae Antiquae*

Kelly, J. N. D. *Early Christian Doctrines* (N.Y., 1960[2])

Kleemann. J. 'Quelques réflexions sur l'interprétation ethnique des sepultures habillées considérées comme vandales' in *L'Afrique Vandale,* 123-130

La Rocca, Christine (ed.) *Italy in the Early Middle Ages*: 476-1000 (O.U.P., 2002)

Lachaux, J.-C. *Théâtres et amphitheatres d'Afrique proconsulaire* (Aix en-Provence, 1979)

Lapèyre, G. G. & Pellegrin, A. *Carthage latine et chrétienne* (Paris, 1950)

Latko, E. *Origen's Concept of Penance* (Quebec, 1949)

Leclercq, H. *L'Afrique chrétienne* (Paris, 1904[2])

Lepelley, Claude & Beaujard, Brigitte 'Du nouveau sur les villes de l'Afrique romaine au temps de saint Augustin' *Revue des études augustiniennes*, 23, 1977, 422-431

Liebeschuetz, J. H. W. G. *The Decline and Fall of the Roman City* (O.U.P., 2001)

Lieu, S. N. C. *Manichaeism in the Later Roman Empire and in Medieval China* (Tübingen, 1992[2])

Llewellyn, Peter 'The Roman Church in the seventh century: the legacy of Gregory I' *Journal of Eccles. History*, 25, 1974, 363-380

——. *Rome in the Dark Ages* (London, 1971)

Lynch, J. H. *Godparents and Kinship in Early Medieval Europe* (Princeton, NJ, 1986)

MacKendrick, Paul *The North African Stones Speak* (Univ. North Carolina Press, 1979)

MacMullen, Ramsay 'Social Mobility and the Theodosian Code *Journal of Roman Studies*, 54, 1964, 49-53

——. *Enemies of the Roman Order: Treason, Unrest and Alienation in the Empire* (Harvard Univ. Press, 1966)

——. *Christianity and Paganism in the Fourth to Eighth Centuries* (New Haven, CT, 1997)

Madoz, J. *Liciniano de Cartagena y sus cartas* (Madrid, 1948)

Maenchen-Helfen, J. Otto *The World of the Huns: Studies in their History and Culture* ed. Knight, Max (Univ. California Press, 1973)

Mansi, John D. *Sacrorum Concilium Nova et Amplissima Collectio* rev. ed. 60 vols (1899-1927)

MacNeill, William Hardy *Plagues and Peoples* (University of Chicago Press, 1976)

Markus, R. A. 'Donatism, the last phase,' in Cuming, C. J. (ed.) *Studies in Church History* 1 (Leiden, 1964), 118-126

—. 'Religious dissent in North Africa in the Byzantine period' *Studies in Church History* 3 (Leiden, 1966), 149ff

—. *Christianity in the Roman World* (London, Thames and Hudson, 1974)

—. *The End of Ancient Christianity* (C.U.P., 1990)

—. *Gregory the Great and his World* (C.U.P., 1997)

Martindale, J. R. *The Prosopography of the Later Roman Empire: AD 395-527* (C.U.P., 1980)

Martyn, John R. C. *A Translation of Abbot Leontius' Life of Saint Gregory, Bishop of Agrigento* (Mellen, New York, 2004)

—. 'Four Notes on the *Registrum* of Gregory the Great' in *Parergon*, 19.2, 2002, 5-38

—. 'Six notes on Gregory the Great' in *Medievalia et Humanistica* n.s. 29, 2003, 1-25

—. *The Letters of Gregory the Great* tr. & notes, 3 vols (P.I.M.S., Toronto, 2004)

—. Gregory the Great on Organ lessons and on the Equipment of Monasteries' in *Med. et Human.* n.s. 30, 2004, 107-122

McEntire, Sandra J. *Holy Tears: The Doctrine of Compassion in medieval England* (Mellen Press, N. Y., 1990)

Merrills, A. H. (ed.) *Vandals, Romans and Berbers* (Ashgate, 2004)

Miller, J. Innes *The Spice Trade of the Roman Empire, 29 B.C.–A. D. 641* (O.U.P., 1969)

Meyvaert, P. 'Uncovering a lost work of Gregory the Great: fragment of the early Commentary on Job' *Traditio*, 50, 1995, 55-74

Moorhead, John 'Boethius and Romans in Ostrogothic Service' *Historia*, 27, 1978, 604-612

—. *Victor of Vita: History of the Vandal Persecution* (Liverpool Univ. Press, 1991)

Moss, H. St.L. B. *The Birth of the Middle Ages, 395-814* (O.U.P., 1963)

Nordberb, Henric 'Athanasius and the Emperor' in *Commentationes Humanarum Litterarum* xxx, 3, 1963, 7-69

Ostrogorsky, G. Geschichte des byzantinischen Staates (Munich, 1963[3]), trans. Hussey, J. M. *History of the Byzantine State* (Oxford, 1956 & Rutgers U.P., 1957)

230 Select Bibliography

Paredi, Angelo *Saint Ambrose: His Life and Times* (Univ. of Notre Dame Press, 1964)

Parsons, Sister Wilfrid (tr.) *Saint Augustine : Letters* (Fathers of the Church vols 12, 18, 20, 30, 32; Cath. Univ. of America Press 1951-6)

Patch, Howard R. *The Tradition of Boethius: A Study of his Importance in Medieval Culture* (N.Y., 1970^2)

Pelikan, J. *The Christian Tradition* vol 1 (Chicago; London: The University of Chicago Press, 1975)

Poschmann, Bernard *Die Abendländische Kirchenbusse im Ausgang des Christlichen Altertums* (München, 1928)

Pringle, D. *The defence of Byzantine Africa from Augustine to the Arab conquest* (O.U.P., 1981)

Procopius: *History of the Wars* see Dewing, H. B. (tr.)

—. *The Secret History* see Williamson, G. A. (tr.)

Rand, Edward K. *Founders of the Middle Ages* (N.Y., 1957^2)

Randers-Pehrson, Justine Davis *Barbarians and Romans: The Birth Struggle of Europe, AD 400-700* (Croom Helm, London, 1983).

Riché, Pierre *Éducation et culture dans l'Occident barbare, 6e-8e siècles* (*Éditions du Seuil,* 1962) tr. Contreni J. J., *Education and Culture in the Barbarian West, sixth through eighth centuries* (Univ. of Carolina Press, 1976)

—. (ed) *Religion and Culture* in honour of R. E. Sullivan

Ross, Anne *Everyday Life of the Pagan Celts* (London, 1970)

Rostovtzeff, M. *The Social and Economic History of the Roman Empire,* revised by Fraser, P. M., 2 vols (O.U.P., 1957^2)

Rowen, Susan *Rome in Africa* (London/N.Y., 1984^2)

Rummel, P. von 'Habitus Vandalorum? Zur Frage nach einer gruppenspezifischen Kleidung der Vandalen in Nordafrika,' in *L'Afrique Vandale,* 131-142

Runciman, Steven *The mediaeval Manichee: a study of Christian dualistic heresy* (C.U.P., 1947)

—. *The orthodox churches and the secular states* (Auckland U.P., 1971)

—. *Byzantine style and civilization* (Penguin, 1975)

Saint, W. P. Le (tr.) Tertullian: *Treatises 'On Penance' and 'On Purity'* (Ancient Christian Authors no. 28, Maryland/London, 1959)

Sherwin-White, A. N. *Racial Prejudice in Ancient Rome* (C.U.P., 1970)

Smith, J. M. H. (ed.) *Early Mediaeval Rome and the Christian West. Essays in honour of D. A. Bullough* (Leiden, 2000)

Stewart, H. F., Rand, E. K. & Tester, S. J. *Boethius: The Theological Tracts and Consolation of Philosophy* (Loeb Series, new ed. 1972^2)

Stroheker, K. F. 'Das spanische Westgotenreich und Byzanz' *Bonner Jahrbücher* 163, 1963, 252-274

Thompson, E. A. 'The Conversion of the Visigoths to Catholicism' *Nottingham Med. Studies*, 4, 1960, 4-35

—. *The Early Germans* (O.U.P., 1965)

—. *The Goths in Spain* (O.U.P., 1969)

Ullmann, W. *The Growth of Papal Government in the Middle Ages* (London, 1970³)

Ure, P. N. *Justinian and his Age* (Penguin, 1951)

Vasiliev, A. A. *History of the Byzantine Empire, 324-1453* (Univ. Wisconsin Press, 1952

Wallace-Hadrill J. M. *The Barbarian West: The Early Middle Ages, A.D. 400-1000*, Harper pbk, N.Y., 1962)

Watts, V. E. *Boethius: The Consolation of Philosophy* (Penguin, 1978)

Webster, Leslie & Brown, Michelle (edd) *The Transformation of the Roman World AD 400-900* (British Museum Press, 1997)

Williams, R. *Arius: heresy and tradition* (Grand Rapids; Cambridge: Eerdmans, 2001)

Williamson, G. A. (tr.) *Procopius: The Secret History* (Penguin Classics, London, 1981²)

Wilson, N. G. *Scholars of Byzantium* (Duckworth, Cambridge Ma, 1996²)

Wolf, Kenneth B. *Christian Martyrs in Muslim Spain* (N.Y./ C.U.P., 1988)

—. *Conquerors and Chroniclers of Early Medieval Spain* (Liverpool Univ. Press, 1999²)

Ziegler, A. K. *Church and State in Visigothic Spain* (Washington DC, Catholic Univ. of America Press, 1930)

NOTICE OF THE PROVINCES AND CITIES OF AFRICA

Names of those Catholic bishops and priests of various provinces who at the King's order came to Carthage to give an account of their faith, on February 1st, in the sixth year of King Huneric.

A. Proconsular Province (54)

Aemilianus of Culsita (Corsica)
Augentius of Uzipparita (exiled)
Aurelius of Clypea (Corsica)
Benenatus (1) of Timidum (Corsica)
Benenatus (2) of Tuburbium
Boniface (1) of Membrosita (admin.)
Boniface (2) of Bolitum (Corsica)
Carcadius of Maxulitum (Corsica)
Carissimus of Gisipum (exiled)
Cassosus of Ausana (here)
Clementinus of Naples (Corsica)
Coronius of Megalopolis (Corsica)
Cresces of Cicsita (exiled)
Cresciturus of Titulitum
Cresconius of Tennonna (died)
Cyprian (1) of Bonustum
Cyprian (2) of Cellae
Dalmatius of Tinnisis (Corsica)
Deumhabet of Thele (Corsica)
Deuterius of Simingum (Corsica)

Eugenius, Archbishop of Carthage (exiled to Tamallenis)
Exitziosus of Verena (Corsica)
Felix (1) of Abaritana (Aures) (exiled)
Felix (2) of Pia, exiled (Corsica)
Felix (3) of Curbita (Corsica)
Felix (4) of Muzua
Felix (5) of Bulla (died)#
*Felix (6) of Carpi (Corsica)
Florentinus of Utica (Corsica)
Florentius of Semina (Corsica)
Fortunatianus of Araditum (Corsica)
Gaius of Uzitum (died)
Gulosus of Beneventum (Corsica)
Hirundinus of Missua (Corsica)
Honoratus of Tagaratum (died)
John of the plain of Bulla
Jonah of Lapdenum (Corsica)
Liberatus of Mullita (Corsica)
Mannucius of Duassedemsaum
Marianus of Hippzariten (Corsica)
Maximinus of Maraggaritum (here)

Arians and Vandals of the 4th-6th Centuries 233

Pascasius (1) of Gunelis
(Corsica)
Pascasius (2) of Migirpis
(Corsica)
Pascasius (3) of Tulanis
Pastinatus of Puppitae (Corsica)
Paul of Sinnarum (exiled)
Peregrinus of Assurita (here)
Quintianus of Urcita
Reparatus (1) of Utimmira
(Corsica)
Reparatus (2) of Puppianum
Sacconius of Uzialum (Corsica)
Victor of Eudalum
Vincent of Zigga (exiled)
Vindemius of Alburita (exiled)

B. Province of Numidia (124)

Abundius of Tididita (died)
Adeodatus (1) of Fesseita (died)
Adeodatus (2) of Nobarbaris
Adeodatus (3) of Idassis
Adeodatus (4) of Sistronianis
(died)
Adeodatus (5) of Zarai (died)
Anastasius of Aquenobis
Annibonius of Vadesita
Antonianus of Mustita
Augentius of Gazaufulis (died)
Benenatus (1) of Lamviritum
Benenatus (2) of Mazacis (died)
Benenatus (3) of Mileu
Candidus of Nobasina (died)
Cardelus of Lamiggigis
Crescentianus of Germanium
Crescentius of Tacaretis
Cresces of Buffadis (died)
Cresconius (1) of Amporis
Cresconius (2) of Tharasis
Cresconius (3) of Zabi

Domnicosus of Tigisis
Domnicus of Caesarea (died)
Domninus of Moxorita (sent to a
mine)
Donatianus (1) of Vaselita
Donatianus (2) of Teglatis
Donatus (1) of Ausuccuris
Donatus (2) of Rusticianis
Donatus (3) of Villadegis
Donatus (4) of Luguris (died)
Donatus (5) of Gilbis
Donatus (6) of Silis
Donatus (7) of Maximianis
Dumvirialis of Damatcoris
(died)
Eusebius of Susicazium
Felicianus (1) from the Ring of
Tarasum
Felicianus (2)
Felix (1) of Bercerita
Felix (2) of Lamsortis
Felix (3) of Matharis (died)
Felix (4) of Gilbis (died)
Felix (5) of Nobasparsis (died)
Felix (6) of Casennigris
Felix (7) of Tabesti
Felix (8) of Suabis
Felix (9) of Garbis (died)
Firmianus of Centurionis (died)
Flavian of Vicopacis
Florentianus of Milidi
Florentius (1) of Nobarbaris
Florentius (2) of Centenarium
Fluminius of Tabudis
Fortunatianus of Naratcatis
Fortunius of Regianis (died)
Fructuosus from the Ring of
Marcellus
Frumentius of Tubusicis
Fulgentius of Vagadis (died)
Gaudentius of Putia

Gedalius of Ospitis
Honoratus (1) of Castella
Honoratus (2) of Fatis
Januarianus of Marculita
Januarius (1) of Jacteris
Januarius (2) of Velesita
Januarius (3) of Legis (died)
Januarius (4) of Centuria
Januarius (5) of Gaurianis (died)
Januarius (6) of Thagaste (died)
Julius Vagarmelita
Junior of Tigillabis
Leontius of Burca
Leporius of Auguris
Marcellinus of Vagrautis
Martial of Giris
Maximus (1) of Sillita (died)
Maximus (2) of Lamfuens (died)
Maximus (3) of Lamigenum
Melior of Fossalis (at a mine)
Mensor of Formi
Optantius of Casensicalanis
Palladius of Idicris (died)
Pardalius of Macomadium
Pascentius (1) of Octabis
Pascentius (2) of
  Cethaquensusea
Pascentius (3)
Paul of Nibis (died)
Peregrinus (1) of Punentianis
  (priest)
Peregrinus (2) of Mulie
Peter of Madis
Ponticanus of Formi (died)
Proficius (1) of Seleucianis
  (priest)
Proficius (2) of Vadis (died)
Pudentius of Madaurus
Quodvultdeus (1) of Calama
Quodvultdeus (2) of Caelianis
  (at a mine)

Quodvultdeus (3) of Respectis
*Quodvultdeus (4) at the Towers
  of Concord (Ad Turres)
Quodvultdeus (5) of Ullita
*Reparatus of Tubunac
Rufinianus of Vadis
Rusticus of Tipasa$
Secundinus of Lamasuis
Secundus of Tamogazium
  (dead)
Servus (1) of Arsicarita
Servus (2) of Belesasis
Simplicius of Vibilita
Stephanus of Sinitis
Timothy of Taguris
Valentianus of Montis (died)
Victor (1) of Cuicul
Victor (2) of Suggita
Victor (3) of Municipis
Victor (4) of Cirta$ (died)
Victor (5) of Gaudiabis
Victor (6) of the Towers of
  Ammeniae
Victorinus (1) from the Noba of
  Caesar
Victorinus (2) from the castle of
  Titulian
Victorinus (3) of Brabris (dead)
Victorinus (4) of Legium
Vigilius (1) of Ressanis (died)
Vigilius (2) of Iziriadis (died)
Villaticus of Casa Mediana
Vitalian (1) of Bocconia
Vitalian (2) of Vazarita

C. Province of Byzacena (109)

Adelfius (1) of Mactaris
Adelfius (2) of Mattaris
Adeodatus (1) of Pederodia
Adeodatus (2) of Praecausa

Arians and Vandals of the 4th-6th Centuries

Albinus of Octabis
Antacius of Median
Athenius of Circinita
Aurelius of Feradimais
Boniface (1) of Maseliana
Boniface (2) of Foratiana
Boniface (3) of Frontonianis
Boniface (4) of Maraguia
Boniface (5) of Filacis
Concordius of Cululis
Cresconius of Temonia (died)
Cyprian of Unuzibiris
Decimus of Theuzita
Domninus of Tarazis
Donatianus of Elien
Donatus (1) of Ermianum
Donatus (2) of Boanis
Donatus (3) of Rufinianis
Donatus (4) of Aggarita
Eubodius of Medidita
Eusebius of Jubaltianis (died)
Eustratius of Sufeta
Fastidiosus of Egnatium
Faustus of Praesidium
Felix (1) of Custris (died)
Felix (2) of Crepedula
Felix (3) of Irpiniana
Felix (4) of Forum Antonianum
Filtiosus of Aggaritum
Flavianus of Buleliana
Florentinus of Tuzirita
Fortunatianus (1) of Leptis
  Minor
Fortunatianus (2) of Cilita
Fortunatianus (3) of Tagarbalis
Fortunatus of Mozotcorita
Frumentius of Telepte
Germanus of Peradamia
Habetdeus of Tamaullina
Heliodorus of Cufrutis
Hilarinus of Trofinianum

Honoratus (1) of Thagari maius
Honoratus (2) of Tizien
Honoratus (3) of Macrianis
  (died)
Honorius of Oppennis
Hortensius of Autente
Hortulanus of Benefum (in De
  Persecutione)
Innocent of Muzucis
Julian of Vararita
Laetus of Nepta (in De
  Persecutione)
Leontius of Decoriana
Liberatus (1) of Amudarsis
  (died)
Liberatus (2) of Aquae Regiae
Mangentius of Ticualtis
Mansuetusof Afulenium
Marcellinus of Tasbalte
Maximus of Gummita
Mensius of Turris
Pascasius (1) of Septimunicium
Pascasius (2) of Tenita
Pacatus of Vicoateria
Paul of Turreblanda (died)
Peregrinus of Materianis
Pirasius of Nationis
Possidius of Massimanum
Praefectianus of Abaradiris
  (died)
Praesidius of Sufetula, exiled
Primianus of Gurgaitis
Proficius of Sublectium
Quodvultdeus of Duris (died)
Quintianus of Casulae Carianae
Restitutus (1) of Thagamuta
Restitutus (2) of Aquiaba
Restitutus (3) of Aquae Albae
Restitutus (4) of Acolita
Restitutus (5) of Segermita
  (exiled)

Rogatianus of Vadentinianum
Rufinianus of Victorianis
Rusticus of Telcita
Sabinicus of Octabia
Saturus of Irena
Secundianus of Mimiana
(exiled)
Secundinus of Garrianis, (died)
Servandus of Putia
Servitius of Unuricopolita
Servius of Arsurita
Servus of Menefessi
Servusdei of Tambeita
Simplicius of Carcabianis
Stephan of Rusfen
Succensianus of Febiana
Terentianus of Tubulbarcis
Tertullus of Iunci
Victor (1) of Nara
Victor (2) of Gauvarita
Victor (3) of Vita (author)
Victorianus of Quaestorianis
Victorinus (1) of Ancusa
Victorinus (2) of Seberiana
Victorinus (3) of Scebatiana
Victorinus (4) of Usulis
Vigilius of Tapsita
Villaticus of Ausegeris
Vindemialis of Capsa
Vindicianus of Marazanae
Vinitor of Talaptulis

Sees without Bishops
(6)

Cunculiana
Dionysiana
Madassuma
Orroea Coelia
Sulianis
Ticibus

D. Province of Mauritania \Caesariensis (120)

Aemilius of Medium
Apocorius of Caesarien
Arator of Catula
Auxilius of Gunugita (died)
Avus of Altabis
Baleas of Villenobis
Benantius of Oppidonebis (died)
Boniface of Rusgunium
Burco of Vardimissis (died)
Caecilius (1) of Minnis
Caecilius (2) of Balianis
Campanus of Bidis
Candidianus of Castris (died)
Cerealis of Castelloripis
Claudius of Vagalita
Cresces (1) of Sestis (died)
Cresces (2) of Tigabita
Cresces (3) of Satafis (died)
Crispinus of Tabadcaris
David of Tadamatis
Donatianus of Usinadis
Donatus (1) of Nobicis (died)
Donatus (2) of Panatorium
Donatus (3) of Tifiltis
Donatus (4) of Subbarita
Donatus (5) of Ternamunis
Donatus (6) of Frontis
Donatus (7) of Voncarium
Emptacius of Siccesita
Eusebius of Obbita
Faustus of Castraseberianis
Felicianus of Idis
Felix (1) of Rusubirita
Felix (2) of Ambium
Felix (3) of Aquisiris
Felix (4) of Flenucletis (died)
Felix (5) of Maxitis (died)
Fortis of Caputcillis

Gaius of Adsinnadis (died)
Gelianus of Reperita
Glorinus of Iunca
Honoratus of Timicita
Honorius of Benepotis
Idonius of Rusadita
Ingenuus of Ubabis
Januarius (1) of Aquis
Januarius (2) of Nasbincis (died)
Longinus of Pamarium
Lucidus of Cartenna$
Lucius (1) of Itis
Lucius (2) of Maturbis
Lucius (3) of Tamazucis
Maddanius of Murconis
Martial of Columpnatis
Martianus of Murustagis (died)
Mattasius of Castelijabarita
Maxentius of Tigamibenis (died)
Maximus of Tuscamium
Mensius of Alamiliaris
Metcun of Rusuccurita
Mingin of Nobis (died)
Nicetius of Castellominorita
Onesimus of Fidolemis
Palladius of Bacanarium
Pannonius of Bitis
Pascasius of Mamma
Passinatus (1) of Masuccabis (died)
Passitanus (2) of Tigisita
Patera (1) of Milianis
Patera (2) of Catabita
Paul of Flumenzerita
Paulinus of Rubicarium
Peter (1) of Oborita
Peter (2) of Castela
Poequarius of Tasaccora$ (died)
Philo of Arsinnarita
Primus of Capri
Quintasius of Mutecita

Quintus of Tabunium (priest)
Quodvultdeus (1) of Tablis (killed)
Quodvultdeus (2) of Summulis (priest)
Reparatus (1) of Girumontis
Reparatus (2) of Bulturium
Reparatus (3) of Tatroportis
Reparatus (4) of Tipasita (killed)
Reparatus (5) of Cissita
Reparatus (6) of Sitis
Restitutus of Florianis
Restutus of Lapidium (died)
Rogatianus of Vannidis (killed)
Rogatus of Sereddelita
Romanus (1) of Sufarita
Romanus (2) of Tamadis (killed)
Rufus of Sfasferium
Salo of Fallabis
Saturninus (1) of Vissalsis (died)
Saturninus (2) of Sertis (died)
Secundus of Maurianis
Securus of Timidanis
Stephan of Zucabiaritum
Subdatius of Sucardis
Subitanus of Idis (killed)
Syrus of Corniculanis
Tacanus of Albulae$
Talasius of Gratinopolita
Teberianus of Quidium
Urbanus of Amauris (died)
Valentinus of the Castle of Tatroportis
Vassinus of Elfantarium (died)
Verecundus of Nobis
Victor (1) of Sufarita
Victor (2) of Taborentis
Victor (3) of Regis
Victor (4) of Icosita
Victor (5) of Caltadrium (died)

238   Notice of the Provinces and Cities of Africa

Victor (6) of Manaccenserita
(died)
Victor (7) of Voncarianum
Victor (8) of Numidia (died)
Vincemalus of Baparis
Vitalis of Castranobis

Sees without Bishops
(6)

Dionysiana
Madassuma
Orroea Coelia
Sulianis
Ticibus

E. Province of Mauritania Sitifensis (42)

Abus of Ficis
Adeodatus of Pribatis
Aemilius of Asvoremixtis
Argentius of Zallatis
Aufidius of Suristis
Clemens of Thamugradi
Constantius Gegita
Cresciturus of Cellis (died)
Donatus of Sitifis$
Domitianus of Igilgita
Emeritus of Macris (died)
Felix of Castella (died)
Festus of Satafis
Flavian of Vamallis
Honoratus of Tamascanium
(died)
Honorius of Aqua Alba
Inventinus of Maronanis
Jacobus of Lemelefis
Justus of Acudifis (died)
Maximus (1) of Covium
Maximus (2) of Thugga Subdita

Montanus of Cedamusis
Pacatus of Equizotis
Pascasius of Saldae
Possessor of Zabi
Redux of Nobalicianis
Restutus of Macrianis (died)
Rogatus of Partenium
Romanus of Molicunzis
Rufinus of Tamallumis
Saturnius of Socium (died)
Uzulus of Thuccis
Vadius of Lesuita
Victor (1) of Horrea (Caelia)
Victor (2) of Jerafita
Victor (3) of Eminentianis
Victor (4) of Flumenpiscis
Victorinus (1) of Serteita (died)
Victorinus (2) of Perdicis
Villaticus of Mozotis
Vindemius of Lemfoctis
Vitalis of Assafis

F. Province of Tripolitania (5)

Callipides of Leptis Magna
Cresconius of Oene
Faustinus Kirbita
Leo of Sabrata
Servilius of Tapacita

G. Island of Sardinia (8)

Boniface from Sanafer
Felix from Porto Torres
Helias from Majorca
Lucifer of Catarina
Macarius from Minorca
Martinianus from the Trojan's
Forum
Opilio from Evusus
Vitalis of Sulcita

Totals

Bishops	374
Killed	88
Total	462
Sees without priests	12

Deaths (Editor)
A 4 B 34 C 10 D 32 E 8 = 88
Exiled/Relegated

Corsica (list)	27 Ed 46
N. Africa	4 Ed 302
Elsewhere	10
Sent to mine	3

Common Names of the Bishops

Felix	26
Victor	22
Donatus	19
Boniface	9
Adeodatus	8
Maximus	8
Januarius	6
Quodvultdeus	6
Cresconius	6

The Bishops of this period of the key administrative centres were:
Apocorius, Bishop of Caesarien
[Mauritania Caesariensis]
Vindemialis, Bishop of Capsa [Byzacena]
Callipides, Bishop of Leptis Magna [Tripoli]
Victor, senior priest of Cirta$ [Numidia]
Fortunatianus, Bishop of Leptis Minor [Byzacena]

For the *Notitia*, see Christian Courtois *Victor de Vita et son Oevre* (Algiers, 1954), App II. He rightly interprets the *prbt* (priest) beside about eighty names as *p(e)riit*. They were all bishops, and over 80 'died' or were killed. But Courtois is very reluctant to credit the historian with the *Notitia* (*op. cit.* p. 9), though the diligent bishop does mention many of

240   Notice of the Provinces and Cities of Africa

them, and is the likeliest Victor active then to have compiled the list, again probably at the request of his patron, the archbishop.

The sign *nam* beside Melior of Fossalis and Quodvultdeus (2) of Caelianis is puzzling, but Courtois seems to be right in his suggestion *n(unc) a(d) m(etalla)*; 'now at a mine,' the fate of Domninus of Moxorita. In Victor of Vita's history, bk. 5, ch. 19, young men and women were sent to 'squalid parts of mines,' by the Vandals.

For the names above, see also Christ. Courtois *Les Vandales et l'Afrique* (Aalen, 1964[2]).